D1448552

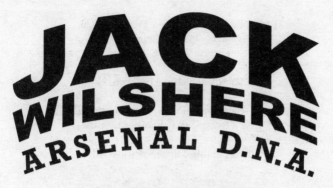

JACK WILSHERE
ARSENAL D.N.A.

THE BIOGRAPHY OF THE GUNNERS' SUPERSTAR

Joe Jacobs

JOHN BLAKE

Published by John Blake Publishing Ltd,
3 Bramber Court, 2 Bramber Road,
London W14 9PB, England

www.johnblakepublishing.co.uk

www.facebook.com/Johnblakepub facebook
twitter.com/johnblakepub twitter

First published in paperback in 2013

ISBN: 978-1-84358-758-3

British Library Cataloguing-in-Publication Data:

A catalogue record for this book is available from the British Library.

Design by www.envydesign.co.uk

Printed in Great Britain by CPI Group (UK) Ltd

1 3 5 7 9 10 8 6 4 2

Papers used by John Blake Publishing are natural, recyclable products
made from wood grown in sustainable forests. The manufacturing
processes conform to the environmental regulations of the country of origin.

Every attempt has been made to contact the relevant copyright-holders,
but some were unobtainable. We would be grateful if the appropriate
people could contact us.

For Noah & Ethan

Cover design by Dan Leydon

Dan Leydon is a self-taught illustrator working from his home studio in Ireland. He mainly illustrates sport but his tastes veer off into literature, film and gaming. Adept at communicating his ideas through a range of vibrant styles, Dan is always trying to outdo the last piece of work he produced. It's rare that a week goes by when he doesn't say 'I think this is my best piece yet'.

His work can be viewed and purchased at the links below:
danleydon.tumblr.com
etsy.com/shop/footynews
@danleydon on Twitter

CONTENTS

INTRODUCTION
The Number 19

Wenger doesn't sell his best players

– PEP GUARDIOLA,
FORMER BARCELONA MANAGER

Holloway Road is alive with noise, fizzing with expectation and anticipation as Bailey patrons down their pints and punters finish off food outside burger vans. On Highbury corner, red and white and yellow and blue jerseys mix with the traffic, clogging up the buzzing thoroughfare as workers navigate the early-evening rush. Crossing the busy junction and across to Highbury fields, ducking under the bars towards the bright lights of 'The Grove', the atmosphere is one of fate – of what will be, will be. Up towards Drayton Park Station, past the giant A-R-S-E-N-A-L lettering where fans pose for photos and programme-sellers jangle change, the sounds of the Emirates Stadium fill the air with that unique sense of anticipation reserved only for European nights.

'*And it's Arsenal… ARS-ENAL F.C.… we're by far the greatest team the world has ever seen!*' Gooners fill the ground with noise as the teams arrive in the tunnel ready for the big game. The stadium emcee reads out the names of the Arsenal first team as the crowd dutifully fills in the blanks. 'In goal, Wojciech…' '…*Szczęsny!*'… 'Number three, Bacary…' '…*Sagna!*' 'Number four, Cesc…' '*Fàbregas!*' The players, meanwhile, walk out into the bright lights of the stadium and onto the perfectly maintained Emirates pitch. Eleven men with one objective… to beat the best football team to have ever played the game.

The match begins in much the same way as the previous encounter 11 months before. Barcelona, replete in cool mint green, dance around the slick Emirates pitch, playing their trademark *tiki-taka* and waiting for the right moment to play the ball through to their talented forwards. On 15 minutes, the Catalans have a glorious chance when Andres Iniesta plays a perfectly weighted pass through to Lionel Messi who, under pressure from Arsenal's Johan Djourou, dinks the ball past Arsenal goalkeeper Wojciech Szczęsny and past the outside of the far post. It's a massive moment early on in the tie and really should have been 1-0 to the Catalans.

Arsenal, though, grow into the game, and resurrect the steel and spirit of generations past by soaking up the Barcelona pressure and reciprocating with direct and formidable counter-attacking football. The Gunners' Robin van Persie, Theo Walcott and Cesc Fàbregas all have chances to put their side on the path to victory, but it is Barcelona who draw first blood in the tie: as Johan Djourou and Laurent Koscielny push up and keep a high line, Gael Clichy remains rooted to the spot and subsequently plays David Villa onside; Messi's through ball is exquisite and true, while

INTRODUCTION

David Villa, as ever, slots home under the onrushing Arsenal keeper, and peels away to celebrate by the corner flag with his teammates.

The second half begins in similar fashion, until the Catalans' high-pressure pressing game begins to show. As Barcelona tire, Arsenal take full advantage, and on 78 minutes their perseverance finally pays off. Arsenal left-back Gael Clichy plays a cunning pass over the heads of Barcelona's attack-minded full-back Dani Alves and Robin van Persie, from a very tight angle, drives the ball past a poorly positioned Victor Valdes to send Arsenal level. Moments later, after good defensive work from a certain 19-year-old Arsenal midfielder in the number 19 shirt, the Gunners peel away from the Catalans again: the youngster begins the move, sliding the ball to Cesc Fàbregas who plays a wonderful ball through to the right flank where it is picked up by Samir Nasri. As Barcelona retreat and regroup, Nasri picks out Andrei Arshavin who is sprinting through the heart of the Barcelona half; the Russian strikes the ball sweetly into the back of the Barcelona net and sends Ashburton Grove into raptures.

'And it's Arsenal... ARS-ENAL F.C.... We're by far the greatest team the world has ever seen!' Arsenal 2 Barcelona 1 – the best scoreline of the season so far, and one of the most significant scorelines of the Number 19's budding Arsenal career to date.

In the 18 months prior to the game, Wenger and the Arsenal faithful had seen the emergence of the most promising talent since the days Fàbregas stepped out against Rotherham

JACK WILSHERE: ARSENAL D.N.A.

United and celebrated scoring his first Arsenal goal by returning home and eating a *Kinder Egg*. The previous March, when Arsenal travelled to the Camp Nou to futilely try and capitalise on a 2-2 first leg home draw against FC Barcelona, young midfielder Jack Wilshere was recovering from a home defeat against Manchester United. The player, on loan from Arsenal, was plying his trade with Bolton Wanderers, contributing to a team that was struggling to keep itself above the Premier League parapet. Intended by Arsène Wenger to be his 'finishing school', Owen Coyle's Bolton Wanderers were slowly turning Wilshere from a boy to a man, and consolidating a process which had begun as a nine-year-old after he was scouted by the North London club. Dextrous, graceful and a true Arsenal lad, he was now, in February 2011, the chief instigator of an Arsenal move which resulted in them scoring the winning goal in a historic victory over one of the best teams for a generation – FC Barcelona.

The boy's rise from promising youth team prospect to the first name on Wenger's team sheet is the stuff of dreams for most 20-year-olds. Young, tenacious, competitive and driven, his presence in the tunnel at the start of the game is, arguably, a microcosm of Arsène Wenger's latest Arsenal project: that is, youth, intelligence and raw, unbridled talent. Comparisons were already being made with Arsenal youth team coach and former player Liam Brady – the chief instigator, no less, of *that* FA Cup final goal against Manchester United in 1979 – and the young man from Hitchin had already etched his name into the playing fabric of the north London club even before taking to the pitch against the Catalan giants.

INTRODUCTION

If that wasn't enough, by the time he was leaving the pitch after helping dispatch the Spanish side 2-1, he was being hailed as one of the truly exciting stars of both Arsenal's and England's footballing future. 'In French academies and African villages Wenger has pursued players capable of executing his vision of what football should be: a game of pace, skill, fluidity, adventure,' said Paul Hayward in an article in the *Guardian*. 'But all he had to do was motor north from the club's training ground at London Colney to a heartland of suburban Arsenal support. There he found the most gifted young English midfielder since Paul Scholes, who made his debut for Manchester United at the age Wilshere is now.' The difference, says Hayward, is that Scholes played Port Vale when he was a 19-year-old wonder kid; Wilshere, on the other hand, is a first team regular and has just received all the plaudits for containing the likes of Xavi Hernandez, Andres Iniesta, Lionel Messi and David Villa. *The Independent's* James Lawton concurred: 'Wenger's men showed strength where there was once weakness… For a while this was mostly a tribute to the pride of Cesc Fàbregas and his brilliant – and dogged – English lieutenant Jack Wilshere. They said no, they would not submit to the ceaseless passing rhythms of Messi and his assistants Xavi and Andres Iniesta.'

The Arsenal manager, moreover, put it slightly more succinctly: '[Jack] was outstanding tonight,' Wenger told *Arsenal.com*. 'He was not fazed by the occasion in difficult periods. He took the ball and got out of the pressure.' Jack was, in fact, slightly overwhelmed by the situation and was too shy to ask his heroes – the very players he shackled for the majority of the game – for their shirts. Responding to a *Twitter* picture of Jack and his dad Andy holding up Xavi and Messi's shirts, captain Cesc Fàbregas tweeted: 'Can't believe i had to go to get Messi's shirt for u. U were so scared…you were MOTM [Man of the Match] so ask yourself next time!'

A few days later, Barcelona coach Pep Guardiola was asked once again whether he was still interested in signing the Arsenal captain – a weekly transfer topic for the Spanish press, especially in the wake of their defeat to Arsenal only five days before. After telling the press that no, Arsenal will not sanction a transfer for Cesc Fàbregas, the eager Spanish press asked the Catalan coach about another certain 19-year-old Arsenal player and whether he might be in Guardiola's long-term plans?

'Arsenal are a wonderful side,' the Barcelona manager said in reply. 'You will not hear me discredit Arsenal – they are a great side with a great coach and they will be a very difficult opponent. [Wilshere] is a great player – a great player for Arsenal… And in any case, Arsène Wenger doesn't sell his best players.'

It was a very telling moment in the career of Jack Wilshere who was signed as a nine-year-old schoolboy at the turn of the century. His rise from promising wonder kid to one of the most influential players in the current Arsenal side came as no surprise to Wenger, Brady or the other coaches who had watched the young man from Hitchin become one of the most talented and technically gifted footballers of his generation. From three successive seasons as captain of The

INTRODUCTION

Priory school football team, through to experienced Arsenal first teamer and England international, it looked as if Jack Wilshere's time had finally arrived.

1 – BEGINNINGS
1991/92

*In which Arsenal are crowned Champions – the Premier League
is formed – Ian Wright tries to stop the rot – Andy Wilshere
keeps one eye on the football scores – we see something of
Hitchin's heritage and the Wilsheres hear the pitter-patter
of a very talented left foot!*

The penultimate 'old First Division' season, 1990/91, was an enormous success in more ways than one for Arsenal Football Club: along with winning the title and losing only one game throughout the campaign, the Gunners conceded only 18 goals – a statistic put into perspective when compared to second placed Liverpool's 40 goals 'against'. Yet football itself was stuck in a rut: hooliganism was rife throughout the country's stadia and the Heysel disaster of 1985 prevented English clubs from entering European competition. Arsenal's ascent to the top of the Championship elite didn't help either: George Graham's side weren't particularly well-renowned for their attacking style and creative finesse, the chant *boring, boring Arsenal* becoming the song of choice for any team visiting Highbury stadium.

Just as George Graham's Arsenal were getting their hands

on the First Division trophy in the summer of 1991, however, the so-called 'big five' of English football were beginning to hatch a plan. Having held talks with both LWT and cable broadcaster Sky – Manchester United, Tottenham Hotspur, Liverpool, Everton and Arsenal agreed that English football required some sort of cash injection if it was to bounce back from its lowest ever ebb. With television becoming the modern way to watch the game, the so-called 'Founding Members' signed an agreement to break away from the current Football League and persuaded the remaining 17 clubs to join a brand new league which was to be funded by investment stemming primarily from television. The 'Founding Members' agreed that this investment, in turn, should be divided equally between the league's elite 22 clubs, instead of being divided out between the 92 clubs of the original football league. The formation of the 'Premier League' – as it was known – thus signalled the beginning of the end for the 'old' First Division. With Sky TV owner Rupert Murdoch seeing an opportunity to turn around his loss-making company, the new Premier League was launched as a premium-rate platform for the top clubs of English football, where a new breed of modern, more cosmopolitan football would be played.

Thus Arsenal went into the last season of the old First Division – 1991/92 – as defending Champions, and it wasn't the start George Graham would have hoped for: an opening 1-1 home draw against QPR was followed by successive losses away to Everton and Aston Villa, before the Gunners finally recorded their first win of the season against Luton Town. The shaky start continued throughout the late summer and it wasn't until mid-September that Arsenal recorded more than two consecutive wins. Indeed it was the first of these victories – against south Londoners Crystal Palace – that George Graham saw the talents of a particular striker. Ian Wright, born in Arsenal's original hometown of Woolwich, was Crystal Palace's player of the season in 1989 and Graham had been tracking the young striker for a few years. Indeed, the game against the Eagles on 14th September 1991 confirmed to the Arsenal manager that Wright was the missing ingredient in a very defensive minded side.

Following a fair amount of courting from George Graham and Vice-Chairman David Dein, Ian Wright signed for Arsenal by the end of September and scored on his debut against Leicester City in a League Cup game. This was followed by a hat-trick away to Southampton, before scoring against Chelsea in a 3-2 win against their London rivals. Arsenal's new star striker – who had cost the club a record £2.5 million – couldn't stop the rot, however, and by the end of November the club found itself sixth in the division. A comfortable home win against Spurs in December, in which Wright and Kevin Campbell scored a goal a piece in a 2-0 win, didn't quash the mini-crisis in form and Arsenal – defending champions with the 'best' defence in the country – found themselves in lowly seventh as 1991 drew to a close.

Just over a month later and a New Year's Day victory against London rivals Wimbledon looked like the perfect tonic for a team supremely out of form. The Gunners had barely registered a point in the league since the beginning of December and were in desperate need of something against a team lying 17th in the table. Forty miles up the M1 in

Stevenage, meanwhile, Andrew Wilshere was keeping one eye on his wife Kerry, and one eye on the football scores on the telly. The former, after all, was in labour with their third child, whereas West Ham United were on a downward spiral towards the bottom of the First Division. The Hammers were playing Leeds United at home and desperately needed something from the game if they were to keep off the foot of the table. Having conceded back to back losses against Aston Villa and Notts County – and only registering a point since the end of November – West Ham had to start the new year with at least a draw if only to stop the rot. But it wasn't to be: by the end of the afternoon the Hammers were 1-3 down to United and hovering dangerously above the relegation zone. Arsenal drew too, not that it mattered to Kerry or Andrew Wilshere: by the time the first division players trudged off the cold pitches throughout the land, they were holding their newborn son Jack in their arms.

Ten miles north-east of Luton sits Hitchin, a market town nestled in a corner of Hertfordshire. Once described by historian Nikolas Pevsner as one of the most visually satisfying towns in the country, it has a population of around 30,000 people and is the hometown of many famous alumni: Bob Hope was said to have family in Hitchin, keeping touch with them right up to his death in 2003; technological guru Kane Kramer was born in Hitchin, and went on to be the inventor of the first ever digital audio player (typically referred to as the iPod); former tennis player and the 'Hurricane of Hitchin' Arvind Parmar was also born there, along with golfer Ian Poulter, and footballers Dave Kitson and Kevin Phillips.

An old market town built alongside the River Hiz and in close proximity to London, Hitchin prospered in the wool trade throughout the medieval period and also holds the dubious record for being the town where the biggest hailstones in history landed during a storm in 1697. Idyllic, suburban, with a very strong sense of community, Hitchin is the town where Andy and Kerry Wilshere settled and brought up their three children – Tom, Rosie and newborn Jack.

Despite the presence of Messrs Palmer and Phillips, Hitchin isn't particularly renowned for its sporting prestige or alumni. The town does have a football team, however, and Hitchin Town F.C. is currently based in the Southern League's central division. The original Hitchin F.C., formed relatively early for a football club in 1865, took part in the inaugural FA Cup in 1872, going on to lose to eventual runners-up Royal Engineers (who were one of the most successful FA Cup teams of the latter half of the 19th century, winning it in 1875 and reaching the final in 1872, 1874 and 1878). In fact, in its original guise, Hitchin F.C. is one of only three existing teams to have played in the oldest football competition in the world. In 1905, furthermore, they were the first team to win away in the 'fortress' that is Stamford Bridge!

Reformed in 1928 under the moniker Hitchin Town F.C., the Canaries held their own in London's Spartan and Athenian Leagues through the early part of the 20th Century (amateur leagues run throughout London and its surrounding districts), but it wasn't until 1958 that one of

JACK WILSHERE: ARSENAL D.N.A.

Hitchin's finest represented their country when Peter Hammond proudly played for England's Amateur side.

Hitchin's relationship with The Arsenal unsurprisingly predates Jack Wilshere: in 1958 – the same year Hammond was appearing in an England shirt – Laurie Scott took over management at Hitchin Town F.C., hoping to develop the club and bring it in to line with other slightly more progressive professional sides. The former international initially played for Bradford City, before joining George Allison's Arsenal side in 1937. Following a stint during the Second World War as an RAF pilot, Scott went on to become one of the best full-backs of his generation, and cemented his place in Gunner history, winning the first division title in 1948. The FA Cup followed in 1950 when Arsenal beat George Kay's Liverpool side at Wembley Stadium, and Scott was subsequently selected for England's World Cup squad in Brazil in 1950 (his appearances were limited, however, by the fact he was Alf Ramsey's understudy throughout the tournament). As a player, the Yorkshireman was among the finest of his generation: 'Scott, who served as a physical training instructor in the RAF during the war, was maturing into a fine all-round player,' read the *Independent* obituary after Scott's death in 1999. 'A crisp and combative tackler, he was quick to recover if a winger had the temerity to give him the slip, his distribution was sensibly safe and he was blessed with a shrewd positional sense.'

Working his way through the various non-leagues of the era, Scott found his way to Hertfordshire, bringing the experience of international tournaments and the class of Highbury to Hitchin: the 1960/61 season saw the Canaries finish in a respectable fifth position in the Athenian League and reach the semi-finals of the FA Amateur Cup. His success was curtailed by behind the scenes wrangling, however, and his departure saw replacement Vince Burgess take the club to second place in 1969 and win the London Senior Cup in 1970. The club meandered in and out of various Southern Division Leagues, right up until 1992/93, when manager Andy Melvin led the club back to the Premier Division by winning the First Division.

Hitchin and its semi-professional football club undoubtedly contributed to Jack's footballing heritage; the local footballing history and enthusiasm for the game can only serve as a strong base for any blossoming talent. The town itself has numerous playing fields and parks, including Windmill Hill with its beautiful views of the surrounding Hertfordshire countryside. Indeed, it was on these very playing fields that Jack Wilshere first kicked a ball; his dad Andy would frequently take his brother Tom and sister Rosie to the local park for a kickabout, and even as a baby who had only just learned to walk, Jack would love to join in with his sporty siblings. His enthusiasm and ability to learn quickly was apparent at a very young age; he would frequently ask his dad to take him out to the local pitch near their semi-detached house on Folly Close in Hitchin for a game of three-and-in or ''66'.

It was, of course, very far away from the flood-lit pastures of Highbury football stadium, and just as Jack was finding his feet in the world, Arsenal were finishing the last First Division season fairly strongly, with five wins and two draws from their remaining seven fixtures. They finished the

JACK WILSHERE: ARSENAL D.N.A.

1991/92 season in fourth position, trailing Sheffield Wednesday, Manchester United and champions Leeds United. Andy Wilshere's team West Ham, meanwhile, were relegated after winning only three games away from home all season.

The Gunners went on to become a prolific Cup side, winning the FA Cup and League Cup in 1993 and the European Cup Winners Cup in 1994. The first division, meanwhile, became the Premier League, and the Highbury faithful had to wait another six or so years before Arsenal were in a position to make another substantial title challenge. By that time Jack was in primary school and Arsenal were under the management of a certain French 'economist'.

2 – BECKHAM-ESQUE
1997/98 – 2001

In which Arsène Wenger makes a shrewd investment
in more ways than one – Liam Brady takes the reigns at the
new 'Academy' – and Jack begins primary school and
joins the LGC Eagles

Half-time at Highbury on 13th December 1997 and Arsenal were a goal up against Roy Hodgson's Blackburn Rovers. A decent display before the interval saw the Gunners take the lead after 18 minutes, when Emmanuel Petit spotted the run of Marc Overmars and played in the Dutchman who slotted the ball gratefully past goalkeeper Tim Flowers. The Gunners were in cruise control, and looking to kick-start their campaign after back-to-back losses against Sheffield Wednesday and Liverpool had threatened to de-rail their season. They were expected to beat Rovers and begin the slow ascent up the table to threaten the reign of defending champions Manchester United – the Red Devils had won four of the past five titles, and were threatening to run away with their fifth. Former champions Blackburn Rovers, however, hadn't followed the script and this particular result towards the end of 1997 would go on to define Arsenal's season in more ways than one.

Despite a decent start to the second half from the Gunners – in which the industrious Overmars very nearly played in Ian Wright only to be thwarted by Flowers – Blackburn forced their way back in to the game. Tony Adams' awful clearance from a corner resulted in Rovers finding Wilcox on the edge of the box and the midfielder converted with glee. Eight minutes later and Blackburn took control of the game: Tim Flowers' goal-kick was flicked-on by Chris Sutton and the ball was chased down the left by Kevin Gallacher, who hit it first time with his left foot. The shot may have been speculative but Gallacher's strike left the scrambling David Seaman with no chance. A late Tim Sherwood goal in the 89th minute sealed the game for Blackburn – the midfielder benefitting from a dubious offside call and beating the Arsenal goalkeeper – which pushed the Gunners to sixth in the league. George Graham's Leeds United, meanwhile, moved above Arsenal into fifth position after drawing 0-0 against Chelsea, while Liverpool comprehensively beat Crystal Palace 3-0 to also move above the Gunners.

The loss to Blackburn was a real kick in the teeth for this Arsenal side. Hotly tipped to challenge Manchester United for the title – particularly after acquiring Emmanuel Petit, Nicholas Anelka and Marc Overmars – Arsenal were now facing a mid-season struggle to keep up with the leading pack. Indeed, in his first full season in charge of the club, Arsène Wenger was facing his first substantial slump in form; a loss at home to the former Premier League Champions wasn't a disaster, but Wenger knew that to win the Premier League he had to turn Highbury into a fortress – a stadium where teams were afraid to play their own game. The Gunners had already lost at home to Liverpool (0-1) and drawn games against Spurs (0-0) and Aston villa (0-0) – both of which the Gunners really should have won. Following the loss to Blackburn, though, Wenger drew a line in the sand. According to *The Independent's* Ian Ridley, the previous loss to the Merseysiders triggered a little soul-searching within the Arsenal dressing room, and Wenger had a full and frank discussion with his playing squad. Adams and the all-English back four wanted more protection from the newly assembled French midfield, and Wenger had to remind Patrick Vieira and Emmanuel Petit of their defensive duties – asking them to alternate between supporting attack and defence.

The discussions did the trick. The loss to Blackburn in December 1997 was to be the last home league defeat for the Gunners in 22 months. Their unbeaten run lasted from December 1997 to September 1999, during which they won their first Premier League title (and their 11th First Division title), beating Manchester United to win the league by a solitary point. It was also the start of a very successful period for the Gunners, with Arsène Wenger cementing his place in the history books in more ways than one.

Success in 1998, however, brought its disadvantages. At the end of the 1998/99 season Arsenal's French superstar Nicholas Anelka was angling for a move out of Highbury. Disillusioned with Arsenal's form in the league – despite the Gunners only missing out on regaining their title by a single point to Manchester United in what turned out to be one of the closest title races of all time – the French striker began to feel unsettled and undervalued. His third full season at Highbury had been his best: 17 goals from 35 starts saw a decent return for the talented Frenchman. Signed in 1996 from Paris Saint-Germain for approximately £500,000, Arsène Wenger saw Anelka as one of the key players in Arsenal's quest for glory in many seasons to come.

Yet Anelka saw things differently. The Frenchman had been alerted of interest from clubs on the continent and began making demands Arsenal simply couldn't meet. Influenced rather crudely by his brother and agent Claude, Anelka wanted to significantly 'up' his wages to make him the top earner in the Premier League. Despite their recent success in the top flight, Arsenal couldn't afford the player's demands, and instead the club decided to cash in on one of their youngest and most talented assets.

By the close season in 1999, Anelka had more or less confirmed he wanted to leave Arsenal and 'Le Sulk' (so nicknamed by disgruntled Arsenal fans) was offered to a selection of top clubs on the continent. He signed for Real Madrid in August for approximately £22.3 million, making Arsène Wenger and Arsenal an astonishing profit of nearly £21.8 million. Not that Vice-chairman David Dein saw it that way: 'I'm not sure who the winner is in all this,' he told *The Guardian* at the time. 'We're receiving a lot of money but that is not what we're looking for. We've lost a talented player.'

Wenger, though, wasn't to be perturbed and with a full programme of Premier League and European football to contend with in the coming 1999/00 season, he immediately drafted in candidates to replace the disgruntled Anelka. His first piece of business was to sign Croat striker Davor Suker – leading goalscorer at the 1998 World Cup Finals in France – for approximately £3.5m. 'I thought he was outstanding in the last World Cup,' Wenger said of the Croat. 'He has quick feet and he is a quick thinker and he is always looking for goals.'

The manager's second piece of business was to shape Arsenal in the coming years in more ways than one.

'*Henry adds to Arsenal firepower*' ran the headline in *The Independent* on 4th August 1999. 'Thierry Henry yesterday became the second international striker to sign for Arsenal within two days when he moved from Juventus for an estimated £11m, a record fee for the Highbury club.' The young French maestro was enduring a tough time at Italian giants Juventus, being stuck out on the wing under coach Marcello Lippi. Wenger, though, saw Henry's clear potential and despite comparisons with the outgoing 'Le Sulk', drafted him in as a replacement for Anelka with a view to turning him into a bona fide centre forward.

By the end of August 1999, Arsenal had seen a world-class 20-year-old striker leave the club and be replaced by a 31-year-old Croat in the autumn of his career and a young, untested and rather enigmatic young winger. With £14.5 million of the 'Anelka money' spent, and approximately £7million of the 'Anelka money' remaining – Wenger, Dein and the Arsenal board turned their attentions to other areas of the club in need of financing: the dilapidated training centre and the youth team.

Arsenal F.C. had operated a youth team as far back as 1894. Indeed, players such as Peter Mortimer – a Glaswegian centre forward – sought 'top level' football at Woolwich

Arsenal, a club with a reputation for blooding youngsters as early as the late nineteenth century. The 19-year-old Scotsman was Woolwich Arsenal's top goalscorer in 1894, scoring an impressive 14 goals in 22 games.

The club's youth team really came into its own in the 1954, however, when the club entered a 'formal' team into the South Eastern Counties League for the first time. The same season the club entered the FA Youth Cup which was eventually won by a dominant Manchester United youth side (the Red Devils beat Wolverhampton Wanderers 5-4 on aggregate in the final). The Arsenal youth side progressed to the 1966 finals of the same competition where they were victorious against Sunderland, beating the Black Cats 6-3 on aggregate. During the same period, the team were competing in numerous leagues across London and the UK, including the London Minor FA Challenge Cup, and the Southern Junior Floodlit Cup. They were very successful too, winning seven South East Counties League titles, six South East Counties League Cups (including three 'Doubles') and four FA Youth Cups.

At the start of Arsenal's double-winning 1997/98 season, the aforementioned youth leagues were replaced by an umbrella Premier League, consisting primarily of the teams from the actual top-flight league. Split into northern and southern divisions, teams were allowed to enter an under-18 side which could include at least three under-19 players per match. A play-off system was integrated into the final part of the season, with teams paired off and playing a knockout game over two legs.

The irrepressible Arsenal youth side won the inaugural FA

Premier Youth League competition in 1998, beating rivals Spurs 2-1 in the final (the goals for Arsenal came from Terry Bowes and Omer Riza, in a team including Ashley Cole, Jay Bothroyd, Richard Hughes and Steve Sidwell). Hoping to build upon this success, Wenger and Dein looked to spend part of the recent transfer revenue on the Academy, with the majority being spent on refurbishing Arsenal's training complex at Hale End.

Wenger charged former Arsenal favourite Liam Brady with overseeing youth development at the club. The Irishman rejoined the North London side in 1996 after brief managerial stints at Celtic (1991-93) and Brighton (1993-95) and oversaw the aforesaid victory over Spurs in the inaugural competition. At the start of the 1999/00 season, as Anelka angled for a move away from Highbury, the Premier League decided to change the youth division's name to the FA Premier Academy League, and Arsenal concurrently renamed their youth development centre the 'Academy'. Brady and Wenger developed a scouting network to compete with the best teams in Europe and, with the youth side firing on all cylinders and Arsenal successful in the top-flight for the first time in 7 years, the club began to look forward to a bright, youthful future.

In the South East corner of Hitchin, just off Stevenage Road, lies Whitehill Junior School, a Hertfordshire County primary school. With around 200 pupils on its books, filling up around seven classrooms, it is a very typical local primary school, one of eleven based in the Hitchin area. 'The goal at Whitehill Junior School,' according to the school brochure, 'is to educate children for their future – a generation who learn how to learn and love doing it, who will look back on their schooling and say "I remember when...".'

Jack Wilshere joined the junior school in September 1997, following in the footsteps of brother Tom and sister Rosie. As with most kids of his age, starting school was a daunting prospect, but Jack was excited by the opportunity to indulge in one of his favourite hobbies. Along with the numeracy and literacy taught in every junior school, Whitehill was also keen on physical education and the school motto would go on to play a big part in Jack's later, footballing life: 'We work together for individual success'.

Always eager to play the game, the five-year-old Jack would relish the opportunity to show off his football skills during P.E. lessons, dominating most matches and hogging the ball in typical schoolboy fashion. Indeed, by the time he was in Year Three, Jack was already the captain of the school football team and his raw talent and natural ability with his left foot caught the eye of even the most diffident of spectators. He was following in the footsteps of his older siblings, with his brother Tom captaining Whitehill Boys football team and his sister Rosie one of only two girls to have also played for the school team. Jack's talents, furthermore, catapulted the team on to even dizzier heights. 'He wanted to win so much,' his former head-teacher Fran Bradshaw said to *The Daily Mail* of Jack's days as a primary school starlet. 'He would get so frustrated with his teammates because he wanted them to be able to do the same things he could. He would cry with frustration if it wasn't going well.'

Whitehill Junior School remains part of the English Schools Football Association, a governing body which was more or less the face of 'grass-roots' football up and down the country. Run by the English FA, it is responsible for developing football competitions for boys and girls at both primary and secondary school level. The organization runs tournaments from junior level upwards, including various trophies such as the Under-11 seven-a-side Schools Cup and ESFA Under-18 Colleges' Trophy. Along with giving young footballers the opportunity to win some local kudos and become heroes within their communities, tournaments run by the ESFA also provide a wider platform upon which young players can display their talent. Scouts employed by numerous top-league sides – from the second division upwards – regularly attend county competitions in the quest to find the next British superstar. Wayne Rooney, for instance, was spotted and monitored by Everton scout Bob Pendleton, netting 99 goals in his final season for Copplehouse Boys' School in the local leagues before being snapped up by the Merseyside Club. Arsenal midfielder Aaron Ramsey, furthermore, was spotted by a scout at an Urdd Tournament in Wales [Welsh Youth Tournament], and duly signed by Cardiff City before eventually transferring to Arsenal.

Premier League football scouts travel the world looking for talented individuals to sign for their respective clubs. They examine general technical ability – such as touch, control and dribbling ability – as well as stamina, position and marking abilities. Intelligence and personality are also a massive factor for many scouts, and Arsenal manager Arsène Wenger has repeatedly referred to footballing intelligence when discussing the necessary attributes of a Premier League player. Once a player is spotted at a particular tournament, the individual is normally recommended to a club who monitor them for part or whole of a season. With the exception of certain players such as Ian Wright – who came to top flight football at the 'old' age of 22 – most top footballers are picked up by scouts relatively young: teenagers Steve Bruce and Alan Shearer, for example, were spotted by legendary scout Jack Hixon, who relayed the talents of Mr. Shearer to (at the time) First Division stalwarts Southampton. Arsenal, furthermore, is renowned for its scouting networks, particularly in South America and Africa. Former Brazilian Under-17s captain Denilson, for instance, was spotted by the club's South American scout Sandro Orlandelli playing for Sao Paulo in 2005 and just over a year later the young Brazilian was lining up in Arsène Wenger's first team having transferred to the club for just over £3 million.

Back in 1997, as part of the Hertfordshire County FA, Whitehill Junior School entered the National Schools Finals, and a five-year-old Jack was chosen as team captain. The young Hitchinian had been gradually making a name for himself as a player at Whitehill, and his winning mentality was catching on within the team. News of Jack Wilshere's talent, furthermore, was spreading throughout the county. 'All the teams had heard of him,' recalls head teacher Bradshaw, 'and the attention was almost Beckham-esque.'

Indeed, Jack's enthusiasm for the game and all round self-belief brought his first foray into school competitions and his first opportunity to show his stuff in front of one or two local scouts. As Bradshaw recalls, the young talisman took his team to the ESFA Under-12s final in Ipswich and came back victorious: 'It was because of him that we got through to the National Schools Finals in Ipswich,' she told *The Daily Mail*. 'His commitment and dedication was extraordinary. He didn't just come in here as a flash player – he had real application and determination. He used to get frustrated that other children weren't seeing what he was. He was so football-intelligent. He just had it.'

The hunger didn't stop there. Away from junior school Jack was busy playing for local side Letchworth Garden City Eagles, a Charter Standard FA Development club based on the grounds of the old Letchworth leisure centre. Founded in 1978 and originally intended as an 'outlet' for boys living on the local Westbury estate in Hitchin, the club was the closest thing Jack had to decent, competitive football at his level. 'It was originally called Westbury Eagles but later changed its name to LGC Eagles as number of teams increased,' recalls club chairman Tony Eden to *Football Focus* magazine. 'I have been involved with Eagles since the early 1990s when my son started to play football, and became chairman in 1995/6. There are now over 450 registered players at mini soccer and junior level… so youth football is very important to the club.'

Attending Whitehill during the school week and playing for Letchworth Eagles at the weekends, it was only a matter of time before the eight-year-old Jack Wilshere was finally spotted by a scout. But for the time being his talent was simply unmistakable to the parents who would come to watch their kids play on the fields of Letchworth and Hitchin: Jack controlled the game from the middle of the park, always wanting the ball, always wanting to play a teammate in and provide them with a goal-scoring opportunity. The schoolboy wanted to win so much he more or less dragged his team through games, showing an ability that was significantly beyond his age and a winning mentality that would endear him to the thousands of Arsenal fans who would visit the Emirates Stadium in years to come. Despite being the top of his class, the young Wilshere was only just starting to play with the 'big boys' and it was the next chapter of his life which was going to prove to be the most demanding. From having a kickabout with his dad Andy on the green, to being captain of Whitehill Primary school, Jack Wilshere's footballing career was only just beginning.

3 – THE CULT OF
DI CANIO
2001/02

*In which Jack is spotted by a scout from a local side – joins the
'cult of Di Canio' – Wenger makes one or two shrewd signings
and promotes a player from the Academy – Steve Rowley jumps
on a train to Luton – Jack is shown around the Hale End
Academy and watches his new team win a trophy*

Luton Town F.C. had hit a brick wall by the turn of the
new Millennium. Over 10 years after the club led by club
legend Brian Stein knocked three past the mighty Arsenal
(and, of course, one of the most renowned defences in the
country) in the League Cup Final at Wembley, the Hatters
were now at a crossroads at the end of 1999. The previous
two seasons saw the club register respectable finishes in the
Football League's second division and even a decent run in
the League Cup in 1998, yet dealings behind the scenes were
taking their toll. Despite the club's relative success in the run
up to the new Millennium, the turn of the new century saw
manager after manager being drafted in to revitalise a team
that had gone stale, along with players being sold to balance
the books.

In the summer of 2000, the club was purchased by Mike

Watson-Challis, who immediately promoted former player Ricky Hill to club manager. The club began to fall down the table, however, and Hill's tenure was short-lived; he was replaced by another former player, Lil Fucillo, who was also sacked a few months later due to a run of bad form in the league. Former Wimbledon manager Joe Kinnear was drafted in to shore up the defence and try and turn things around, but Luton Town F.C.– for the first time since 1968 – were relegated from the Football League's Second Division.

Naturally, it was the start of a difficult decade for the team and the constant managerial shift and changes in playing staff would affect the club for years to come. The club's youth system, however, was beginning to reap dividends, and in 2001, whilst playing for his primary school, Jack Wilshere's footballing career became briefly intertwined with the ups and downs of the Hatters.

While putting in one of his characteristic shifts for Whitehill Primary school, Jack was spotted by a Luton Town Youth Scout who immediately looked into signing the kid to the Bedfordshire outfit. Despite its parent club's relative troubles in the football league, Luton Town's youth system was immensely respected by footballing bodies throughout the domestic leagues, and Jack was simply the next talented footballer to catch the eye of Luton Town's ever-watchful scouts. Luton Town's development programme is second to none and Jack was following in the footsteps of numerous other players before him who made the step up from schoolboy to youth team football. Former Arsenal centre-back Matthew Upson joined the Hatters youth team in 1999 after stints at his hometown clubs, and West Ham midfielder

Matthew Taylor also played for the Luton Town Youth Team, having impressed playing for his school team and Oxford United.

Luton Town's youth development is more or less exclusive to Britain, with scouts concentrating their efforts in and around the local football pitches of London, the Home Counties and much of the North. Based on a pyramid filtering system which encourages young talent to the top, around 25 scouts work under a Recruitment Officer, each of whom separates the 'talent' from the 'deadwood'. Basing its 'pupils' within 12 regional football centres which are filled out by approximately 1,000 talented young footballers, coaches and scouts select around 25% of the top crop to be sent to the Centre of Excellence with a view to gaining a coveted place in the Luton Town Youth Team.

According to *IMScouting.com*, in recent years the Luton Town Youth Team has generated large dividends for the club, 'with around £20 million generated by the club through the players they have produced in the last 25 years'. Along with Upson and Taylor, the likes of Curtis Davies, Emmerson Boyce and Jerome Thomas can all count themselves as graduates from the Hatters' youth team set-up and the club is considered to be one of the most consistent and reliable youth teams in the country. Indeed, *IMScouting.com* – formerly one of the leading scouting facilities on the web – acknowledges the talent Luton Town Youth Development have provided for numerous top teams throughout the football league: 'There is no room for complacency at Luton, with coaches constantly pushing the players to move on to the next level. The progression to the youth team is clear for all recruits to see, and the first-team manager's readiness to pick young players into his first-team squad is an added impetus. Luton Town is seen as a great chance for young players who, if good enough, will invariably be given every opportunity to break through.'

In fact, in August 2010, the Premier League commissioned a report to find out the origin of each player in the division. Luton Town, according to the report, were especially highlighted as having an exceptional record, with eight graduates now plying their trade in England's top division. Luton Town F.C. – a member of the Blue Square Premier division at the start of the 2010/11 season – were placed in the official top five, just under Premier League stalwarts Manchester United (22 graduates), West Ham United (16), Manchester City (11) and Everton (9).

Luton Town youth scout Dean Rastrick spotted Jack while he was still in primary school. The future 'performance manager' at Tottenham Hotspur, Rastrick also had previous stints as assistant academy manager at Norwich City, where he unearthed numerous young prodigies of varying footballing abilities. It was during a game playing for Letchworth Garden City Eagles that Jack was spotted by Rastrick: the young Hitchinian's boundless energy, ability, and self-belief caught the eye of the Luton scout, who immediately signed him to the Hatters' academy.

This was 2001 – when Jack was only nine – but the boy wonder already had plenty of football under his belt and his eagerness to play and express himself on the pitch was close to boiling point: 'I played rugby and hockey but nothing came as easily as football,' Wilshere would later recall to *The*

Times. 'It came naturally, I think. I was always playing with my brother and his older mates when I was three or four and against older people, because they're more developed, you have to learn to handle yourself physically and to beat them using a trick. I practiced – everybody has to – but I didn't find skills difficult.'

The Premier League was nine seasons old in 2001, and Jack would watch the highlights on *Match of the Day* religiously, taking notes from the likes of Bergkamp, Beckham and Zola and imitating his heroes on the pitch whilst playing for Letchworth Eagles. There was one player in particular, however, who really stood out for Jack, and he played for his dad's favourite team.

In January 1999, Paulo Di Canio signed for West Ham United for £1.7 million. The 31-year-old had played for numerous club sides across the continent, beginning his career with boyhood club Lazio, before moving to giants of the Italian game Juventus; this was followed by stints at Napoli, Milan, and Celtic, before Di Canio joined Sheffield Wednesday for £4.2 million. The Italian made an immediate impact for the owls in the 1997-98 season, scoring 14 goals to become top goalscorer and was named 'player of the season' by fans of the club.

A massively popular figure both on and off the pitch, Di Canio's success was tainted by various controversies, with an incident in a game against Arsenal a particular lowlight in an otherwise celebrated career in English football. The game at Hillsborough in September 1998 was nicely balanced, with the two teams scrapping to get a footing in an otherwise indifferent contest. Arsenal were on a high, having beaten title rivals Manchester United 3-0 in front of the Highbury faithful in an early-season showdown; the Owls, on the other hand, had started the season inconsistently, winning only two of the first seven games of the season and conspiring to lose the rest.

Just before half time, Arsenal's Patrick Vieira was hauled to the ground by Wednesday's Wim Jonk, and the Frenchman retaliated by shoving Jonk. The Dutchman went to ground rather theatrically and a 10-man brawl ensured, with Paulo Di Canio seemingly leading the march against Vieira and his Arsenal counterparts. The Italian, recalls *The Independent's* Phil Andrews, 'was clearly seen to aim a kick at the Arsenal centre-back [Martin] Keown, whose only offence seemed to be to defend himself against the onslaught.' Spotted by referee Paul Alcock, Di Canio was immediately sent off and the Italian responded by 'giving the referee a petulant two-handed shove in the chest that sent him staggering back to end up sprawled on the pitch.' The British media immediately jumped on Di Canio's outrageous reaction to the red card, with many newspapers running headlines alluding to English football 'returning to the dock' only a few years after the rebranding of the game by the English Premier League. 'I just don't know what went through [Di Canio's] mind,' Sheffield Wednesday manager Danny Wilson said after the game. 'His emotions were very mixed up and the best thing to do was to get him down the tunnel and out of the ground as quickly as possible.'

Indeed, it was Di Canio's emotional attachment to the game and the way he wore his heart on his sleeve (alongside the badge of whichever club he represented) which drew fans to the 'cult' of Di Canio, and only five months after the referee-shoving incident at Hillsborough, Di Canio was offloaded to West Ham United. It was a move which suited all parties: Wednesday wanted rid of a troublesome player who divided the dressing room, West Ham acquired a much needed striker to bolster their strike-force, and Di Canio remained a Premier League player.

West Ham were struggling to find form in a very competitive league prior to Di Canio's arrival in January 1999: despite a respectable start to their season which culminated in a win against Tottenham that sent the Hammers second in the league in November 1998, a run of bad results against Leeds, Middlesbrough, Arsenal and Manchester United dropped the Hammers back down to earth with a bump. In fact January 1999 was awful for the East End club, with three losses (including two at home) and a draw pushing the team as low as ninth in the league. Di Canio's transfer, however, triggered a period of decent form in the latter half of the season, and West Ham fulfilled Harry Redknapp's ambitions, finishing the league campaign in fifth position – their highest league position since they finished third in 1986 – and with a European spot to boot (a place in the now defunct Intertoto Cup).

It was during the 1999/2000 campaign, however, when Di Canio inspired a very young and very impressionable Mr. Wilshere, and the volley scored against lowly Wimbledon on a sunny day in March 2000 is one of Jack's favourite Premier League goals of all time. The sublime strike in front of the Upton Park faithful was awarded

'Goal of the Season' by Match of the Day in the summer of 2000, and was also dubbed 'Goal of the Decade' by Sky Sports News in 2009: Trevor Sinclair's perfectly weighted ball to Di Canio deep inside Wimbledon's box was met with a perfectly struck – and rather audacious – volley straight into the corner of The Dons' net. Di Canio's manager Harry Redknapp would go on to say that Paulo Di Canio 'did things with the ball that made you grasp' and this was one such example. Wilshere concurs: 'I used to look up to him for some of the goals he scored.'

For the young Wilshere, the West Ham of the Di Canio era was his 'first' team in terms of education and inspiration: 'My family have always been West Ham fans, so growing up I used to go and watch them and so I was a West Ham supporter,' he told *The Daily Mirror*. 'I remember my first game was against Coventry, in 2000, Di Canio scored a hat trick and they won 5-0 so I enjoyed it.' In fact the game against the Sky Blues capped off a relatively decent month for the Hammers, which began with a 2-1 win against Wimbledon at the end of March and ended in the comprehensive win against Coventry in front of Jack and his dad Andy. Inconsistency was the story of West Ham's season, however, and despite this late surge in form, the Hammers conspired to lose their next three games (against Middlesbrough, Arsenal and Sunderland) and draw their final game against Leeds. They finished the season in ninth position – not as respectable as their fifth place finish in the previous season, but a decent finish nevertheless.

Jack, meanwhile, had a few decisions to make. After meeting with Dean Rastrick and the Luton Town Youth

Development program, the nine-year-old kid and his father Andy discussed the possibilities of leaving Letchworth City Garden Eagles and taking up a post with the Hatters. There were advantages and disadvantages: at Letchworth, Jack was talk of the side and the first name on the manager's team sheet, the playmaker of the team and the hero of countless wins over numerous teams from the same area. His fame locally was almost 'Beckham-esque' and teams feared his talent and vision when he was on the ball. If, on the other hand, Jack left the Eagles and took up a position at Luton, he'd be a small fish in a big pond – another talented playmaker with bags of talent but with everything to prove; he'd have to demonstrate his boundless ability to a new head coach and gain respect from his new teammates. Most importantly, though, it was a *massive* opportunity: Luton Town's youth development program was immensely respected throughout the country and Jack's dad Andy knew that this was a big step towards something incredible. Yet with the slate clean and new obstacles to face, it was time for Jack to commit fully to the game he loved to play.

Finishing second to Manchester United for the third time running, Arsenal manager Arsène Wenger sought to bring in some fresh faces to revitalize his squad at the start of the 2001/02 season. Following Nigel Winterburn's sale to West Ham in 2000, Wenger's primary concern was replacing an aging yet dogged (and very successful) back four. Steve Bould left Arsenal in 1999 to spend a season at Sunderland; Tony Adams and Lee Dixon were thinking of retiring at the end of the 2001/02 campaign.

Wenger thus alerted his scouts across the globe to begin the search for world class talent to fill the void left by the famous 'back four'. The manager's trusty network came up with two relatively unknown centre halves: Greek defender Efstathios Tavlaridis and Ivory Coast international Kolo Touré. Both untested in the English top-flight, Wenger hedged his bets and sought an experienced defender to shoulder the responsibility alongside Tony Adams in what would be his last season at the club. Looking no further than the end of the Seven Sisters road, Wenger made one of his most astute and controversial signings of his Arsenal tenure.

In January 2001 Sol Campbell was locked in to contract negotiations with Tottenham Hotspur and his agent, Sky Andrew, was touting the player around many of Europe's top clubs. The player, however, was adamant that he wanted to remain a Tottenham player and win things at the North London club: 'I can assure everyone that I won't be signing for another club while I am still a Spurs player. There have been numerous times when I could have just walked away and said "I've had enough, I'm leaving." I haven't done that because I want to be here. It annoys me that people question my loyalty to the club... I want to win the Premiership and I want success in Europe but, most of all, I want to believe I can achieve that here.'

Seven months later, Wenger signed Campbell to Arsenal on a free transfer. In a move that outraged one half of North East London, Campbell came to an Arsenal side pressing for honours and looking to build on the recent league successes only a few years earlier. Campbell was one of the very few players to have made the jump from the north end of the

Seven Sisters Road to the south; it was a move which underlined the growing sense of player power within the Premier League – that is, players moving not primarily for the love of the club, but more for the quest of silverware. Campbell would be vindicated by the end of the season, of course, but his move was to prove a symbolic moment in the modern history of the Arsenal-Tottenham rivalry. Wenger, pleased to have found a natural replacement for Adams, now turned his attention to another pressing problem in his squad: the left back position.

It was the purchase of a young, talented Brazilian full-back which precipitated the sale of Nigel Winterburn only a few seasons earlier. Signed from Corinthians in 1999, Sylvinho was a lightning-fast, attacking full-back, and brought a fresh approach to an Arsenal back four which was impeccable defensively but limited creatively. Displacing Winterburn for the majority of the 1999/2000 campaign, the Brazilian had a mixed career with the Gunners: he was on the losing side when Arsenal crashed out of the UEFA Cup Final on penalties; he also missed a penalty for the Gunners against Middlesbrough in the League Cup. It wasn't to be his playing style which capped a short Arsenal career, however: in 2001, Portugal notified Arsenal that they had no record of Sylvinho's dual Brazilian-Portuguese nationality and even went as far as allegedly accusing Sylvinho of forging passport documents. Not wanting to enter murky waters with the Portuguese Immigration, Arsenal offloaded the Brazilian in the summer of 2001, selling him to Celta Vigo for an undisclosed amount.

Waiting in the wings was an 20-year-old left back from

Tower Hamlets. Ashley Cole – an Arsenal fan who had grown up watching the likes of Kenny Samson and Nigel Winterburn – was a graduate of the Arsenal Academy, and had been recommended to Wenger by youth director Liam Brady. Part of the team which won the Under-18s FA Premier Academy League after the influx of cash from the Anelka sale in 1999, Cole was reportedly on the verge of joining Crystal Palace when Arsène Wenger drafted him in to the first team squad for the start of the 2001/02 season. The young Cole was more or less fully integrated with the first team, watching his heroes train from afar as a 14-year-old youth team player, before making his way in to the Reserves.

His subsequent promotion to the first team was to prove a masterstroke, and Ashley Cole turned out to be the most successful Arsenal Academy graduate to date. When asked by the magazine *Soccerlens.com* which player has been the Academy's biggest success story, Liam Brady concurred: 'Ashley Cole. It was very satisfying for myself and my colleagues because when we signed him initially he wasn't one of the more highly rated boys. At 14 or 15 we never thought that Ashley was going to be a superstar and play for England. What he did possess was a real passion to play the game and real dedication for it. He also had the speed and aggression needed and that enabled him to take off once he got into the first team.'

Tower Hamlets-born Cole's ascension to the first team was a real testament to the ongoing development within Arsenal's youth teams ever since becoming an Academy. His promotion represented the excellent work done by

Wenger's domestic scouts, and with the addition of locally 'sourced' Sol Campbell, it also underlined the (at the time) unfashionable notion that local talent was good enough to fill the void left by an attacking Brazilian full-back.

Speed, aggression and self-belief, as Brady notes: all ingredients for success at the top level. Around about the same time Cole was making his first team debut for the Gunners in the summer of 2001, Liam Brady was alerted to the talent and unheralded self-belief of a certain nine-year-old dazzling for the Luton Town youth side.

With a promising mix of young talent mixing with the old guard, Arsenal's start to the 2001/02 season was rather unusual. By the end of August, the Gunners had played three games, scoring nine goals in the process, but still found themselves in sixth position in the league. They opened the campaign with a decent win against Middlesbrough at the Riverside Stadium, beating 'Boro 4-0, with goals from Thierry Henry, Gilberto Silva and a brace from Sylvain Wiltord.

Three days later Leeds United arrived at Highbury for an evening kick-off. The Whites had travelled to north London looking to disrupt Arsenal's flowing, direct style, and with four yellow cards inside the first 18 minutes for David O'Leary's team, it looked as if their tactics might just pay off when Ian Harte scored the opening goal. Sylvan Wiltord's reply just after the half-hour mark did little to cool an already tempestuous affair and by the middle of the second half – with the Gunners now trailing 2-1 due to a Mark Viduka goal – no less than 8 players were on yellow cards. Arsène Wenger brought on Giovanni Van Bronckhorst and Francis Jeffers to no avail, and by the time the referee blew the final whistle (having booked a total of nine players and sent off Leeds United's Lee Bowyer), Arsenal had suffered their first defeat of the season only two games in to the campaign.

Despite the shaky start, Arsenal found some form going in to September, and went on a relatively long unbeaten run until November, beating the likes of Fulham, Derby County and Southampton, while drawing with a resurgent Chelsea at Stamford Bridge, Blackburn Rovers and Sunderland. Talk of the title was kept to an absolute minimum, however, as Arsène Wenger sought to keep his team focused on keeping themselves in the mix and see where they are as they headed into the New Year and the final stretch of the season.

Jack, in the meantime, was dividing his time between playing for his new club Luton Town and watching West Ham struggle to put together a win in the first half of the 2001 season. Opening their campaign with two losses against Chelsea and Leicester City, the Hammers went on a dreadful run which saw them only win one of the first 10 fixtures of the season. By the beginning of December, the Hammers languished in 16th position in the league, two positions above the relegation zone – at the time occupied by Southampton, Derby City and Ipswich Town (the latter two of the three would eventually be relegated) – although five points clear of the Saints in 18th. Andy and his son would go to a few games here and there, but playing the game soon became the most important thing in Jack's life.

The young Mr. Wilshere was now plying his trade for new club Luton Town Youths after switching from Letchworth Garden City Eagles. It wasn't an easy decision to make since the boy was very popular with the local side and the coaches had contributed a lot to his playing style and overall confidence. Yet when Dean Rastrick appeared at the Letchworth Garden training centre with an irresistible offer of unlimited game time and first class coaching, Jack and his dad Andy couldn't resist, and a few months later, Jack joined Luton Town's 'School of Excellence'.

Luton Town's reputation, of course, attracted scouts from across the country. Indeed, by 2001, Premier League clubs were employing hundreds of scouts and spending millions in the pursuit of the next Michael Owen or David Beckham. The ambition of the clubs, coupled with the international appeal of Premier League football, had propelled scouting into the big time, and it was only a matter of time before fans of the club were scouring their own scout-fed Youth Teams to find out about the players of tomorrow. At the turn of the new Millennium – almost 10 years after the Premier League was introduced in 1992 – the English top division was only just starting to realise its full potential in terms of both entertainment and finance. The arrival, furthermore, of Wenger more or less began (or heavily contributed to) the influx of the 'foreign' in to modern day football and arguably triggered the Premier League's proud international appeal. Of course, the continental heroes of Cantona, Schmeichel and Anelka had already made a massive mark on the game throughout the nineties. The Premier League in the turn of the 21st Century, however, had become obsessed with worldwide talent scouting and the enduring quest for rough diamonds hidden in amongst the minor leagues of South America, Africa and South East Asia.

JACK WILSHERE: ARSENAL D.N.A.

Naturally, the Arsenal scouting system had already been markedly developed since Arsène Wenger's arrival in 1996. Prior to the Frenchman's tenure at the club, scouts were rarely sent outside London to find talent to play for the team, let alone to Europe or even further afield. When Wenger arrived, the contacts the Frenchman had built up across the world allowed the Arsenal scouting network to expand internationally.

The change brought about by Wenger can be illustrated by one of Arsenal's longest serving members of staff. Head scout Steve Rowley had been working for the club for over 30 years and his discoveries included the likes of a very young Ray Parlour. His job changed considerably, though, once Wenger came on the scene: 'Previously, a trip outside the home counties was considered an event for an Arsenal scout', writes *The Telegraph's* Jonathan Northcroft of Rowley's involvement in Wenger's revolutionary scouting system. 'At their first meeting, Wenger said: "Steve, this weekend I want you to go to… Teresina." It is a city in northern Brazil, requiring a journey to Rio de Janeiro, then a further five-hour flight to reach it. Rowley had travelled no further than Spain on holiday. Now he has more air miles than the Space Shuttle.' Rowley, according to Northcroft is very, very thorough, and 'insists on watching every youngster personally before he is recommended to Wenger.'

Rowley himself gave an insightful interview to *YoungGunsBlog.co.uk* in 2008, in which he divulged how Arsenal arrange their scouting system to find talent for the club. Using a mixture of veteran scouts and former players already versed in the 'Arsenal way', Rowley heads an internationally renowned scouting system with an impeccable reputation amongst the elite clubs of Europe. Geographically, says Rowley, Arsenal's scouting system is second to none: 'I have 12 scouts based in the UK,' he told the website, 'and we have a worldwide network… We have our former left-back Danny Karbassiyoon in America, and he covers Mexico too. Then we have Sandro Orlandelli who looks after the scouting in Brazil, Argentina and the rest of South America, along with Pablo Budner and Everton Gushiken. Bobby Bennett does all of Scandinavia, where he has been doing a great job for seven years. We have Francis Cagigao who does Spain and Portugal while Gilles Grimandi does France and Switzerland. Jurgen Kost covers Germany, Czech Republic, places like that. Then we have Tony Banfield in Italy, Slovenia and Croatia. Finally we have Peter Clarke, another of our former players, who is based in Holland.'

All bases were covered at Arsenal and Wenger would seek constant updates from Rowley and his network of cosmopolitan scouts. Yet despite such a grand expansion both geographically and financially, Rowley didn't need to look much further than their own back yard to find one of the most promising youngsters to emerge on the scene since he signed-up an 11-year old Tony Adams in the early 1980s.

Sean O'Connor had alerted Rowley about a certain young man playing for the Luton Town Youth Team. A member of Rowley's 12-man strong domestic scouting team, O'Connor had been monitoring players at Luton for years and relaying all information back to Rowley at Hale End via a scouting database. He had also built up a rapport with the coaches, players and other scouts at the club, constantly discussing a certain player's development and potential. Alerted to a certain player by a domestic scout, Rowley would usually ask his scout to continue watching the player. 'There is no set number of times we watch a player', Rowley told *YoungGunsBlog.co.uk*. 'For [Cesc] Fàbregas, for example, you watch him once or twice and that's enough. Other players though may play in a poor league, so you need to watch them more when they come up against a good team.'

O'Connor was very impressed with one player in particular at the club and implored Rowley to come out to Bedfordshire to assess him. Rowley, always trusting of his scouting staff, hopped on the next train to see what the fuss was about. He didn't have to wait long. It was in a youth game against Arsenal's traditional pre-season first-team opponents Barnet that a nine-year-old Jack Wilshere proved to Mr. Rowley he had what it takes. It turned out that another of Arsenal's domestic scouts was the referee.

Having only played a few games for Luton Town, Jack was already at the heart of the midfield, pulling the strings much in the same way he did for the Letchworth Garden City Eagles. Versatile, athletic, and incredibly passionate, Wilshere stood out amongst his teammates as being a player of genuine ability. Above all else, he had intelligence – a commodity that Arsenal and Wenger ultimately place above all other attributes: 'Wenger believes footballers must tick four boxes,' writes Northcroft. 'Only two relate to the physical; intellect and mentality are the others. Players with brain-power, he feels, analyse themselves and improve quicker.'

Encouraged by what he and his fellow scouts saw, Rowley

immediately reported back to Wenger. Rowley normally tries to gather all of the available information on the player – from his best playing positions, to where he is based and how long he has been playing the game: 'After I've watched the player', Rowley told *YoungGunsBlog.co.uk*, 'I compile a dossier for the manager, and also a video which contains the player's good and bad points. The manager is so, so good at assessing a player that he can say straight away whether he likes what he sees or not.' Wenger, wanting only the very, *very* best for the Youth Team, drew on O'Connor's contacts to look into Jack's background and assess whether he would fit in to the Arsenal set-up at Hale end, and then, 'when [Wenger's] made the decision,' says Rowley, 'we move quickly to seal the deal.'

With the nod from Wenger and Liam Brady, Rowley approached Luton and Andy Wilshere with a view to signing Jack to the Arsenal Academy. Jack had only just left Letchworth Eagles to join Luton and settle with the Bedfordshire side; he'd made loads of new friends, and was enjoying his new surroundings and playing against other players of similar ability. The approach was totally unexpected and came as a complete shock to Jack and his family.

Indeed, the choice presented to Andy and his nine-year-old boy was rather overwhelming; only a few years previous, Jack was the captain of Whitehill Primary School football team – a little, local 'legend', content with the ball at his feet and his feet firmly on the ground. Now, in the presence of Arsenal Youth Director (and footballing legend) Liam Brady, and with the opportunity of signing for the

Academy at one of the biggest clubs in the world, Jack had to make a decision which would no doubt affect the rest of his – and his family's – life. Leaving the Letchworth Garden City Eagles was difficult enough; to up and leave Luton Town – a club with an amazing youth reputation in its own right – and join Arsenal F.C., with its tradition, history and heritage, and meet some of the greatest names in contemporary football, *and* play within touching distance of Adams, Petit, and Henry, was something not even the most ambitious nine-year-olds would ever dream of. But here was Jack Wilshere, a kid from Hitchin, suddenly with the world at his feet.

The Arsenal scouting team, meanwhile, couldn't believe their luck. 'Everyone connected with those very young age groups felt Jack was exceptionally gifted,' Liam Brady told the BBC a few years later. 'He had instant control, a good football brain, a lovely left foot and he could beat people. Even from those early days he showed tremendous determination to make it.'

Jack's dad Andy, naturally, had a list of questions to ask the Arsenal representatives before Jack committed to the club. His main concern was where Jack would live while training and playing at Arsenal's Hale End Academy. He also wanted to know about the current set-up and how a kid of Jack's age could progress at a club with such a talented playing squad. Hoping to allay any concerns, Rowley showed Jack and his dad around the Arsenal training facilities at the Hale End Training Centre, and introduced the pair to youth team coach Roy Massey. A former Arsenal youth apprentice and centre-forward at Rotherham United, Leyton Orient and Colchester United, Massey re-joined

Arsenal in 1999 following a coaching tenure at Norwich City. Head Coach for all levels from the Under-9s through to the Under-16s, Massey manages approximately 120 kids at the Hale End Training centre and is responsible for integrating new recruits in to the club. The man would be the first point of call for Jack and the first in a long line of Arsenal and England Coaches who were to develop Jack's raw footballing talent.

Meeting Jack for the first time at the age of nine, Massey wasn't surprised by the young man's ability – in fact it merely emphasised the good work being done by Rowley and the Arsenal scouting system: 'It amazes me how good our scouts are,' Massey told the *Waltham Forest Guardian*. 'If you're looking at a lad who is six or seven [years old] you're looking to see if he can run. Then you're looking to see if he's got some spirit, if he's got some personality to play in the game. Then you might look to see if he's got some sort of intelligence when he's got the ball.'

Jack, unsurprisingly, had it all – the pace, the winning mentality and, of course, the intelligence – so he was the right fit for Arsenal. But Jack and his dad Andy were wondering whether Arsenal was the right fit for the Wilsheres.

Speaking to *The Times* eight years after joining Arsenal, Jack recalls his hesitations about joining the Arsenal youth set up: 'When I had to pick between Luton and Arsenal, it sounds stupid but I didn't choose until the last day of the [registration] window. Arsenal was further away and I had mates at Luton.' Indeed, Jack waited until the very last day of August to sign for the North London side – understandably hesitant about moving away from his family and friends. Yet, just like his move from primary school to Letchworth City Garden Eagles, and then on to the Luton Town Youth Team, Jack and his family agreed that rejecting an approach from one of the greatest institutions in the English game would be unthinkable.

With assertions from the Arsenal set-up that Jack would be taken care of at the Hale End training centre, Jack finally signed for the Gunners late in the summer of 2001, amid celebrations from his family and friends. Speaking about his short stint at Luton Town sometime later, Jack admits he still has a lot of time for the club and still follows their progress in the English youth leagues: 'I'm often in the area, and a few of my mates still play there so I keep in touch,' he told *Arsenal* magazine nearly a decade later. 'Luton Town are quite a big club for the area, going up to under-16 level I think, and as far as I know they're still going strong.' He goes on to talk about his former teammates, many of whom he kept in touch with despite signing for Arsenal: 'They were all my friends and we got on well, worked together well and managed to win things.'

Leaving Luton, Jack was immediately placed under the tutelage of Roy Massey and fellow youth team coach Neil Banfield. The latter joined the Arsenal youth system in 1997 after an undistinguished playing career and guided Ashley Cole and the youth team to the Under-17 Premier League Youth Title in 1999/00. Massey and Banfield were the primary authorities at the Hale End Academy, and Jack was expected to report to either of the two coaches on a daily basis to evaluate his playing progress.

Turning up for his first day training in the late summer of

2001, another Arsenal coach also caught Jack's eye – a tall, friendly and familiar-looking bald former centre-half. As mentioned, Steve Bould left Arsenal in 1999 in search of first team football. Two years later, he retired from playing the game and opted to pursue a coaching career at the club where he spent the majority of his playing days. He joined the Arsenal youth setup the same summer as Jack, and the young midfielder would later acknowledge the former centre half as being one of the central influences in his development. '[Bould and Banfield] deserve a lot of credit,' Jack said of his initial days as an Arsenal youth team player. 'People say, "Arsenal's youth set-up is good", but they're good coaches as well. They're focused. You wouldn't want to muck around or let them down.' It was to become a prevailing theme in Jack's development as a player: he'd look up to his mentors, learn from them and treat them with boundless respect.

Another important issue stipulated by the Wilshere family was that of Jack's ongoing education. His parents were worried that all this excitement and football development might get in the way of Jack's studying. As a nine-year-old, Jack was close to joining secondary school and his parents wanted reassurance that his studies would be attended to alongside his football playing. Wholly experienced with tutoring youths in the ways of football, the Arsenal youth team reassured the Wilsheres that Jack's football would not get in the way of his schoolwork. The boy was to stay in school in Hitchin, but would be a full-time youth player at the Arsenal Hale End academy.

And thus, with a place at the Arsenal youth team and a

spring in his step, Jack sidled up the path towards his first game in the Arsenal colours.

Wednesday 8th May 2002. Manchester United 0 Arsenal 0, in the penultimate Premier League match of the season. The Gunners travelled up to Old Trafford, five points ahead of the Red Devils, with only two games remaining. Liverpool, the closest challengers to the top two, had 74 points, and required the Gunners and the Red Devils to lose at least one game each for the Merseyside team to win their first top division title since 1989/90.

Arsenal had one simple objective: win the game and put an end to three consecutive years of Manchester United dominance; win the game, moreover, and they would be crowned Champions for the second time in Arsène Wenger's tenure. The Gunners played themselves into astonishing form in the closing months of the season, winning every single fixture since late February. Massive victories against Everton, Newcastle and Aston Villa away was topped with a symbolic 2-1 win against Spurs that put Wenger's team in the driving seat heading towards the business end of the season.

They'd also beaten Chelsea in the FA Cup final only five days before their Premier League game against United, seeing off the Blues with two late goals from Ray Parlour and Freddie Ljungberg. The game – held for the second time at the Millennium Stadium whilst Wembley was rebuilt – was Arsenal's second FA Cup final in what would become a run of four finals in five years. More importantly, though, they exorcised the demons left behind a year previously when Michael Owen slotted home his 88th minute winner to take the FA Cup to Merseyside.

Wenger thus sent his men out for the league game against United knowing he was on the verge of his second double in four years, and only the third in Arsenal's existence. It was a massive moment in the history of the club.

As with the FA Cup final a few days before, Jack watched the game on TV with his new Academy teammates after training. He hadn't had the chance to meet any of the Arsenal first-team squad yet, but he was still rooting for the team as they marched out of the Old Trafford tunnel and in to the early summer light. He'd obviously followed the Arsenal first team closely ever since he signed for the youth team the previous summer. From time to time, Massey and Banfield would allow the Under-9s, 10s and 12s to head over to the new London Colney training centre to watch the Reserves and the first team train. Jack would watch from afar as the likes of Henry, Vieira and Ljungberg would play what Arsène Wenger called the 'Arsenal way' – direct, attacking football, constantly passing and moving and making every play count. The boy would see how Henry wasn't simply the goalscorer in the team – he was also an important cog in the team's play – always available, making space, looking for ways to win. Jack would watch on as Tony Adams and Martin Keown would work on defending set pieces and see how the two centre-halves and full backs Cole and Lauren would organise themselves into a strong defensive unit. He'd watch Robert Pires and Dennis Bergkamp create space and always think one pass ahead. Jack, no less, would watch the heart of Arsenal – paid professionals working hard to play for the team they love and respect. It was a life and career he coveted from the first time he saw this great team, and Jack knew he had a real chance to make the most of the opportunity he'd been given.

Back in Manchester for the 'title decider', lining up with veteran Martin Keown stood former Spurs centre half Sol Campbell, who'd had an impressive first season with the Gunners; at right-back stood the industrious Cameroonian Lauren; and at left-back Ashley Cole – the most recent Academy graduate, who over the course of the season had grown into one of the most respected left-backs in the Premier League. Ray Parlour, Edu, Patrick Vieira and Freddie Ljungberg made up the Arsenal midfield, with Sylvain Wilton and Nwankwo Kanu replacing the injured Thierry Henry and Dennis Bergkamp respectively.

It was a very edgy first half, played very much in the vein of a 'cup tie': both teams were tentative, neither team wanted to make the first move. Two teams who had been at each other's throats for nearly four years, United and Arsenal, played out the game in good spirit and various players agreed that it was one of the most intense competitive fixtures they'd ever played in. Legendary captain Roy Keane later recalled to the *Telegraph* just how much such occasions meant to a professional player. 'Those games were brilliant, absolutely fantastic, the best. You would give anything to play in one of those games again.' His Arsenal counterpart, Ray Parlour, agreed: 'Without doubt [those were the best games], and I really enjoyed my battles with Roy Keane – he was a very fair player, a very honest player. If you kicked him, he got straight back up, and if he kicked you, you got straight back up. We respected each other. It was fantastic, it was a great atmosphere – the fans knew it would be a fiery affair. For us that was always the crunch game, you talk about Arsenal and Tottenham and that was a massive game, but Manchester United was always the one for the league title.'

The game was 0-0 at half-time. Someone had to turn the screw, and the 'ginger-Pele' rose to the occasion with aplomb. In the 55th minute, Manchester United's Juan Sebastián Veron conceded possession to Ray Parlour in the middle of his half. The Arsenal midfielder fed an onrushing Sylvain Wiltord who darted in to the heart of the Manchester United half. Spotting Freddie Ljungberg sprinting across the United back four, Wiltord played the ball to the Swede, who managed to slip the ball past Laurent Blanc and set up a one-on-one chance against Fabien Barthez. Ljungberg forced a save from the United keeper, but the Frenchman could only parry the ball into the path of Wiltord, who gratefully slipped the ball into the United net.

It sent Wiltord, Parlour, Ljungberg, and the travelling Arsenal fans into raptures, and even Arsène Wenger leapt off the bench to celebrate Wiltord's goal. Back at the Hale End Academy, the Under-10s celebrated like they'd just won the league themselves, jumping around and chanting the names of their heroes. As the game wore on, Jack kicked every ball with the Arsenal team – heading every ball directed in to the Arsenal box and intercepting every United attack. Arsenal, on the ropes for much of the last 30 minutes, finally won the game 1-0, with their defence garnering particular praise for their dogged display at the end of the game. Jack Wilshere, meanwhile, much like Ashley Cole years before him, looked on admiringly, having seen a team display full of heart and soul; he watched one of the greatest Arsenal sides of the modern era celebrate another league and cup double success, and was simply proud to be even a tiny part of such an amazing club.

4 – YOUNG, GIFTED
AND INVINCIBLE
2003/04

In which Jack starts secondary school – Wenger signs the next generation – Arsenal are tormented by Jack's mentor in waiting – Jack learns what it means to be Invincible

Encamped just off the A600 and nestled in-between north eastern Hitchin and the town of Letchworth, the Priory secondary school has been educating local kids for over 20 years. A mixed-gender, multi-faith, multi-cultural institution, it has over 950 pupils in attendance in ages ranging from 11 to 19, most of whom hail from the surrounding towns of Hitchin, Letchworth, and neighbouring Stevenage.

One of three secondary schools in the local area, the Wilshere family were adamant that their youngest son would get a decent education while he was plying his football trade at Hale End Academy with Arsenal. Jack, naturally, just wanted to play football, but his parents knew that success (or even a wage) at the top level was by no means guaranteed; they also acknowledged – along with Jack himself – the importance of school in terms of his football development: it provided structure to what could become an indulgent hobby and allowed their young boy to develop important qualities which couldn't be learnt by running around on a football pitch. Leadership, responsibility for oneself and others, and selflessness were just as important as a sweetly struck shot into the bottom-corner, and the Priory's reputation and popularity throughout Hitchin made it the natural choice for Jack and his family. One of the Priory school's aims is 'to prepare [pupils] for their future lives and occupations by helping them to achieve the necessary knowledge, skills and understanding in all their areas of study, including the physical, mental, moral, social, cultural and spiritual.' While Arsenal (along with certain other Premier League sides) was to become Jack's footballing 'finishing school' for football, it was at The Priory where he began to understand what it really meant to be a responsible adult.

An 11-year-old Jack started secondary school in September 2003, a few months after the new football season began in earnest. A lot had happened at the club since Jack signed for the Arsenal in the summer of 2001: most significantly his coach Roy Massey had given him the opportunity to train with the Under-11s only a few months after he'd joined as a nine-year-old. It was a massive opportunity and triggered the extraordinary pattern which would prevail throughout Jack's football career: for the next 10 years Jack would always be at least two steps ahead of his nearest contemporary.

Arsenal, meanwhile, were entering the new season once again toe-to-toe with Manchester United. The previous season, 2002/03, was bittersweet to say the least: Arsenal led for most of the campaign, only for their title aspirations to collapse in shocking fashion towards the end of the campaign. The Gunners, two points behind United going in to the final three games of the season, had to entertain a relegation-threatened Leeds United at home; the Whites, in free-fall off the pitch due to Peter Ridsdale's financial dealings, had to win the game to guarantee Premiership survival.

Thus, when Harry Kewell scored within the first five minutes, the Highbury faithful were understandably worried, and Arsenal, with a rather 'makeshift' back four (including the much-since maligned Oleg Luzhny), took a while to find their way out of first gear. Most neutrals would have bet on a home win once Arsenal equalised through Henry, but tired legs – combined with an unfamiliar defence – meant Arsenal were always going to be vulnerable against an experienced side battling relegation. And so, by the time Mark Viduka fired home the 88th minute winner, Arsenal's title hopes for the season were all but over. 'It was Arsenal's last punishment in the Premiership to relive in miniature the torments that have torn the title from them,' wrote *The Guardian's* Kevin McCarra after the game. 'Here again, in a transfixing match, was the élan in attack that could not quite atone for fragility in defence. There was delirium in the Highbury stands over an exquisite winner but the joyous pandemonium came in the visitors' corner of the stadium… It was… the moment when Arsenal's dream of creating history by retaining their Double died in its first instalment.'

It was tough result to swallow for Wenger, the team and, of course, the fans. It wasn't only the league which was on the line, it was history, as McCarra points out, and Viduka's strike would go on to live long in the memories of those were there to witness it.

But it wasn't all doom and gloom for the Gunners. Two weeks after the shock defeat to Leeds they played Southampton in the FA Cup Final, which turned out to be the perfect remedy for their Premier League trauma. Taking a second gamble on the unreliable Oleg Luhzny, Wenger's line-up was more or less identical the one he sent out against Leeds two weeks before. The game against Southampton, however, had a completely different outcome.

The Gunners went in to the game as favourites to retain the FA Cup, following their triumph against Chelsea in 2001/02. Despite their shock defeat in the league against Leeds and also having to throw together an unfamiliar defence, fans and pundits alike couldn't see Arsenal losing against the Saints in the final at the Millennium Stadium (the third time it was used for the FA Cup Final). The Gunners, buoyed by the thrilling form of Robert Pires and Player of the Season Thierry Henry, felt they deserved something from a season which had promised so much but had so far delivered so little. Wenger, furthermore, believed this current Arsenal team could go down in history as one of the best-ever. Many pundits thought Wenger's confidence in the team was rather misplaced; after all, it was only eight months before that Wenger said his team could go through the season unbeaten – a statement which looked like a pale act of hubris when the Gunners went on to drop nine points in their last six games (not including the loss to Leeds United) of the season, while Manchester United won seven and drew one. Yet Wenger knew that this Arsenal side – made up of tough veterans and talented youngsters – were only just beginning to realise their full potential, and that the double winning season of 2001/02 was the beginning of something truly special.

The final against Southampton was over after 38 minutes. 'Southampton had settled well to their task without seriously troubling [David] Seaman,' reads the BBC's report of the game, 'but Arsenal swept forward in typically stylish fashion to break the deadlock seven minutes before the interval. Henry played in Bergkamp, and when Freddie Ljungberg's shot was blocked, the rebound fell invitingly for Pires to sweep home from eight yards.' It was really that simple. An hour later, Arsenal were crowned FA Cup winners for the ninth time in its history.

Thus they began the 2003/04 season as the 'nearly men' of the league, hoping to repeat the amazing achievements of 2001/02 by becoming champions for the third time under Arsène Wenger. The summer saw a few comings and goings at the club: defender Oleg Luhzny was sold to Wolves, while young English prospect Jermaine Pennant was sent out on loan to Leeds; Giovanni Van Bronckhorst was loaned to Barcelona for the season, and 'fox in the box' Francis Jeffers returned to Everton with his tail between his legs.

Looking ahead to the future, Wenger had one of his busiest summers yet and signed numerous young players who were to shape the future of Arsenal for years to come: 16-year-old La Masia graduate Francesc Fàbregas was signed from FC Barcelona; Robin Van Persie was brought in from Dutch side Feyenoord; Gael Clichy was signed from

Cannes; Swiss centre-back Philippe Senderos was signed from Servette; goalkeeper Jens Lehmann was brought in from Borussia Dortmund; and Spanish forward José Antonio Reyes was drafted in from Atletico Madrid for a club record fee of £10.5 million. The first four players were signed purely on potential and immediately placed in the club's youth and reserve systems; Lehmann and Reyes were bought for the first team, the former of the two replacing club legend David Seaman, who was sold to Manchester City at the end of the previous season.

Meanwhile, an 11-year-old Jack began his education at The Priory School in Hitchin, watching from afar as Arsenal began the new season with massive expectations. As a youth team player, it was unlikely Jack would hear about the comings and goings in the first team, but he and his father would have certainly kept track of the club's dealings in the transfer market. The first team, after all, were his mentors and heroes, and the dealings of star players such as Thierry Henry and Patrick Vieira would have had a domino effect on all of the playing staff at the club, from the Reserves right through to the Under-12s.

Arsène Wenger, meanwhile, was locked in a battle of wills with Alex Ferguson. The former's assertion that Arsenal could go through the league unbeaten had come back to haunt him when they lost to Leeds on that sunny day in the preceding May. The Frenchman's overconfidence at the beginning of the season simply made Ferguson's eighth title all the more sweeter. Yet Wenger, stubbornly ignoring the previous season's mistakes and heaping pressure on to himself and his players, stood by his claim that a team could go unbeaten in a domestic season in the modern game and charged his players to deliver the Premier League trophy without recording a loss by the summer of 2004.

The Frenchman was also receiving criticism from all quarters regarding the ongoing influx of foreign players in to the game. Following England's disappointing showing at the 2002 World Cup and with the European Championships on the horizon at the end of the 2003/04 season, the English press became rather fixated on the 'talent' being fed to the English side by the Premier League's top sides. In 2002, Arsenal sent three players (Ashley Cole, Sol Campbell and Martin Keown) to the World Cup held in Japan and South Korea; two years later, at the European Championships in Portugal, the number was reduced to two (Ashley Cole and Sol Campbell) – the smallest in comparison with the other big four sides in the league. In addition, the number of young English players Wenger was fielding at the start of the 2003/04 season was dwindling. Having sent a fair number of his English youth prospects on loan or sold them to other clubs, Wenger was criticised for replacing them with young foreign stars such as Fàbregas, Clichy and Van Persie. It was clear that the talent in English football was receding, but whether it was the responsibility of the clubs to supply talent to the national side remained to be seen. What was obvious, however, was that the demand for immediate success in one of the world's richest and competitive leagues wasn't helping the 'English' cause.

The Frenchman's situation at Arsenal proved to be the tip of the iceberg, however; other big clubs – including Ferguson's title-winning United side – were beginning to field foreign-heavy sides. Indeed, in the summer of 2003, Ferguson brought in five players to strengthen the squad: Frenchman David Bellion; Cameroonian Eric Djemba-Djemba; American goalkeeper Tim Howard; Brazilian playmaker Kleberson; and Portuguese wonder kid Cristiano Ronaldo. Meanwhile, a total of nine English players were either sold or sent out on loan from Old Trafford before the autumn of 2003. Such dealings, coupled with the English FA's appointment of its first ever foreign manager, hardly set much of a precedent for the game's top flight league. Hence it wasn't simply Wenger's or Arsenal's problem.

Champions League pretenders Chelsea, furthermore, were the first English club to field an all-foreign side – against Southampton in 1999/00 – and in the close season of 2003, Ken Bates made a deal which would significantly change the Premier League's relationship with foreign players and, more importantly, foreign ownership for good. With the West London side facing a financial crisis in 2003, owner Bates sold the club to Roman Abramovich for approximately £60 million. Bates, ever the businessman, went on to buy a bankrupt Leeds United for an undisclosed fee (he reportedly made a £17 million profit on the Chelsea sale) while Abramovich bought the London side with a view to indulge in one of his favourite hobbies. The Russian oligarch – with numerous international business interests ranging from oil distribution to politics – wanted to transform Chelsea F.C. into the Real Madrid of the Premier League. Having taken a particular interest in the *galacticos* side which won the Champions League in 2002 and La Liga in 2003 (one of his favourite games was reportedly Real Madrid's Champions

League quarter-final against Manchester United in which the Brazilian striker Ronaldo scored a wonderful hat-trick), Abramovich was happy to flood the transfer market with millions of pounds in the hope it might attract the best stars on the planet to West London. In the summer of 2003, the Russian oligarch sanctioned the purchases of some of the world football's most sought-after players, outlaying approximately £111 million in total: Claude Makelele and Geremi were bought from Real Madrid; Joe Cole and Glen Johnson were signed from London rivals West Ham; and winger Damien Duff was brought in from Blackburn Rovers.

It turned Chelsea into the richest club (in terms of footballing assets) in the world and one of the most competitive in Europe, and had a direct impact on the dealings of their London neighbours. Thierry Henry, for instance, was at the height of his powers after coming off a season in which he registered 24 league goals (and 23 assists) and won the Player of the Season award. Boundless Abramovich, of course, licked his lips in anticipation of signing the best striker in Europe – particularly from arch-rivals Arsenal. Here was the best player in the world playing in potentially the most lucrative league on the planet – why would he not choose to play for the wealthiest club of all time?

The Gunners, though, saw things differently and immediately rebuffed any approach from the Russian billionaire; they felt that Thierry Henry was irreplaceable and utterly priceless. 'Henry is not for sale at any price,' Arsenal vice-chairman David Dein told Spanish newspaper *AS* after Chelsea tabled a bid thought to be between £40-£50 million. 'Not to Real Madrid, not to Chelsea, not to any club,' he added. Wenger echoed his vice-chairman's stance, taking a characteristically philosophical view: 'When you have the money but not the players it does not help you a lot,' he told BBC Radio Five Live. 'The target is not to have a bank full of money but good players on the pitch... People will never understand if you sell your best players. That would be the wrong signal to send.'

Yet Abramovich's offer did send a signal, albeit in a slightly different way. The Russian's willingness to pay whatever it takes to get whoever he wanted certainly transformed the Premier League, not just in terms of transfer but with regards to talent. With Abramovich shooting £50 notes at Arsenal (according to Chairman Peter Hill-Wood) and in the Chelsea boardroom demanding success *today* not tomorrow, this was bad news for players pushing through the youth ranks of some of England's top sides. Other clubs had to adapt to the changes in the market and with one side hoovering up expensive talent across the world, it meant Arsenal would have to dig even deeper to find equal talent at a fraction of the price. Indeed, in 2003, Chelsea had hot prospects such as Jermaine Beckford and Carlton Cole in their ranks. The arrival of Abramovich simply bloated transfers and increased wages, effectively making it even harder for a young Englishman to break into the domestic top flight. The bottom line for any football club is success and for a club with no financial constraints, this simply meant the best player in every position, regardless of where they were born.

The changing climate of British football didn't really

register on young Jack Wilshere's radar. He was busy beginning his first full term at The Priory, attending school during the week and playing as much football as he possible could during the weekends. From the moment Steve Rowley introduced Jack to his coaches at the Hale End Academy, the boy was told about the importance of hard work and determination. Being a decent football player was one thing, but to earn a living at the highest level took self-sacrifice and determination, and Jack would have to fully commit himself to his favourite hobby if he wanted to play for the Arsenal first team. School was a very important part of this development, and Jack's Arsenal coaches would encourage their students in both footballing and academic studies. Arsène Wenger, in fact, would say the two areas aren't mutually exclusive, and to be a successful football player you need both talent and brains.

The same month that Jack began his school life at The Priory, Arsenal were hoping to assert their authority in what was shaping up to be one of the most significant Premier League campaigns since United's 1998/99 treble-winning season. After a home victory against Everton on the first day of the season, the Gunners put together a formidable set of results which cemented their place at the top of the table; in fact, come November, they had played 13, won 10, drawn 3 and lost 0. Only Abramovich's Chelsea – managed by Claudio Ranieri – could keep up with the Gunners, losing only once to the North London side in an otherwise decent start to their campaign.

Wenger, of course, learning the lessons of the previous season, kept his predictions to himself. The manager knew that the important 'talking' came on the pitch and 'mind games' were only employed in desperation; he also knew that this was Arsenal's best ever chance of winning the title without losing a game (but this time wouldn't admit it out loud!). In 13 games, the Gunners had shipped only six goals and simply didn't look like they even *knew* how to lose. With Sol Campbell forming an effective partnership with Ivorian Kolo Touré at the back, Arsenal were tearing teams apart with their direct, no-nonsense defending and formidable attacking play. With full-backs Ashley Cole and Lauren supporting the likes of Robert Pires, Dennis Bergkamp and Freddie Ljungberg, Arsenal looked more and more unbeatable as the season wore on. The team were hungry, determined, organised and – most galling for Chelsea's Roman Abramovich – supremely entertaining. Thierry Henry was having another fine season and putting the finishing touches on some of the best moves the Premier League had ever seen. By the end of the calendar year – despite a slight 'dip' in form when they drew two in a row – Arsenal were in the driving seat for their 13th title and Arsène Wenger's third Premier League triumph. With 2002/03's self-destruction still in recent memory, the question on everyone's lips was: 'Could they stay the course?'

Jack began school in September eager to get involved in the Year Seven football team. He arrived at The Priory with a big reputation for an 11-year-old. His games for Letchworth Garden City Eagles were often reported on in the local *Comet* newspaper, plus Jack's move to Luton Town after being 'scouted' also went down in local legend. But it was his affiliation with a Premier League football club which impressed the most; only a month or so before he joined The Priory, Jack was signed up by Arsenal F.C. – one of the most respected and indeed popular football clubs in the world. Jack thus arrived at his new school with a rather large reputation to live up to. He was a local lad with a local upbringing, but it wasn't every day that one's classmate was on the books at one of the biggest football clubs in the world. He was only in the Under-11s, of course, but once Jack got on a football pitch, his classmates and teachers quickly recognised that the Wilshere 'myth' was fully justified.

To get on to The Priory's Year Seven football team Jack had to go through the same procedures his fellow schoolmates had to go through: try-outs. Students were separated into 'A' teams and 'B' teams and played against each other. Jack, naturally, was in the 'A' team and certainly didn't shun the opportunity to impress. Even though there was a massive amount of pressure on his shoulders, he played his game and controlled the midfield as if he'd been playing there all his life. It was quite startling to see a boy of Jack's age comprehensively out-class the majority of the other players on the pitch. Of course, Jack's fellow players hadn't applied themselves quite in the same way Jack had done over the previous six years, but the kid's natural talent was undeniable. 'From the first time I saw him at 11, I always thought he would make it,' Jack's former P.E. teacher Jack Nearney told *The Sun*. 'There was no comparison with any other pupil I have seen.' Jack's initial games for the Year Seven football team confirmed to the staff at The Priory that they had something very special on their hands, and even

JACK WILSHERE: ARSENAL D.N.A.

Jack's teammates knew that their new centre midfielder had what it takes to get to the top. '[Jack] was always an inspiration, he led by example,' continues Nearney. 'He was always all over the park; he had such an amazing engine. Despite his size, he was still the strongest player on the pitch.'

The spirit Jack first displayed at Whitehill Junior school – when he would cry in frustration when his teammates would fail to pick out the best pass or play the ball intelligently – certainly hadn't receded with a change of scenery; his commitment to the game continued to be second to none: despite playing for the Arsenal youth team every weekend and training at the Hale End Academy as much as he possibly could, Jack was fully committed to his school team and always turned out for the local clashes against other schools in the area. From the first time he pulled on a Priory jersey, Jack was fighting for the cause. 'What is really good about Jack,' said Priory teacher Nearney, 'is that, even though he was with Arsenal, he never missed a single school game from the age of 11 to 15.' In his first full year at The Priory, Jack, on average, was playing a couple of games a week and training in between; it was this kind of commitment which separated Jack from most of his contemporaries both at The Priory and the Hale End Academy. He was simply *obsessed* with the game of football. The new workload would eventually turn him into a workaholic, an issue which would come in to greater focus when his career really took off some seven years later. For now, though, Jack was happy to dominate and dictate the heart of the Priory midfield while making a real impression in and around the Hale End academy.

Jack's school life would revolve around Arsenal. His day would normally consist of waking up and eating breakfast with his family, heading to school for his morning's lessons and having a kickabout at lunchtime, before heading off to the academy for training in the late afternoon when school finished. His dad Andy would normally pick up his son from The Priory and drive up to Hale End. Andy, of course, would watch Jack train – trying his best not to interfere in Roy Massey's carefully planned coaching sessions – before taking his boy back home to Hitchin. In the car Jack and Andy would evaluate the day's training and talk about Jack's strengths and weaknesses throughout the 2-3 hour long session. They would discuss Jack's technique, how many chances he created, how many opportunities he might have missed, how many errors he might have made and how he can make an improvement on his day to day game. Andy, of course, was very careful not to put too much pressure on Jack's shoulders; he knew, after all, that confidence at Jack's age was more or less like a house of cards – it could collapse at any given moment. Andy needn't have worried, however; his son's self-belief was to become arguably the jewel in the Wilshere crown.

Jack, now a fully-fledged Year Seven student at The Priory School, settled in to his new routine with glee. He was worried that the start of secondary school might spell the end of playing football day in, day out. This, of course, was far from the reality as the winter of 2003 progressed: Jack was playing the game at school during lunch breaks, after school with his mates, in school for the Year Seven team, and most importantly at the Hale End Academy for Arsenal.

JACK WILSHERE: ARSENAL D.N.A.

Things were looking up for young Jack Wilshere and, perhaps more importantly, the tides were turning at the Premier League club which snatched him out of the hands of Luton Town only a few months before.

Come January 2004, Arsenal were once again grappling with Chelsea and Manchester United for top spot in the Premier League. After beating Southampton away on 29th December, Arsenal resumed their campaign in the New Year with a draw against Everton at Goodison Park, a result which allowed United to creep in to a one-point lead at the top. It was an uncomfortable evening for the Gunners, who were looking to protect their unbeaten run in the league. Nwankwo Kanu opened the scoring for Arsenal, taking full advantage of the slip in concentration in Everton's back line to slip the ball past Nigel Martyn. The Gunners, however, couldn't hold on to their lead for the full 90-minutes, and when David Moyes sent the returning (on-loan from Arsenal) Francis Jeffers into the fray, the Merseysider relished his opportunity to put a dent in his parent club's Premier League campaign. The Press Association's Paul Walker described the game's exciting dénouement: 'When Kilbane limped off, Everton's response was another striker with Jeffers introduced to the fray... And it was he who played a major part in Everton's deserved equaliser on 74 minutes. Ferguson's header wide sent Jeffers scampering away on the right and when his fierce cross-shot was palmed away by Lehmann, Radzinski was coming in unmarked on the left to angle his shot into the unguarded net'. Jeffers' goal allowed United – who had beaten Bolton away – to leapfrog the North London side to the top of the league, while Chelsea faltered at home to Liverpool in a loss which arguably signaled the beginning of the end for Claudio Ranieri.

The draw against the Toffees meant that Arsenal were now playing catch-up with a Manchester United team who had barrels of experience in seeing out the final half of the season. The hurt, of course, of 2002/03 was still fresh in the mind of this Arsenal squad and Wenger was determined not to let the mental weakness of the previous season interrupt what had been a fine campaign throughout the latter half of 2003. Indeed, it was only 15 months previously that Arsenal were dealt an even bigger blow by a certain young Englishman playing for the same Merseyside club. Arsenal's tormentor that day was going to become one of the defining players of his generation.

Travelling to Goodison Park the previous season on 19 October 2002, the Gunners were in the midst of another remarkable unbeaten run, which stretched far back in to the latter stages of the 2001/02 season. Arsenal, two points above nearest challengers Liverpool and a massive nine points above eventual champions Manchester United, arrived at Goodison Park to not only consolidate their place at the top of the Premier League, but to also reassert their total dominance in English football. The 30-game unbeaten run began on 23rd December 2001, when a 10-man Arsenal beat Liverpool (the previous game was a 1-3 home loss against Newcastle). It ran throughout the remainder of 2002 – during which Arsenal picked up he Premier League trophy – up until kick-off against Everton on 19 October 2002.

In Everton's starting line-up that day was a certain young

Englishman who would go on to become one of Jack Wilshere's mentors in his subsequent career at the top level. Wayne Rooney was born on 24 October 1985 and had risen through the Everton youth system to become one of the most exciting talents in English football. The boy had grown up supporting Everton and idolized players such as Duncan Ferguson and former Arsenal midfielder Anders Limpar; he won over the affections of the Everton faithful, moreover, when he celebrated scoring against Aston Villa in the FA Youth Cup Final by displaying a t-shirt which read 'once a blue, always a blue'. By the time the game against Arsenal rolled round, at the start of his debut first-team season at the club, Rooney was already a firm fan favourite and one of the most sought-after young players in English football. He had already made a real name for himself within the youth programmes on Merseyside, scoring a massive 99 goals in one season while playing for Copplehouse boys' club in a local league; 114 goals in 29 games for the Everton Under-10s; and eight goals in eight games on the run up to the FA Youth Cup final in 2002. The one thing that was missing from Rooney's record, however, was a Premier League goal.

In terms of background and football development, Wayne Rooney doesn't necessarily have a lot in common with Jack Wilshere. Yet his debut Premier League strike against Arsenal in October of 2002 certainly shared the audacity and imagination which would go on to become one of Wilshere's early trademarks when he finally broke in to the Arsenal first team nearly a decade later. Rooney, on for Thomas Radzinski in the 80th minute, controlled Thomas Gravesen's pass with ease, turning away from a retreating Lauren at right-back. Almost out of nowhere, the young Englishman whipped the ball past a stranded David Seaman, and into the Arsenal net – just as the clock reached stoppage time. The Everton faithful were in raptures as Arsenal's 30-game unbeaten run came to a truly dramatic close. Clive Tyldesley, the ITV commentator at the time, was simply astonished by the audacity of the shot and summed up the goal by saying: 'A brilliant goal! Remember the name… *Wayne Rooney.*'

After the game Wenger was rather magnanimous in defeat and admitted that his team couldn't go unbeaten forever. He acknowledged, moreover, that the winning goal was more or less a once in a lifetime strike from a truly talented individual: 'Rooney is the biggest England talent I've seen since I arrived in England. There has certainly not been a player under 20 as good as him since I became a manager here.'

There's no doubt Wenger's words would have pricked the ears of the *Match of the Day*-obsessed Jack Wilshere. He watched the Premier League highlights every weekend, looking to emulate his idol's moves on the school pitch at The Priory and the training pitch at Hale End. Little did he know that one day he would be lining up alongside Wayne Rooney in an England shirt at Wembley Stadium. Rooney, of course, has been a major inspiration for Jack and there's no doubt that the kid would have seen the Rooney goal against his parent club in 2002 and thought, 'I can do that!' Rooney was simply another player – just like Paulo Di Canio – who contributed to the modern-day footballer that is Jack Wilshere. Even as an 11-year-old schoolboy, Wilshere was learning the ways of the game and understood the raw emotion of every goal and every victory. Indeed, it's unsurprising that Jack's favourite players share numerous attributes – unmatched skill, technique, hunger and intelligence – but perhaps the most common link between Di Canio and Rooney was their heart and their absolute desire to play the game they love.

Returning to 2004, following the away draw against Everton, Arsenal had a decent chance to get back on track by playing Middlesbrough at home. The Teessiders were having a respectable season in the Premier League and in Steve McClaren had a decent manager who knew the English top division intimately; his team, furthermore, would go on to affect the 2003/04 title race in more ways than one (plus they knocked Wenger's men out of the League Cup that season).

The Arsenal team sought to put the previous draw behind them in the game against Boro and they knew that any further slip-ups would more or less hoist a white flag above Highbury aimed in the direction of Alex Ferguson et al. Thankfully for Arsenal, though, Boro simply didn't turn up. Gareth Southgate and his fellow centre half Ugo Ehiogu had been relatively impenetrable at the back for parts of the season, but this particular game was certainly one to forget for Boro's defence. Arsenal created numerous chances during the game, and were it not for Mark Schwarzer's talent between the Boro sticks, the Gunners would have scored at least half a dozen goals against McClaren's men. A penalty from Henry got the ball rolling for Arsenal after Vieira was brought down by a clumsy Ehiogu challenge; his conversion from the spot was even more impressive after

Boro's Danny Mills thought he'd give the Arsenal man some words of encouragement before he stepped up to take the penalty. The penalty set the tone for the rest of the afternoon: Arsenal were both exquisite and profligate, while Boro were lethargic and defensive. With the introduction of their Brazilian ace Juninho after half-time, Boro fashioned a consolation goal in the dying minutes of the game; the Brazilian played Massimo Maccarone in to the box and the Italian was duly brought down by Jens Lehmann. Maccarone slotted the ball home to make it 4-1 – a rather flattering scoreline for Middlesbrough given the amount of chances Arsenal failed to convert.

Yet it was a win for the Gunners, and only the second time since November that Arsenal had scored more than one goal in a match (the other a 3-0 victory against Wolverhampton Wanderers in December). Results indicated that Arsenal were sailing rather close to the wind and Wenger would have enjoyed a comprehensive 4-1 victory over a well-drilled mid-table team. Manchester United, meanwhile, were beginning to find a mid-season squabble for top-spot in the league a little too much to take: they had started the New Year well with an away win against Bolton, but the form which took them to the top of the league at the back-end of 2003 had hit a brick wall. While Arsenal were grinding out victories and comfortably beating Boro, United surprisingly drew 0-0 with Newcastle at home. They subsequently lost to Wolves on their travels, before chalking off a pair of very tight wins against Southampton and Everton. By the time their home fixture against Middlesbrough rolled around at the beginning of February,

Arsenal were five points ahead of United, having been one point behind them at the start of the New Year.

United's game against Middlesbrough thus became a must-win. Yet Ferguson's men were leaking goals. Their previous wins against Southampton and Everton were tight to say the least: they'd beaten the Saints 3-2 at home and ground out a 4-3 victory against Everton at Goodsion Park. In total, United had scored 9 and conceded 7 goals since the start of 2004 – not title winning form. And with the injury to £30 million signing Rio Ferdinand, Ferguson's defence went from bad to worse. When McClaren's Middlesbrough arrived for their game at Old Trafford, Ferguson knew that another loss would see Arsenal march further off into the distance and their title dreams over. Thankfully for Wenger and Arsenal, McClaren's men did a better job of defending at Old Trafford then they did at Highbury: Boro won the game against United 3-2, with Juninho scoring twice and Joseph-Désiré Job grabbing the winner. It damned United to their fifth Premier League defeat of the season, whereas Arsenal remained unbeaten.

United faded in the latter half of the season and Chelsea failed to really find any kind of title-winning form: the Blues' mid-season slump – which began with a draw away to Leeds and culminated in a loss at home to Liverpool – significantly hindered their opportunity to overhaul Arsenal at the top of the league, and the west Londoners remained second or third throughout the remainder of the 2003/04 season.

It was Arsenal's season – and what a season it had turned out to be. Jack would have watched Arsenal dismantle some of the best teams in the country, combining guile, intelligence, and determination with supreme mental and physical fortitude. The young Mr Wilshere – 12 years old on 1st January 2004 – would travel to Hale End on those early spring evenings to train with the same club who had recently dispatched the likes of Chelsea 2-1 at Stamford Bridge. He would come home after training on a Saturday afternoon, watch *Match of the Day* with his dad and see the likes of Pires, Vieira, Ljungberg and, of course, Thierry Henry, stick four past Liverpool and three past Leeds. The boy would watch in awe as the Arsenal defence kept their heads and refused to panic, even if they were a couple of goals down to a side battling relegation. Jack would see what it was like to be *invincible* – to be part of a cub in which winning was a habit and losing was only something other clubs could do.

It was, of course, a landmark moment in the history of the club, but it was also a significant moment in the youth players who were coming through the ranks. Wenger's team of 2003/04 had set the standard for any side: subsequent Arsenal teams would always be compared to the wonderful team which graced stadia up and down the country – a team which played 38, won 26, drew 12 and lost 0. Young players such as Cesc Fàbregas and Gael Clichy – both of whom were squad players during the campaign – knew they would have to reach a whole new level if they were to better the 2003/04 season. Jack, no doubt, would have been overwhelmed by the audacity of Arsenal's performances during the season, and in years to come would be constantly compared to the glory days of 2004 when Gilberto and Vieira graced the centre of midfield with physicality, heart and intelligence.

JACK WILSHERE: ARSENAL D.N.A.

There's no doubt, however, that those performances were at the forefront of Jack's mind when he would emerge as Arsenal's pivotal player some five or so years later.

In 2011, during Jack's breakthrough season, Arsenal blogsite *Arsenalcolumn.co.uk* published an article comparing the Arsenal side of 2003/04 with the Arsenal side of 2010/11. The article – entitled 'Arsenal 2011 vs The Invincibles' – posed the question: what would happen if both teams played each other? The idea, of course, was illogical, but it represents the standard by which Fàbregas, van Persie, Wilshere and any Arsenal player will always be judged. The article makes for a fun and illuminating read, and goes some way towards highlighting the major footballing differences between the two sides:

Rumours that Patrick Vieira tried to rile Cesc Fàbregas in the tunnel but failed to get a reaction out of him are unfounded, nevertheless the teams were immaculately led out. The Invincibles were sent out in a 4-4-2 with Dennis Bergkamp playing off Thierry Henry and the two wide men looking to support them as often as possible. Behind them, Vieira and Gilberto formed a solid midfield base that allowed the attacking players to get forward with assurance as their primary job was to help retain the shape of the team in and out of possession. Arsenal of 2010/11, meanwhile, had more of a 4-2-3-1 shape: Cesc Fàbregas had the main creative duties in front of a double pivot of Alex Song and Jack Wilshere while Robin van Persie played as a focal point of the attack, allowing Theo Walcott in particular, to take up a forward role by drifting inside from the right... While [the

Invincibles] *held most of the possession, Arsenal of 2010/11 became unstuck against old-fashioned resilience and organisation and their lack of experience told in the end. However, there are some positives they can take out of the encounter and it's that they dominated a very good side over both legs. Their style is more suited to Europe but if they can add a couple more robust individuals they can be a force in the league for the next coming years. The Invincibles showed again why they are a great side as their football bordered on the impossibly quick at times and defended astutely.*

It's a fun insight in to what separated the team of 2003/04 from other Arsenal sides and offers a glimpse of what it is like to be a player in a modern-day Arsenal side – forever judged in the context of 2003/04.

The Invincible season, of course, was a landmark in both Arsenal's history and the history of English football. Only Preston North End at the top end of the 19th Century had accomplished such a feat and it is sure to live long in the memories of even the most diffident of football fans. As mentioned, the side of 2003/04 would also become the yardstick by which every subsequent Arsenal side is judged: in the years following the momentous campaign – just as Jack was climbing the ladder of the youth teams, B-teams, A-teams and reserve teams – pundits would constantly hark back to the season 2003/04 when Vieira et al would refuse to 'roll over' and would always 'grind out results'. Despite the once-in-a-lifetime achievement, the Invincible season therefore became a type of poisoned chalice – a unique achievement that some of the best teams in English top flight history couldn't even repeat (indeed, even the treble-winning United team of 1999 lost to Arsenal, Sheffield Wednesday and Middlesbrough in the league that season!).

The captain of the side, Patrick Vieira, reflected on the feat in 2011, saying that despite the amazing achievement, the team of 2003/04 wasn't, in fact, that different from the contemporary Arsenal side which features Wilshere at the heart of its midfield: 'There is a big difference between the Arsenal team now and the one I played in,' he told the *Daily Mail*. 'It was a big, physical team. We could play as well but I honestly believe that the Arsenal team now are playing better then we ever did. The difference is we put silverware on the sideboard. That is what people remember, not how you play.'

The season was a milestone for Arsenal, but even Jack was beginning to feel a change in the air: he had finished his first full term at school and his first full season at Arsenal, and his coaches had started to allow him more access to Arsenal's training facilities at London Colney. This, of course, meant the chance to meet the stars of the Invincible campaign and perhaps even train with some of his favourite Arsenal players. All this was to come, however; as Jack settled in to the summer of 2004, he knew he needed to be patient and he'll get his chance. The same summer, an 18-year-old Wayne Rooney completed his £25.6 million move from Everton to Manchester United, and Jack realised that anyone – even a young boy who'd grown up playing the game just for fun – could make it at the top level if they wanted. All he needed was ambition, dedication and, of course, a little patience.

5 – THE NEXT FÀBREGAS
2004/05

In which Jack and his friend Jake make names for
themselves on the fields of Hertfordshire – and Arsenal
lose a hero but gain an apprentice

Jack was eager to get back to the training fields of Hale End as soon as he possibly could at the end of the summer. It wasn't that he didn't enjoy his time off – he'd had a great six weeks in the sun – he simply wanted to get back to playing the game he loved regularly. He had spent the summer of 2004 with his family, going on holiday with his parents Kerry and Andy, and kicking a ball with mates on the playing-fields of Hitchin. Jack loved to show his siblings all the new tricks he learnt at London Colney and talk about the different tactics he'd been taught over the past 12 months: he'd showboat in front of his brother and sister, flicking the ball over their heads and 'nutmegging' them whenever they'd try and get the ball from him; he'd also show his family just how many 'keepy-uppies' he could do (more or less an infinite amount – or at least until he got too tired!).

Jack would talk at length about 'give and go's and 'man-to-man marking', both confusing and annoying his siblings who just wanted to kick the ball around the park.

He and his brother Tom would even re-enact favourite Premier League goals (such as the Di Canio volley against Wimbledon a few seasons back), incorporating Andy, Rosie, Tom, and, of course, a little imagination. Thierry Henry's goal against Spurs in 2002 – when he bypassed the whole of the Tottenham midfield and defence – was a particular favourite: Jack would play the role of Thierry as he darted through the middle of the park while a hapless Stephen Carr (Tom Wilshere) would try to intervene; 'Henry... chance for a break-out', Jack would say, imitating the commentary, 'Wiltord to his right, Bergkamp to his left... they'll do well to catch up with Thierry Henry though... *HENRY!*' The boy would smash the ball perfectly in to the bottom-left hand corner, past a helpless Neil Sullivan (Andy Wilshere) just as his hero Henry did only a few years before. He'd then run down half the pitch to celebrate in front of the Spurs fans (the bushes), sliding on his knees just like the imitable Frenchman.

The *real* Henry, meanwhile, was a month or so in to the new Premier League season when Jack went back to The Priory for this second year. The Frenchman and his Arsenal teammates had finished the previous season as unbeaten Champions of England and were just getting into their stride at the start of September 2004. A tricky away fixture to old foes Everton was navigated with style, with the Gunners leaving Goodison with a 4-1 victory under their belts. Comprehensive wins against Middlesbrough (5-3),

Blackburn Rovers (3-0), Norwich City (4-1) and Fulham (3-0), furthermore, sent the Gunners to the top of the table and on course to defend their Premier League title for the first time under Arsène Wenger.

What was most astounding to Wenger and the Arsenal management, however, was the sheer attacking force of this Arsenal team: by mid-September Arsenal were two points clear of second-placed Chelsea, with a goal difference of +14. Jack's favourite Frenchman Thierry Henry and his fellow Arsenal teammates had netted a massive 19 goals in five games since the first fixture of the season – one of the most impressive strike rates the Premier League had ever seen. What's more, the majority of their goals had been scored away from home – 11 goals for, 2 against – and Arsenal showed no sign of letting up. They were still unbeaten, of course, and were looking to capitalise on such wonderful form as the winter months set in.

Jack had also started the year where he left off. He was back at the Hale End Academy, training hard and enjoying his football; his dad Andy continued to take him to Arsenal after school, talking his son through each and every pass, tackle and shot. Jack was well integrated into the Arsenal way now and his dad Andy could see the clear development in his son's game. Where once he would try and dribble through defenders – many of whom were far bigger than the diminutive Jack – the kid would now look for a player in space and knock the ball square. Where once Jack would hesitate when a teammate was in space, he would now wait for the very last possible moment to play a fellow player in, feeding the ball into space instead of passing it aimlessly.

JACK WILSHERE: ARSENAL D.N.A.

Where there was once drive, heart and pure, raw talent, Andy now saw a killer instinct in his son's game. Roy Massey and his fellow coaches at the Hale End Academy were having a clear effect on Jack's game, and Jack was responding well to the incessant coaching too. It looked as if Arsenal and Jack suited each other: Jack's drive and open-mindedness certainly complemented Arsenal's rather technical and high-tempo approach to the game.

All of which came in handy when Jack was asked to captain the year eight football team for the second time in a row. It came as a surprise to Jack, even though he had been captain of the year seven team; he didn't expect the Head of P.E. to ask him to be captain again, particularly since there were loads of other talented youngsters in The Priory's football team. Nevertheless, Jack was really excited about the year ahead: he was settled at school and at Arsenal. And he was also ready for his first taste of 'competitive' football.

Arsenal travelled to Old Trafford under rather unusual circumstances on 24th October 2004. They were 49 games unbeaten in the league – undefeated in 2003/04 and currently unbeaten in 2004/05 – and top of the league. Chelsea were their nearest challengers, two points behind the Gunners in what was a decent start to their campaign. Indeed, Roman Abramovich had made a rather bold statement of intent in the close season of 2003/04: the Russian oligarch sacked the dithering Claudio Ranieri and in his place appointed a 41-year-old Portuguese manager who had recently taken lowly Porto to Champions League glory the first time of asking. José Mário dos Santos Félix

Mourinho came to represent everything good and not so good about Chelsea: he was confident, arrogant, intelligent and cunning; he was also a shrewd tactician and turned out to be one of the most entertaining and effective characters the Premier League had ever seen. The man also took Chelsea by the lapels and dragged the team exactly where Abramovich wanted them – to the top (or near the top) of the Premier League.

Manchester United, meanwhile, were struggling to find form when Arsenal came calling at the end of October. Fifth in the league under Everton and plucky Bolton, Ferguson's side had lost their 'mojo' after Arsenal marched to Premier League victory in such an overwhelming manner the previous season. They'd already lost to Chelsea on the opening game of the 2004/05 season (another satisfying victory for Mourinho, who had dispatched United as manager of Porto on the way to Champions League glory the season before), and consecutive draws against Blackburn, Everton and Bolton saw United languish mid-table for the opening weeks of the season.

Nevertheless, Manchester United were always up for games against Arsenal. Plus this fixture had added spice not only because of the ongoing rivalry (Ferguson and Wenger had been at each other's throats for nearly a decade now), but also because Arsenal had were proud owners of a rather distinguished unbeaten record. And records, of course, were there to be broken.

The Arsenal and United teams knew each other well. Their rivalry had built up nicely since Wenger's arrival back in 1996 and games between the two clubs always culminated in some sort of fallout. Arsenal, of course, had won the league at Old Trafford in 2002 after putting together an astonishing run of form to clinch the title from Ferguson's grasp. During the equivalent fixture the previous season (2003/04), Arsenal travelled to Old Trafford defending their budding unbeaten record, only to concede a dodgy penalty to United in the last minute of the game. The controversy, as ever, arose due to Ruud Van Nistelrooy's dubious dive and Martin Keown's angry response following the Dutchman's miss from the spot. The ill-feeling was consolidated by Van Nistelrooy's previous attempts to get Arsenal captain Patrick Vieira sent off, after which Wenger and his captain more or less brandished the Dutchman an out and out cheat.

Thus it was a massive Premier League fixture – a game, no doubt, Jack would have watched from the comfort of his own home back in Hitchin. There was pride at stake at Old Trafford and Alex Ferguson knew that a win against Arsenal would not only stop them from reaching the half-century of games unbeaten, it would also prove a massive morale boosting win for a team in need of direction following a bad start to the season. The problem for Ferguson, however, was that his team couldn't find a way to cope with Wenger's men: the Arsenal side of 2004 was quick, intelligent, nimble-footed and cunning, and had arguably dominated English football since Wenger's second double success in 2002. Ferguson's treble-winning team of 1999 had been through a number of guises since its success in Munich and the Scotsman had done well to keep his team as competitive as possible; but with his retirement on ice and a third-place finish in United's most recent Premier

bove: Already a mainstay in the Arsenal Youth Team setup, Jack Wilshere made is debut for the Arsenal Reserves in February 2008, scoring the only goal of the natch against Reading.

elow: His skill, creativity and dominating presence in midfield saw Arsène /enger call the 16-year-old up to the Arsenal First Team where he played in a re-season fixture against Barnet at Underhill Stadium. He's pictured here with llow youth team players (*from left to right*) Jay Simpson, Rui Fonte, Nacer arazite, Francis Coquelin and Mark Randall.

Above: Wilshere made his competitive debut in the Premier League against Blackburn in September 2008, making him Arsenal's youngest-ever league player he celebrated ten days later by scoring Arsenal's fifth goal against Sheffield United in the Carling Cup.

Below: Wilshere was soon rubbing shoulders with Arsenal's first team regulars, including (*from left to right*) Kieron Gibbs, Carlos Vela, William Gallas, Samir Nasri and Alex Song.

Above: Arsène Wenger had other ideas, however, and allowed Steve Bould to re-draft Wilshere into the Arsenal Youth Team setup, where he was instrumental in taking his team to the Youth Cup final – beating Aston Villa, Wolves, Sunderland and Tottenham Hotspur along the way.

Left: Wilshere tussles with Manchester City's Abdisalam Ibrahim in the semi-final of the Youth Cup in March 2009.

Above: Jack celebrates scoring his team's second goal in front of a packed Emirates crowd in the FA Youth Cup final first leg against Liverpool.

Below: Wilshere takes on Liverpool's Jack Robinson in the FA Youth Cup second leg at Anfield…

..Before celebrating the historic win with team-mates Jay-Emmanuel Thomas and Sanchez Watt.

Following his Youth Team triumphs, Wilshere was recalled to Arsène Wenger's first team in the summer of 2009 and scored in the Emirates Cup game against Glasgow Rangers (*top*), taking home the Man-of-the-Match award (*bottom*).

bove: Wilshere's international career was boosted when he received a call-up to
uart Pearce's Under-21s Squad at the age of 17; he's pictured here alongside
*eddie Sears (*left*) and Andy Carroll (*right*).

elow: Wishere takes on Netherlands' Vurnon Anita whilst playing for England's
nder-21s in August 2009.

Jack returned to Arsenal with a view to breaking into the First Team on a more regular basis. He's pictured here taking on former Arsenal forward Emmanuel Adebayor in the League Cup.

League campaign, people were beginning to question whether the Scotsman had it in him to create yet another attack-minded, stylish side.

In fact, the United side of 2004/05 were rather brutal in their response to Arsenal's attacking play. For every intelligent through-ball or cunning flick from an Arsenal player, there was a nasty tackle or a cynical foul in reply. Gary Neville, Paul Scholes, Roy Keane and even new boy Wayne Rooney were all eager to assert themselves on Arsenal – a tactic not wholly approved of by Ferguson, but never entirely discouraged.

And so Arsenal's game against Manchester United on 24th October rocked the Premier League for various reasons: United's eventual 2-0 win abolished Arsenal's unbeaten record; the Gunners attacked stylishly but with no end product; United won a penalty from a referee who had given the same team seven penalties in the seven previous games he had refereed at Old Trafford; an 18-year-old Wayne Rooney won the aforesaid penalty and scored the second goal; the game ended in acrimony as Arsenal refused to shake the hands of their opponents amid accusations of gamesmanship. But perhaps the most infamous incident of the fixture occurred in the tunnel after the game. According to reports, various objects such as pizza, coffee and even pea soup were thrown at the United manager and players. 'The Battle of the Buffet' match would go down in history as a microcosm of the most cherished rivalry in the Premier League, a rivalry which incorporated love, hate and grudging respect.

A twelve-year-old Jack would have found out all he

needed to know about competitiveness watching such a legendary game. Wenger, of course, cited gamesmanship as the reason Arsenal didn't make it to 50 unbeaten games; Ferguson, on the other hand, cited passion and defensive quality as the reason United won the game. Either way, Jack would have watched the game and pined for the day he could pull on an Arsenal jersey and win trophies for the team. He knew he had it in him to play for Arsenal and was so eager to play for the side that he would beg coach Roy Massey to let him go over to London Colney and train with the first team. Even after big games such as the one against United, a few Arsenal first teamers would return to North London the next day for light training or to see the physiotherapist. Jack was eager to ask the likes of Campbell, Ljungberg and Reyes – the latter of whom had a particularly rough night at Old Trafford – what it was like to play in such a massive game. Massey, of course, declined Jack his request, but the boy was determined to meet his heroes one day.

Meanwhile, the same autumn of 2004, The Priory School began their National Schools Cup campaign. Jack was used to the FA-affiliated cup campaigns, having captained the Whitehill Junior team at under-8 level; the under-14s competition, however, was treated more seriously by schools up and down the country, and it proved to be yet another platform for Jack to demonstrate his range of skills. Captaining the side, Jack led the Priory team out against various teams within the district from October through to Christmas. It was a busy schedule for the youngster: he would train with Arsenal at weekends and play against various school sides on weekday evenings. The school games allowed Jack to try out his new-found tactical insight against par opposition: he would teach The Priory's back-four the offside trap and how to implement it in a game situation; he would also instruct his team to 'keep their shape' and keep the ball moving, hoping they might be able to fashion some sort of chance. Jack, of course, would remain in the middle of the pitch, dominating the midfield from box-to-box; indeed, even as a twelve-year-old he had a great engine and was invariably the last player to stop running at the end of the game. He was also a match-winner: 'Whenever there was an influential goal to be scored', Jack's former P.E. teacher Dan Nearney told *The Sun* newspaper of the boy's days as The Priory's school captain, 'it was Jack who got it.'

Jack was insatiable playing for The Priory school team; his hunger had grown since he started playing for Arsenal, and he was now ready to step up and take responsibility for winning 'big' games. His drive rubbed off on his fellow teammates and by Christmas, The Priory Under-14s were on their way to the district finals which were to take place at the beginning of the new term.

While Jack was making a name for himself on the playing fields of Hertfordshire, Arsenal were licking their wounds following defeat to Manchester United. As the New Year came and went – and as Jack's District Cup finals date approached – Wenger's team finally emerged from a crisis of confidence which saw them slip to second in the league and a rather daunting five points behind Mourinho's Chelsea. Following the shock 'Battle of the Buffet' defeat to

United at the end of October, Arsenal went on to win only twice in the next seven games; they drew to Southampton, Crystal Palace, West Bromwich Albion and Chelsea, and lost to Rafa Benitez's Liverpool (a team, of course, who famously went on to pick up the European Cup the following summer). Only a result at White Hart Lane could remedy the malaise, with Arsenal winning an astonishing match 5-4. The team managed to scramble a few wins together at the back end of the New Year, but as 2005 arrived, the formerly 'Invincible' Arsenal side were now looking at a potential run-in with one of the most talented Chelsea sides the first division had ever seen.

It wasn't all doom and gloom for Wenger and the Arsenal management, however. Another particular – albeit minor – attribute of the team in 2004/05 was the emergence of an Arsenal talent who would go on to define the way the club (and Jack) would play the game in years to come. During the aforesaid 5-4 win over Spurs in November 2004, a certain young Catalan midfielder made a goal out of nothing: tackling a defender on the edge of their box, Cesc Fàbregas retrieved the ball and fooled the whole of the Spurs defense by sending a sublime reverse-pass in to the path of Freddie Ljungberg. With Arsenal already 3-2 up (following goals by Henry, Lauren and Vieira), the goal more or less sealed the result for Arsenal and sent the red half of North London into raptures.

Fàbregas was fortunate to be in the team on that chilly night in November. Gilberto Silva sat out the majority of the 2004/05 season with severe back pain and returned to his native Brazil to receive specialist treatment. In his absence,

Fàbregas seized the opportunity to make a name for himself in the team: after signing a professional contract in September 2004, Fàbregas began to start games in the Premier League, and not before long he began scoring – and creating – goals. His first contribution came early on in the season against Blackburn, precipitating the following acclamation from club legend Bob Wilson: 'The player who has created so much excitement and generated so much interest... is the young boy Fàbregas. He is another diamond that Arsène Wenger has unearthed. From everything I've seen and everything I've heard about him, it is clear that Fàbregas is going to be an absolutely massive, massive star player. I think Fàbregas is one of the best young players there has ever been.'

It was a ringing endorsement for a truly talented youngster. Moreover, it was a ringing endorsement for the club's scouting and academy system, the former of which spotted Fàbregas as a 15-year-old playing for Barcelona's celebrated La Masia Youth Academy. Francis Cagigao, the scout who discovered the Spanish maestro during a training game in Les Cortes, said of Cesc: 'Even when he was 15 I was captivated by his intelligence. He was mature which is hard to find in young players.'

Fàbregas joined Arsenal in 2003 and was immediately placed in the Reserves. After a few months training and adapting to his new life in London, Fàbregas was given his big chance in a League Cup game against Rotherham United in October the same season, scoring a goal to make him the youngest ever player to score for Arsenal (and celebrating by returning home and eating a Kinder Egg!). From that point on the talented Catalan never looked back; by the end of the 2003/04 season he was knocking on the door of the (Invincible) first team and managed to claim a spot on the bench for the 2004/05 Community Shield.

It was a speedy rise to the top and his journey would only serve to encourage youngster Wilshere as he quietly got down to business in the lowly youth squads. He could only look up to Fàbregas and marvel at what the Spaniard had achieved in such a short space of time; from being a no-one in a Barcelona youth side, to pushing for a first-team berth in one of the best teams in England, was no mean feat, and Jack knew it took guts, determination and brains to get to the top. Nevertheless, Jack was equally determined to make a name for himself at Arsenal and Fàbregas' quick progression through the ranks only confirmed to the young Hitchinian what he really knew deep down: that he was at *the right club* at *the right time*.

First things first for Jack, however; he had the small matter of captaining his school side for the National Schools Cup finals in February 2005. It was the first of many such outings for the young central midfielder and the games allowed Jack to sharpen his ability within the context of a competitive fixture. At Arsenal, of course, he played in various youth club fixtures, usually against the likes of Chelsea, Crystal Palace and West Ham youths; playing for the Priory school team, though, meant a lot to the boy who had grown up showing off on the playing fields of Hertfordshire. During this time he played alongside Jake Argent-Martin, a young midfielder who had grown up in the same area of the county as Jack. Jake and Jack became close and developed a decent understanding of the each other's game on the pitch: when Jack would go on and attack, Jake would sit in front of the defence and shield the team from any prospective counter-attack. When Jake, on the other hand, would press ahead, Jack would support the midfield from the base and act as its focal point for developing a new attack. It took a lot of discipline for a pair of 13-year-olds, but Jack and Jake were mature and intelligent enough to understand that you couldn't do *everything* during the game. Indeed, it was perhaps the first genuine 'partnership' of Jack's career; he would go on to play alongside many established central midfielders – including Aaron Ramsey, Santi Cazorla, Mikel Arteta and, of course, Cesc Fàbregas – but the partnership with Jake taught Jack a lot in terms of the necessity of good work-rate and communication.

Following their stints in the Priory school team, Jake and Jack would take rather different routes to the top of their respective games. Argent-Reeves was eventually picked up by Leyton Orient in the summer of 2010, after making a name for himself in the 'O's' prolific youth system. After signing professional terms for the east-London side, however, Jake severely injured his knee ligaments in a pre-season friendly, and was forced to retire from the game at the age of 19. The two Hitchin locals remain great friends and have stayed in touch despite their differing fortunes at the top of the game.

The Priory had had a decent season on the pitch and Jack had done well to captain the team to success for a second successive season. It wasn't all about the football, however, and Jack also had important exams at the end of the school year. One of the issues for Jack's parents while he was running the midfield for both club and school was that of his schoolwork. Andy and Kerry were worried that his obsession with football and his dedication to the Arsenal youth team might intrude on his learning. Arsenal, of course, had given every assurance that their coaching wouldn't impinge upon Jack's schoolwork, and his day-to-day learning wouldn't be affected. Jack, however, was rather bloody-minded about the whole situation and was keen to put football first with everything else second. As winter became spring, and as Jack reveled in The Priory's football success, it was getting to the stage when Jack's parents were wondering whether so much football would benefit their 13-year-old's long-term future.

Arsenal, meanwhile, continued to threaten Chelsea at the top of the league through the early period of 2005. It was a difficult start to the year, with Arsenal losing to Bolton following a home draw against Manchester City. It was, as ever, against the red side of Manchester when Arsenal really began to lose faith in retaining their title for the first time in their history. Following the 'Battle of the Buffet' in October, Manchester United arrived at Highbury for the return leg on 1st February 2005, with Arsenal a massive 10 points behind Chelsea. It was Arsenal's opportunity to avenge United for their gamesmanship in the previous contest and perhaps more importantly to reignite a championship charge which had seen Chelsea more or less run away with it. The game fizzled with acrimony before the game even kicked off: according to reports, Arsenal captain Patrick Vieira had words with Gary Neville, following the United defender's treatment of José-Antonio Reyes in the previous fixture. United captain Roy Keane took umbrage with Vieira and the two captains squared up in the Highbury tunnel with referee Graham Poll having to separate them.

It wasn't the best advert for the game prior to kick-off, but the remaining 90 minutes turned out to be one of the best contests the Premier League had ever seen. Despite neither team being within touching distance to Chelsea at the top, both United and Arsenal produced six astonishing goals and demonstrated that the true league rivalry remained between the red half of London and Manchester. New boy Cristiano Ronaldo scored both the equaliser and the winner for United to make it 3-2 (John O'Shea sealed the deal for United with a chip over Manuel Almunia's head to make it 4-2), but the game would undoubtedly be remembered for the quality of football on show. Both teams bristled with intention and Arsenal's Cesc Fàbregas had another decent game lighting up central midfield. Again, Jack would have watched in awe as an 18-year-old Fàbregas held his own against the likes of Keane, Giggs and Scholes, and would have taken notes from the passing and movement of some of the best central midfielders in the world.

United's win placed them just above Arsenal as the Premier League hit the business end of the 2004/05 season. United's form, however, saw them drop even more points towards the end of the campaign, and Arsenal in fact finished above Ferguson's men, ending the campaign five points ahead (although an insurmountable 12 points behind champions Chelsea).

There was to be one final chapter in Arsenal's ongoing

rivalry with Manchester United – at least as far as Roy Keane and Patrick Vieira were concerned – when the two teams met at the Millennium Stadium for the FA Cup final on 21st May 2005. In arguably one of the most one-sided finals in recent memory, Arsenal took Manchester United to extra-time after being more or less outplayed by Ferguson's team. Arsenal's Thierry Henry – who had recently broken Ian Wright's goalscoring record for the Gunners – was unfortunately out injured, so Wenger opted to play Dennis Bergkamp as a lone striker up-front, with Vieira and Fàbregas providing the support. It was a plan which arguably backfired, with United dominating most of the play during both halves of the game.

One of the more intriguing sub-plots to the final centred on Patrick Vieira's impending move away from Highbury. The Arsenal captain had been linked with various moves away from the club throughout his tenure, and the build-up to the FA Cup Final had been marred by strong rumours of Vieira's imminent departure to Italian giants Juventus. Ever the professional, Vieira denied the rumours, but many felt the FA Cup Final would be his final game for the club. With the emergence of the talented Fàbregas, Arsenal fans knew they had a top-class replacement for one of the most successful captains in Arsenal's history, but there was worry that his drive and determination would be massively missed in the dressing-room for years to come.

Regardless, Arsenal managed to push the game all the way to penalties, and with Paul Scholes the only player to miss, it was up to Patrick Vieira to win Arsenal's tenth FA Cup. In what was to prove the last kick of his Arsenal career,

Vieira smashed the ball into the bottom-right hand corner and won the game for the Gunners. Arsenal were crowned FA Cup champions again and Vieira joined the manager and his teammates in celebrating Arsenal's latest triumph.

It all seemed rather jaded, however. With the rumours circulating that Vieira was to leave in the summer, and various other members of the 2003/04 Invincible side also linked with moves away from the club, fans and pundits alike were beginning to question how long Arsenal's remarkable period of success would last. Where would Wenger find another Patrick Vieira to steady the Arsenal ship when they were up against it? Who would captain the side to yet another Premier League triumph?

Wenger, of course, had his plans, and when Patrick Vieira did eventually leave Arsenal in June 2005, it became apparent where Arsenal's future lay – in youth, potential and Cesc Fàbregas. The Spaniard had gone from strength to strength during the early period of his Arsenal career and it was apparent that Wenger put a lot of faith in the youngster, starting him in over 33 games during the course of the 2004/05 season. Despite handing Thierry Henry the captaincy following Vieira's departure, it became more and more obvious as to which direction Wenger wanted to steer the club after such a protracted period of success: although he had an experienced, successful team, Wenger decided that the close-season of 2004/05 was the right time to beginning investing in the future.

Jack, as ever, wouldn't have been privy to Wenger's team selection as he watched Arsenal's FA Cup success at the Hale End Academy. Of course, he would have noted

Fàbregas' rise to the top and seen other players – such as right-back Justin Hoyte and Phillipe Senderos – pushing for a starting place. But as he broke up from school for the summer, Jack could also sense that the chances of breaking into the Arsenal team were beginning to look more and more likely. He naturally began to wonder, if Fàbregas is next in line, who would be the 'next Fàbregas'? With Wenger ushering out Vieira and asserting an under-30 player policy – in which any player who is over the age of 30 would only be granted a one-year extension to their contracts – it looked as if a new era had begun at Arsenal. And Jack sensed he was destined to be part of it.

6 – A NEW GENERATION
2005/06

*In which Arsenal say goodbye to their old home and hello to
their new one – Jack continues to make an impression at school
and at Hale End – Fàbregas becomes the heart and soul of the
Arsenal midfield – and Jack goes along for the Champions
League ride*

In November 1999, just as Jack was impressing the locals
while playing for Whitehill Junior School, the powers that
be at Arsenal F.C. announced a deal which would change
the club forever. With rumours circulating that Arsenal were
planning a move outside their traditional Highbury home,
Peter Hill-Wood and the Arsenal board announced that
Arsenal would be relocating to a new 60,000-seat stadium
within the boundaries of N1. The move, they said, was to
take place in the close season of 2002/03 and part of the
board's plans included the dismantling and reselling of the
great Highbury stadium.

Six years later and Arsenal were still at Highbury, having
just won the FA Cup for the tenth time in their history. Jack
had just finished his second year at The Priory secondary
school and second year as captain of the school football

team. As the close-season set in and Jack holidayed for six weeks with his friends and family, it was confirmed that the forthcoming 2005/06 season was indeed going to be Arsenal's last at Highbury, with the new stadium ready for use for the 2006/07 campaign.

The relocation was a massive project for the club. Privately the board had been discussing such a move throughout the 1990s, yet was put off by both the financing and the impracticalities of the project. At the forefront of stadium design when it was built in 1913, the enduring popularity of Highbury (or, to give the official title, The Arsenal Stadium) and her marble halls couldn't withstand the demands of modern, financially-led, *Premier League* football. The stadium was relatively small and enclosed between terraced housing which left little room for expansion; its 38,000 seat capacity, furthermore, was one of the smallest among Europe's elite clubs, and the Arsenal board came to realise that if they were going to compete with the biggest clubs in the world then the team would require one of the biggest platforms upon which to perform. Yet it wasn't a straightforward decision to make: Highbury was, of course, adored by the fans, and it came to symbolise the history of Arsenal F.C. – from working-class beginnings, to the swagger of Wenger's Arsenal, all via the magic and vision of Mr. Herbert Chapman. It was also home of many a memorable victory, from the amazing league campaigns of Chapman's sides which included wins over the likes of Liverpool and Bolton at the back end of the 1937/38 season to seal Arsenal's fifth league championship, to the wondrous displays towards the end of the 2001/02 campaign when the

A NEW GENERATION

Gunners rocked home to win their 12th title at Old Trafford before returning for the victory parade in and around Highbury fields. The stadium had style, character, and above all, a proud history, and Arsenal supporters had certainly seen some amazing football surrounded by Archibald Leitch and Claude Ferrier's art deco façades.

Yet the club had to progress. With the acquisition of Chelsea in the summer of 2004, along with the Glazer takeover of Manchester United in the close-season of 2005, the Premier League was beginning to look more like a stock market than a sports division. The injection of television money back in the heady days of 1992/93 had slowly but surely begun to reap dividends, and with the influx of talented, foreign players, the Premier League was fast becoming the most popular and lucrative league in the world.

The Arsenal board was weary of the club being left behind in their rivals' financial wake and thus sought ways to transform the club from domestic stalwarts to internationally renowned super-club. Thankfully they were blessed with the most successful (and economically savvy) manager in the history of the club and one of the most talented teams the club had ever produced; they were also blessed with a proud and dedicated fan-base with an enormous season ticket waiting list. What the club therefore required was a suitable platform upon which the team could perform – a stadium which would continue the traditions Highbury had so proudly established, while at the same time tap in to a potentially massive revenue stream. They spent nearly a decade mulling over the decision, but towards the end of 1999, as Arsenal were playing their

Champions League matches at the old Wembley Stadium, the Arsenal board decided the time was right to give the project the green light: Arsenal announced plans to move to the new 60,000-seater stadium, located, fortunately enough, only a quarter-mile or so down the road next to Drayton Park train station.

But moving a football club from the home it had occupied for nearly 100 years was never going to be a simple task. It required planning, preparation, patience, and above all, money. In the initial press release announcing the building of the new stadium on the Ashburton Grove site, Arsenal confirmed that the final project cost was expected to be in the region of £357 million 'which includes the stadium build [and] the relocation of businesses' and various community-centred initiatives (such as the construction of a brand new recycling centre) in and around Highbury and Islington. 'The Stadium facilities', it continued, 'comprise £260 million of senior debt to be provided to Ashburton Properties Limited' by various banking groups, along with an additional loan which was secured against 'the contracted amounts receivable from Wilson Connolly PLC in respect of certain completed property development transactions.' Essentially, the club planned to secure financing for the new stadium project against the land upon which Highbury was built, turning the old stadium into brand-new apartments to sell on the real estate market. This, in turn, gave the club access to the loans which precipitated the building of the new stadium, but left the club with a rather large financial noose around its neck. For the next five or so years – as the club completed the project and sold the brand new flats in

Highbury – Arsenal Football Club would have to live very carefully within its means.

Like any business, such a financial code would have a knock-on effect on the staff. Everyone from Arsène Wenger down to the match-day steward would have felt the effects of moving to a new stadium. Even Jack would have felt the transformation within the club: he could sense the rumblings at the back-end of last season and noticed a slight change in policy when it came to certain aspects of the coaching system. His coaches would still not allow him to go over to London Colney to meet his heroes, but Jack noticed that more and more young Reserve players were being integrated into the first team. Indeed, Arsène Wenger seemed to be taking a slightly more eager interest in the youth prospects at the club, and the promotion of players such as Cesc Fàbregas from lowly deputy to out and out first-team regular suggested a subtle change of direction in terms of youth policy.

The most significant transformation for the younger generation of Arsenal players during the summer of 2005, however, was that of their manager's dealings in the transfer market. As the 29-year-old captain Patrick Vieira followed 24-year-old goalkeeper Stuart Taylor and 22-year-old winger Jermaine Pennant out the door, Wenger brought in four new players in their place: 17-year-old goalkeeper Vito Mannone was transferred for approximately £350,000 from Italian side Atalanta; 15 year-old left-back Armand Traore was brought in from Monaco, and 17-year-old centre-forward Nicholas Bendtner was purchased from F.C. Copenhagen. Out went players with an average age of 25; in came players with an average age of around 18. The plan, of course, was to blood the likes of Mannone, Bendtner and the young Traore alongside experienced players such as Jens Lehmann, Ashley Cole and Thierry Henry, yet Wenger's dealings during the summer were no doubt encouraging for the younger playing staff at the club. As the final beam was placed atop the Emirates Stadium in August 2005, it certainly looked as if Arsène Wenger himself was also building for the future – buying raw, promising talent on the 'cheap' in the hope they would grow up to become world class players in the mould of Thierry Henry et al. For players like Jack Wilshere – 13 years old and on the cusp of the Under 14s/15s at both club and school level – the new policy was simply another reason to play harder and better than anyone else.

As the new season approached and Jack prepared to go back to school, Wenger brought in another player to further augment his plans for the future. Alexander Hleb, a ball-playing attacking midfielder, was purchased from VTB Stuttgart for approximately £11.2 million. Unproven in any of the top leagues on the continent, the Belarussian was a decent winger and would serve as deputy to the likes of Freddie Ljungberg or the aging Robert Pires; he was also a very capable playmaker and fitted with Wenger's plans for a more continental game based around the talents of Spanish protégé Cesc Fàbregas.

For Wenger, Fàbregas was the future of Arsenal: he was short, athletic, technically gifted, driven, ambitious and mature. He also had an astonishing 'football brain' which Wenger felt would become the metronome of his next

Arsenal team. The young Catalan had just come off the back of a very successful breakthrough season at the club, enjoying 46 first-team appearances, setting up five goals and scoring twice. He had also played a big part in Arsenal's FA Cup success only a few months before and was seen by many at the club as a truly exciting prospect for the future. After years of success, Arsenal fans were rather disconcerted about how Wenger might replicate the wonderful period between 1997 and 2005 when he won the club seven major trophies. With Fàbregas as the beating heart of the midfield, they needn't have worried: Vieira may have been the battling, seasoned veteran, but Cesc Fàbregas – as far as Wenger was concerned – was the future.

Jack restarted school at the beginning of September, hoping to impress again on the playing fields of Hitchin. The boy had somewhat of a breakthrough season as captain of The Priory school football team the previous year and he was eager to get back to winning ways as the new term kicked off and try-outs began in earnest. Jack, of course, was a shoo-in for the school captaincy again, but he had to get in to the team just like any other school football player, and he was eager to once again show the school – the whole district in fact – how good he was at playing his favourite game.

With new signings in tow, Arsenal began the last ever season playing their home matches inside the historic Highbury stadium. Jack – just like anyone else connected to the team (he was, after all, a de facto fan, after his beloved West Ham United) – had a lump in his throat as Arsenal kicked things off against Newcastle in front of the Highbury faithful. The 38,000 or so people packed in to the stadium that Sunday afternoon knew that something was going to be lost in the move up the road to Ashburton Grove; what that 'something' was nobody knew, but deep in their collective gut the Arsenal faithful sensed that the coming campaign was going to be momentous for more than just historical reasons. And Jack sensed it too.

Arsenal won that game 2-0, with late goals coming from Thierry Henry and the young Dutchman Robin van Persie. It was a nice start to the campaign, particularly winning the opening game in front of the Highbury faithful in the final season at the stadium. Despite the fear and worry, Vieira's departure didn't seem to hit Arsenal as hard as everyone had predicted: Fàbregas settled very well into his new first-team berth; Gilberto Silva was the perfect foil for his Catalan counterpart, proving to be the ball-winner in what was slowly becoming an intricate midfield; even Thierry Henry – promoted to captain following the departure of his French counterpart – was rising to the challenge and seemed to relish the new responsibility he had on his shoulders. Indeed, the Arsenal of 2005/06 didn't seem that different from the title-winning team of a few years ago and it looked as if Wenger had done a very sound job in integrating the younger members with the more experienced players on the pitch.

The optimism wasn't to last long. Just as Arsenal dispatched Graeme Souness' Newcastle United, the following weekend they travelled to Stamford Bridge for an early-season clash with reigning champions Chelsea. The Blues had undergone a rather large personnel change in the last few seasons, and while Arsenal and Manchester United were battling it out for FA Cups, Chelsea had 'quietly' gone about their business and won their first ever Premier League title in 2004/05 with an impressive (and rather formidable) 95 points. Abramovich's money had finally paid off: they had the best goalkeeper in the world, world-class defenders and midfielders, and in Didier Drogba they had one of the most powerful centre-forwards the Premier League had ever seen. In the dugout sat the manager José Mourinho – a character who had slowly but surely left his mark in English game's top division, disregarding the 'history' of the Wenger/Ferguson rivalry and gleefully knocking the two teams off their perch with organised, pragmatic football.

Thus when Arsenal played Chelsea in the second game-week of the 2005/06 season, the Gunners knew what kind of match would be served up: tight, powerful ball-playing football from the boys in blue, with a garnish of 'mind-games' from their manager served neatly on the side. Indeed, Arsenal lost the game 1-0, with substitute Didier Drogba's second-half strike enough for Chelsea to grind out a victory and see them join the one and only Tottenham Hotspur at the top of the Premier League. For Arsenal, though, it spelled a bout of early-season soul-searching not seen since before the days of Patrick Vieira. The Gunners had been garnering a reputation for starting strongly in recent league campaigns – they had only lost two games in their opening eight fixtures in every season since Vieira became captain of the side in 2002 through to 2005 – so were understandably worried when their early season tempo was disturbed by an unstoppable Chelsea side.

Things unfortunately didn't get any better in the

subsequent weeks: they followed their trip to Chelsea with a 4-1 win over Fulham at Highbury, before going on to lose at Middlesbrough, beating Everton and drawing at West Ham United. By mid-October, Arsenal had played eight, won four, lost three and drawn one – certainly not title-winning form from the red and whites – and results which sent them to eighth in the Premier League.

It was surprising for Arsène Wenger and his management team. Of course, losing one of the most successful midfielders the club had ever employed was always going to have a knock-on effect on the remainder of the playing staff. But with everything nicely in place during pre-season, and with Arsène Wenger having sold Vieira – on the manager's terms and at what he believed to be the right time – it looked as if Arsenal were embarking a brand new chapter in its history, this time without one of its most successful ever captains. The new team had Fàbregas and Gilberto in the heart of the midfield – a balance in the centre of the park not seen since the aforementioned captain and Emmanuel Petit governed the Highbury field. But as Arsenal faltered and their league rivals progressed, fans began to wonder whether Wenger was, in fact, rather premature in his selling of the club talisman and captain.

It could only be a good thing, though, for the captain of The Priory school Under-14s. Not that Jack didn't idolise Patrick Vieira, or think he was one of the best players he'd ever seen play for Arsenal, but he'd be lying if he thought Vieira's exit from the club and Fàbregas' promotion into the first team wasn't a good thing for his own future at the club.

Plus Jack was already honing his skills in Patrick Vieira's

and Cesc Fàbregas' position on the pitch. Youth team coaches Roy Massey and Steve Leonard had been advising Jack on which position suited him best and they both agreed that he'd be most effective in the middle of the park. His dad Andy had also been giving him some tips too and agreed with his coaches that Jack's best position would be in the middle, dictating the game and developing possession. Their reasoning was as follows: first and foremost Jack was comfortable with the ball at his feet facing towards the opposition's goal; his direct style of play – he'd always look to go forward – meant he'd always advance with the ball looking for an attacking pass. Secondly, he was very calm in possession and enjoyed taking his time on the ball; this was a very valuable asset to have at such a young age and Massey sought to develop this part of Jack's game even further. Lastly, the boy had amazing vision and naturally understood the flow and pace of the game; when there was a chance to progress play he would choose to do so, when the game needed slowing down or the team had to keep possession Jack would simply revert to what he and his fellow Arsenal youths knew best – to pass and move and keep the ball. He knew instinctively when to move the ball on to a teammate or when to take a few more touches to slow down the play, and this was very impressive for the team of coaches teaching him how to play the game.

Another valuable asset of Jack's style of play – an attribute that Massey had only just began to notice – was his rather odd physique. He had very short legs and a longish torso which meant he had a very low centre of gravity, allowing him to turn his body more fluently. It was a physique similar to that of the senior side's new signing Alexander Hleb; the Belarusian's ability to turn quickly and weave in and out of play allowed him to slow the pace of the game and also pick out the goal-scoring assists so valuable in top-flight football. Jack, of course, was only 13 years old and was in the midst of developing both his game and his physique, but coaches Massey, Bould, Steve Leonard and his dad Andy all knew that if Jack was to fulfill his potential and become a first team player, he'd have to play in the middle of the pitch.

As the Premier League season rolled into the winter months and the Arsenal first team desperately tried to regain some sort of form, Jack kicked on with his fledgling Arsenal career. He was doing his utmost to make an impression on anyone who might happen to be watching him play at the club, from his teammates right up to the coaches Bould, Massey and Leonard. Jack was instrumental in every game he played in and would regularly win the unofficial 'Man of the Match' award normally bestowed upon him by his fellow teammates and opponents (and of course his Dad!).

Arsenal, however, were underachieving in the league. By the New Year, they were in sixth position, having lost six of their first 20 games. They were behind Chelsea, Manchester United, Liverpool, Spurs and, rather shockingly, Wigan Athletic, and were looking like being drawn into a battle for the final, highly coveted Champions League spot. They had already lost to Chelsea, Middlesbrough and West Bromwich Albion in the league, and a barren run of form in December 2005 – in which they lost three times in a row against Bolton Wanderers, Newcastle United and Chelsea – meant they were facing one of their worst campaigns under Arsène Wenger's stewardship.

Ironic for Arsenal, though, was their respectable run in the Champions League group stages. Wenger had opted for a rather more continental system in Europe throughout the 2005/06 European Cup campaign, utilising Thierry Henry as a lone striker ahead of two wingers (or inside-forwards) and the chief-orchestrator Cesc Fàbregas. It worked wonders for the team, and by the start of 2006 Arsenal had won all but one of their group games in the tournament (against FC Thun, Sparta Prague and Dutch giants Ajax), booking their place in the knock-out stages with points to spare.

The imbalance in league and European form continued, and by the end of February Arsenal had just knocked Spanish giants Real Madrid out of the Champions League, having come off the back of successive defeats in the Premier League (against Liverpool and Blackburn Rovers). While they were riding high in Europe – and being drawn against quarter-final opponents Juventus – Arsenal were struggling to keep up with the chasing pack, languishing in seventh position below teams such as Bolton Wanderers, Blackburn and Champions League pretenders Spurs. It was disconcerting to say the least for Wenger and his management team, even more so when Arsenal were travelling to the likes of the Santiago Bernabeu and getting a result and failing to replicate the form on their domestic travels. But a cup run is a cup run, and Wenger knew that the system he was using in Europe might get this Arsenal team as far as the final in Paris.

Jack, of course, was watching the team with glee. During

the game against Real Madrid, Thierry Henry had scored one of the best goals Jack had ever seen, slaloming three or four Real Madrid players before slotting the ball past Iker Casillas in the Madrid goal. What stood out for Jack, though, was Cesc Fàbregas' assist. The young Spaniard had really made an impression on the Arsenal first team and Jack was flabbergasted by how many attacks the young Spaniard was involved in. On a game by game basis, Jack would be really happy with 20 or 30 decent passes, an assist here or there, and maybe even a goal; during Arsenal's European fixtures, though, Jack could see just how much more work was needed to even get close to the level of Cesc Fàbregas. For example, in the build-up to the goal, Fàbregas got the move going by picking the pocket of a stranded Thomas Gravesen, and played a short, simple pass to Thierry Henry who did the rest. It was almost too easy, thought Jack, who knew only too well how the best players would normally make the difficult things look very easy indeed.

Arsenal, Henry and Fàbregas continued on their quest for European glory, drawing a heavily experienced Juventus side in the quarter-finals. Their Premier League form had picked up too and the team managed to string together a series of wins to restore some semblance of confidence in the league. The first leg against the 'old Lady' of Italian football was played at Highbury on 28th March 2006. It was a massive opportunity to say goodbye to the old stadium in what may have been the last ever European home game played there and Arsenal took it with aplomb. It was also a massive opportunity for the team to show Patrick Vieira that life did indeed go on after his departure in the preceding summer, the former captain returning to his old club with a Juventus team that included experienced internationals such as Gianluigi Buffon, Fabio Cannavaro, Emerson, David Trezeguet, Lillian Thuram, and, of course, Alessandro Del Piero.

Jack settled down to watch the game with a couple of youth team friends. He was intrigued and massively excited about the fixture, curious to see how Vieira might play in front of the Highbury faithful. He was also interested to see how Cesc Fàbregas might perform against the former captain, especially since many Arsenal fans (himself included) believed Cesc Fàbregas was Vieira's natural successor in central midfield. Either way, Jack knew this was one of the most important games in the history of the club – a match which could go on to define not only a season, but a generation.

The game began rather statically given the occasion. Arsenal went toe to toe with Juventus, with Wenger's assertion that European ties are invariably settled in the first leg still ringing in his team's ears. A few minutes before the end of the first half, a tenacious, untypical Robert Pires tackle dispossessed the lumbering Patrick Vieira; his compatriot retrieved the ball and advanced up the pitch, spotting Thierry Henry in the heart of the Juventus half. He made a sharp pass to Henry who slowed the tempo before playing in the onrushing Cesc Fàbregas on the edge of the Juventus box. The Catalan took two touches to take the ball beyond the highly-experienced Lillian Thuram, before sliding the ball into the reverse corner, beyond the reach of Gianluigi Buffon.

It was a massive goal for the Gunners. It might have been a slender lead in what was a very competitive tie, but it was also a psychological victory for Arsenal and, of course, Cesc

Fàbregas. From Vieira's dithering in the middle of the park, to the ecstatic celebration of the Catalan who ran the length of the pitch to celebrate with his teammates, the goal represented a changing of the guard at the heart of the Arsenal midfield, and finally ended the fading legacy that was Patrick Vieira's captaincy at the club. It was as if Patrick Vieira had effectively passed the proverbial baton to Cesc Fàbregas and the Highbury was witnessing the birth of a new legacy right before their eyes. 'A reunion with old acquaintances can turn into a disturbing experience,' agreed Kevin McCarra writing in *The Guardian*, 'and so it was for Patrick Vieira, who came back to Highbury and found himself, along with the rest of the Juventus midfield, overshadowed by the superb 18-year-old Cesc Fábregas.'

Jack, obviously, was over the moon with the team, and by the time Thierry Henry scored a late penalty to make it 2-0, the kid knew a place in the Champions League semi-finals was on the cards. Fàbregas started the move once again in the Arsenal half, passing the ball to Thierry Henry who played a first-time pass to Alexander Hleb on the wing. Fàbregas, meanwhile, continued his run into the Juventus box and duly received a perfectly weighted pass from Hleb; after drawing the two Juventus centre-halves, Fàbregas slotted the ball back to a slightly off-balance Thierry Henry who squeezed the ball into the back of the net.

It was a wonderful goal and Jack and his mates all acknowledged that this was the game when Fàbregas became the new heart of the Arsenal midfield. Jack could only dream of replicating such play for the Arsenal first-team, but took heart from seeing an 18-year-old youth prospect become the centerpiece of a Euro-conquering side. *'We've got Cesc Fàbregas'* chanted the Highbury faithful, as a 14-year-old Jack Wilshere watched on in both awe and genuine excitement.

Arsenal, of course, still had a lot to do in the competition, let alone take a 2-0 lead to the Stadio delle Alpi – a difficult place to go and keep a clean sheet whatever the occasion. But the late sending-offs of Mauro Camoranesi and Jonathan Zebina, along with the suspension of Patrick Vieira following his fifth yellow card in the competition, was a massive boost for the second leg. 'The poise of Arsenal was remarkable,' continued McCarra, 'just as it had been when they claimed the goalless draw required against Real Madrid on this ground in the previous round. They have faith in the philosophy instilled in them by Wenger and that ought to reinforce them at the Stadio delle Alpi.'

The second leg was indeed a massive test for Arsenal, but they managed to return to London with a 0-0 draw and a place in the semi-finals of the Champions League. Excitement was building in and around the Arsenal training grounds (indeed, Jack and his fellow youth team players were already looking into travel arrangements for the final in Paris), but Arsène Wenger was careful not to put too much pressure on this Arsenal side, particularly since their league form was severely faltering. Following the quarter-final games against Juventus, the Gunners managed to string together a mini-run in the league in March, beating Fulham, Liverpool, Charlton Athletic and Aston Villa, to send them within two points of fourth place Spurs and the coveted Champions League spot. But their local rivals were going strong under Dutchman Martin Jol and were looking to register their highest league finish in many a season and indeed knock Wenger and Arsenal off their perch.

It was a strange situation for the team. On the one hand they were on course to become the first Arsenal side to lift the European Cup, and also the first London side to taste success at the top table of the European elite. Yet they were also on the cusp of a relatively disastrous season, potentially finishing below Spurs for the first time since the Premier League was formed and facing a season in the 'lowly' UEFA Cup. Wenger, as ever, knew that the team's progress in the Champions League would be dictated by their form in the league; the manager saw that a string of decent results in the league would obviously aid any kind of progress in European competition. But as the season reached its climax, it was looking more and more likely that Arsenal would have to qualify for the 2006/07 Champions League by winning the competition. Spurs had invested sensibly in their squad at the start of the season and were in pole position to qualify for Europe's premier competition for the first time in their history; Arsenal, on the other hand, were getting used to the wistful reality that their current run in the Champions League might turn out to be their swansong in the competition.

The stakes were thus extraordinarily high as teams entered the business end of the 2005/06 season. Following a string of strong results in March, Arsenal took on old foes Manchester United in the league on 9th April, only 10 days before the first leg of the Champions League semi-final. United were seven points behind leaders Chelsea when Arsenal arrived at Old Trafford, eager to stay in touching distance of Mourinho's blues and perhaps dent Arsenal's faltering Champions League hopes. Unlike previous contests, it proved to be a relatively easy task for United: Arsenal clearly had their minds on the upcoming Champions League games and were easily dispatched 2-0 following goals by Wayne Rooney and Ji-Sung Park.

Returning to North London with their tails between their legs, Arsenal could finally turn their full attention to what was perhaps the biggest game in the club's history, the Champions League semi-final. The Gunners were drawn against La Liga's Villarreal, managed by the talented and well-respected coach Manuel Pellegrini. His side was built around the talented Argentinean midfielder Juan Román Riquelme; a playmaker at heart, the former Boca Juniors star had recently resurrected his career at Villarreal following an unsuccessful stint at Barcelona, and was now in the heart of the Villarreal midfield. For a player learning the trade like Jack Wilshere, Riquelme represented everything needed to be a truly world-class central midfielder: he had vision, creativity, technical ability, intelligence and an eye for goal. He could also slow down or speed up the tempo of the game with a single pass – an attribute Roy Massey noticed in Jack from a young age.

Thus, when Villarreal arrived for the first leg of the Champions League semi-final on 19th April 2006 – the last European game ever to be played at Highbury stadium, no less – Jack wanted to keep his eye firmly on Riquelme in the hope the Argentinean maestro might teach him a few things about the art of the playmaker. He wasn't to be disappointed: after only a few minutes the Argentine midfielder burst into life, dictating the course of the game and directing Villarreal's flowing style. But it was the home team who nearly got the breakthrough goal – after 11 minutes, Thierry Henry calmly slotted the ball into the back of the Villarreal net, only to be judged offside by the linesman. The Spanish side began to retreat and even Riquelme's probing passes weren't reaching the desired recipient. Then, more or less out of nowhere, the Argentine produced a blistering shot which was saved by Jens Lehmann, before setting up former Manchester United forward Diego Forlan, whose shot was also parried by the athletic German keeper. That's how you dictate a game, thought Jack, as the Villarreal player swaggered around the Highbury pitch looking to create yet another opening in the Arsenal defence.

But it wasn't to be for Villarreal. Four minutes before the interval, Thierry Henry played in Alexander Hleb, whose cross was slotted into the back of the Spanish side's net by Kolo Touré. Jack and his dad Andy, along with the rest of Highbury, all celebrated like Arsenal had just won the European Cup itself, but the Gunners still had work to do. The second half was a nail-biting performance from an Arsenal point of view, and even though there were chances for both teams to alter the score line, neither could take them. Goalkeeper Jens Lehmann managed to parry a screaming shot from defensive midfielder Marcos Senner and Dennis Bergkamp very nearly scored Arsenal's second but was denied by canny goalkeeping at the other end of the pitch.

All in all, the Highbury faithful and the Wilshere family

were pleased to take a 1-0 lead to the El Madrigal stadium, knowing that a clean sheet the following week would take Arsenal into their first ever European Cup final. As *The Guardian* journalist Kevin McCarra succinctly wrote: 'Arsenal showed the maturity of a team that belongs in the Champions League final. Having scrambled Villarreal's wits in the first half with a high-speed approach that achieved the breakthrough, they assumed a more contemplative style to protect that lead. It might well have been increased, but a 1-0 win, thanks to Kolo Touré's first goal of the season, is a better result than appearances suggest.'

But there was still work to do. Arsenal had to travel to the El Madrigal stadium in the province of Castellón with a valuable 1-0 win to protect, and the league fixtures were coming thick and fast for Wenger's men. After losing to Manchester United and drawing against relegation battlers Portsmouth, Arsenal entertained Spurs in the final North London derby at Highbury in what was touted as a Champions-League six-pointer. The Gunners were four points behind Tottenham with a game in hand and were eager to hedge their bets just in case the dream of winning the Champions League – and therefore qualifying for next season's competition – didn't materialise. Tottenham, meanwhile, were confident that a win or even a draw against their oldest rivals would more or less secure Champions League football and condemn Arsenal to the ignominy of playing in the unfashionable UEFA Cup.

Wenger had a few choices to make before the game. The manager opted to drop talisman Thierry Henry to the bench for the defeat against Manchester United only a few weeks earlier, fully aware that his pace and guile would be more valuable in the Champions League semi-final; the manager bravely did the same against Spurs, putting faith in youngsters Robin van Persie and Emmanuel Adebayor and looking to nick a win against a Spurs side boasting the likes of Matthew Dawson, Aaron Lennon, Jermaine Defoe and Robbie Keane. He also rested Cesc Fàbregas, choosing instead to shore up the midfield with the slightly more defensively-minded Abou Diaby, sacrificing creativity for solidity.

It was a gamble for the Arsenal manager. Up until that point, Arsenal had won only two of the eight fixtures Thierry Henry had not started in and Wenger appeared to be putting all his eggs in one basket by initially omitting the Frenchman from the Arsenal team sheet. It was a decision which very nearly backfired for the Arsenal manager: bolstered by the omission of the Arsenal captain, Spurs were the superior side for much of the game and went in for half-time with the wind in their sails. Wenger responded by throwing on Fàbregas and Henry, only for Robbie Keane to score more or less straight after their substitutions. Kicking into action, Thierry Henry reacted like any world-class forward should – he set up a few chances and scored one of his own: bringing the ball under control from an Adebayor pass, the Frenchman controlled and finished into the bottom-right corner of Paul Robinson's goal. It was to be the highlight of the match which eventually finished 1-1; Arsenal remained in fifth position, four points behind Tottenham Hotspur, the latter now odds-on to qualify for the Champions League 2006/07.

For a youth-team player like Jack, Thierry Henry

represented everything an Arsenal player needed to be: graceful, intelligent and psychologically invaluable to his team. Before and after the game, Wenger was criticised for leaving Cesc Fàbregas and Thierry Henry on the bench, a decision which arguably backfired after Spurs left Highbury with a draw, to which the manager retorted: 'People will criticise because Thierry Henry didn't start, but at the end of the day I think if Tottenham had not stolen that goal we would have won.' The criticisms simply represented the importance of Thierry Henry (and, to a lesser extent Cesc Fàbregas) to this Arsenal side: the Frenchman's presence on the pitch simply changed the game and Jack would have noted the importance of individual responsibility after Henry's idiosyncratic goal and celebration. The youth player would have also noted, though, Henry's sense of collective responsibility after the game, backing the boss' decision to omit him from the starting line-up and emphasising the importance of the Arsenal *team* in winning football matches: 'I don't like [being a substitute] but you have to accept it,' Henry told *The Guardian*. 'In the past I didn't accept it and I got upset. When the boss used to ask me how I was, I'd say I was fine all of the time. But fine all of the time doesn't work well… If you want to be fresh and sharp then somewhere along the line you have to take a break from games. I didn't play at Manchester United but in the past I've not played against them and we've won. I didn't play against Tottenham last year and we won and against Liverpool last year and we won.' Despite the result – and the daunting likelihood that Arsenal might have to qualify for the Champions League by winning it – Jack went home happy to have seen an Arsenal great like Thierry

Henry demonstrating that sometimes individual brilliance is simply invaluable in the game of football.

Four weeks later Arsenal were poised to play in their first ever Champions League final, thanks largely to a heroic late penalty save from Jens Lehmann in the dying minutes of the semi-final in Castellón. Villarreal had been knocking on the door throughout the return leg at the El Madrigal stadium, only for Gael Clichy to stick out a leg and bring down substitute José Mari in the box. The responsibility fell to Juan Román Riquelme who – thankfully for Jack and the remainder of the Arsenal faithful – blasted the ball straight at the diving German goalkeeper and thus booked Arsenal a place in the final in Paris.

The dust had also settled on the Premier League run-in which had seen the Gunners – more or less out of nowhere – qualify for the 2006/07 Champions League. On the final day of the season, Arsenal entertained Wigan at the final game at Highbury, while Spurs travelled the short distance to play a relatively decent West Ham United side (the Hammers finished in a respectable ninth position in 2005/06). Going into the weekend, Arsenal were one point behind Spurs and required their rivals to either draw or lose against the Hammers to ensure any chance of qualification. Jack, obviously, would have had one eye on the Spurs game, hoping his boyhood team might come out on top against Arsenal's greatest rivals.

It was a very odd end to the Premier League season for both North London sides. Firstly, Arsenal were saying goodbye to the stadium which had been home for nearly 100 years; it was a massive moment in the history of the club, with an almost carnivalesque atmosphere inside and outside the stadium, and various heroes of old taking their seats to watch the boys in red and white play for the final time on a unique footballing stage. Fans wore red and white shirts and chanted classic Highbury songs, full in the knowledge that qualification for the European Cup would be the perfect send-off for Archibald Leitch's classic edifice. It was an even bigger occasion for the team as a whole since they knew they required some sort of result against a Wigan side who had nothing to play for.

Meanwhile, over in east London, Spurs were staying in the Marriott Hotel in Canary Wharf in preparation for their game against West Ham: 'As is Martin Jol's custom for London matches,' wrote journalist Mihir Bose in the *Telegraph* newspaper at the time, 'A buffet dinner was laid out in a specially booked room and Jol was feeling particularly happy. Many of the players who had been carrying knocks were now fit, including [Robbie] Keane and [Michael] Carrick.' Then, out of nowhere, things turned to the worse for Martin Jol's team. 'From about 1am,' continued Bose, 'virtually Tottenham's entire team were violently sick... [Michael] Carrick, the most ill, was hardly able to walk. Early in the morning chairman Daniel Levy was informed that the Premier League would have to be asked for a postponement.'

It wasn't granted. Spurs' game against West Ham United – a game which would decide whether or not the club will be playing lucrative Champions League football for the first time in their history – was to go ahead with the other matches in the Premier League that day. Arsenal, replete in their season long claret colours, kicked-off against Wigan, while Spurs, depleted in numbers and feeling very under the weather, kicked off against West Ham. The latter of the two fixtures had an added subtext, given that West Ham were due to play in the FA Cup final the following weekend and manager Alan Pardew planned on resting a few of the Hammers' big players. But the possibility of facing a 'weaker' West Ham side (which featured talents such as Nigel Reo-Coker, Matthew Etherington and future Arsenal loanee Yossi Benayoun) certainly didn't help Tottenham's malaise: the North London side went 1-0 down in the space of 10 minutes after Carl Fletcher scored a rasping 30-yard goal. The visitors responded with a goal of their own – former Hammer Jermaine Defoe scoring a goal equal to the West Ham's efforts – and, having had a West Ham penalty saved by goalkeeper Paul Robinson, Tottenham left the pitch at half-time still in a decent position to qualify for the Champions League.

Over at Highbury, with one eye on Tottenham's plight and on West Ham's endeavor, Jack Wilshere and dad Andy watched the progress of the Arsenal team. It was a disconcertingly open game: Robert Pires had put Arsenal a goal up on eight minutes, striking from close-range in front of the Highbury faithful; Wigan equalised via Paul Scharner and then drove panic into the hearts of the spectators in the East, North and Clock End stands when they went ahead 2-1 in the 33rd minute with a David Thompson goal. The panic was soon quashed by Thierry Henry who put the Gunners back on level terms going into half-time, but Arsenal knew that it would take a stroke of fortune to allow them to qualify for the European competition next season.

Fortunately, a combination of sickness and grace sealed it for the red half of north London. Despite their best endeavours, Tottenham went behind to a crafty Yossi Benayoun goal on the 80th minute, allowing Arsenal to play-out the remaining 10 minutes of their own match with some semblance of calm. Of course, being 4-2 up against Wigan at home – in the last ever home match at one of the most iconic stadia in the country – certainly helped and Thierry Henry's hat-trick against the Latics eventually sealed Arsenal's qualification for the European Cup at Tottenham's expense.

What an afternoon it was for the Gunners. Jack had seen Arsenal win, qualify for the Champions League over Spurs, say goodbye to Highbury with a glorious victory and seen Thierry Henry kiss the pitch after putting the finishes touches on his farewell hat-trick in the stadium. Thierry Henry was the last in a long-line of Arsenal players to have shared a truly special bond with Highbury Stadium. Ian Wright broke Cliff Bastin's scoring record there, Tony Adams sealed Arsenal's first Premier League title in glorious fashion in front of the Arsenal faithful, and the Invincibles etched their legends in and around the marble halls of the magnificent stadium. Players, of various standards, had appeared on the Highbury turf – from the majesty of Marc Overmars through to the ignominy of Francis Jeffers or Eddie McGoldrick – and Jack could only feel privileged to have seen the such a legendary group of Arsenal players sign off on the hallowed turf. Of course, he was disappointed not to have played at Highbury, but he sensed a new dawn beginning at Arsenal and hoped the move to the

Emirates stadium, and all that came with it, would provide the first-team opportunities he so eagerly craved.

Back in Paris, Arsenal were preparing for the Champions League final. They faced Catalan giants Barcelona, a team which had recently strolled to the La Liga championship. Managed by Dutch football legend Frank Rijkaard, the Catalan outfit boasted FIFA World Footballer of the Year, Ronaldinho, along with a formidable midfield dominated by the illustrious Deco and anchored by the aging Brazilian defensive midfielder Edmilson. Barcelona also had a very strong defense, with the likes of Carlos Puyol and Rafael Marquez governing central defense, with support coming from full-backs Oleguer and former Gunner Giovanni Van Bronckhorst.

The Catalans were strong favourites going into the game against Arsenal, having dispatched the likes of AC Milan, Benfica and Chelsea on their way to the Stade de France final. They'd also had an immense season in La Liga, scoring 80 goals and finishing eight points clear of bitter rivals Real Madrid. Arsenal, on the other hand, had struggled to regain entry to the following season's Champions League, and were coming off the back of one of their most inconsistent seasons in recent history: the team had lost 11 times in the Premier League that season, shipping 31 goals home and away and losing to the likes of Middlesbrough, Blackburn Rovers and West Bromwich Albion in the process. The one consolation for Wenger et al – and it was possibly the biggest surprise for both Arsenal players and fans alike – was that Arsenal had gone through the Champions League knockout stages without conceding a goal. A makeshift back-four of Matthieu Flamini, Phillipe Senderos, Kolo Touré and

A NEW GENERATION

Emmanuel Eboué had kept out teams such as Real Madrid, Juventus and Villarreal to advance Arsenal through the upper echelons of the competition, and Arsenal goalkeeper Jens Lehmann was also having perhaps one of his best-ever spells between the Arsenal sticks.

As a resident of the Hale End Academy and a regular spectator in the London Colney training complex, Jack knew the secret to Arsenal's defensive invincibility during their run the final in Paris. At the end of the 2003/04 season, Martin Keown decided to hang up his playing boots and begin a tentative coaching role at Newbury Town. The former defender had obviously stayed in touch with the coaching staff at Arsenal, most notably youth coach Steve Bould, a fellow defender in George Graham's formidable Arsenal sides between 1993 and 1996. Wenger, conscious of the problematic nature of an unfamiliar back-four, had asked Keown to temporarily return to the club to train the new line, and Jack had seen the former defender at the Arsenal training complex, chatting to Steve Bould and walking to and from the London Colney training pitches.

It was shrewd placement: the Arsenal back four didn't concede a goal in 995 minutes of Champions League football – a record which still stands. The team went from September 2005 to May 2006 without letting a goal in, and with a back four consisting of one first-choice player and a utility player in the left-back position (Flamini) this is no mean feat. Arsenal, thus, went into the game against Barcelona as underdogs but with the knowledge that another 90 minutes of defensive invincibility might, *just might*, win them the European Cup.

JACK WILSHERE: ARSENAL D.N.A.

Jack watched the Champions League Final with his Arsenal-supporting family, but the final itself couldn't have started worse for the Gunners. Sent through on goal by a sublime pass by Ronaldihno, Barcelona striker Samuel Eto'o was hauled down by the onrushing Jens Lehmann and the German goalkeeper was sent off. Robert Pires was sacrificed for Arsenal's substitute goalkeeper Manuel Almunia, and the Gunners had to play the remaining two-thirds of the final with 10 men. Despite the disastrous start, Arsenal responded surprisingly well: a fortunate free kick won by Emmanel Eboué on the edge of the Barcelona box resulted in Thierry Henry floating in a wonderful cross, for a leaping Sol Campbell to plant a head on the ball and send it beyond Victor Valdes and into the Barcelona net. Arsenal led the game 1-0 going in at half-time and the support inside and outside the stadium was wondering whether a 10-man Arsenal side could possibly keep out such a creative Barcelona side. Their fears were confirmed when Barcelona substitute Henrik Larsson set-up Sammuel Eto'o to equalise and, only five minutes later, Juliano Belletti nipped in front of Arsenal's back-line to score the winning goal for the Catalans.

It was a great night for Barcelona, but for Arsène Wenger and Arsenal it seemed to signify not only a missed opportunity, but the end of an era: Arsenal, with the remnants of the great Invincible team of 2003/04, were playing at the top end of the game, against the best teams in Europe; they were also saying goodbye to their Highbury home of 93 years and looking at an uncertain near future where the possibility of building another great side was becoming more and more unlikely. Wenger was told, prior to going into the 2005/06 season, that the finances at Arsenal would be rather limited for the next few seasons – due mainly to the financing of the Emirates Stadium deal and all that comes with moving stadiums – and, standing by himself on the soaking wet pitch in the Stade de France on 17 May 2006, Wenger seemed to cut a solemn figure who knew he simply had to start again. With Thierry Henry's head already turned by Barcelona, the new Champions of Europe, Robert Pires seemingly off to join Villarreal, and with Gilberto, Sol Campbell and Jens Lehmann not getting any younger, the Arsenal manager knew that a new team was needed to compete with Manchester United, Chelsea, Liverpool and the top teams of Europe: with emerging talents such as Robin van Persie, Gael Clichy and Cesc Fàbregas coming through the ranks, Wenger also knew that a new, more financially stringent policy was required to steer Arsenal through the uncertain times ahead.

'We will be back, of course,' said the Arsenal manager after the game. 'I believe this team has grown a lot this season. We have plenty of good young players behind this team and I would like to thank them all because they have been fantastic. We are already strong and sometimes if you can transform your frustration at defeat in such a game as this then you can come back stronger – and we will do that.'

Arsenal returned to north London with their heads held high. The team went into the close season with a proud Champions League campaign under its belt and with another season in the European top flight to look forward to. The club said goodbye to Highbury for the last time and looked ahead to the first competitive game at the Emirates

JACK WILSHERE: ARSENAL D.N.A.

Stadium as the new Premier League season kicked off in earnest in the late summer. It was announced that the first game at the new stadium would be Dennis Bergkamp's testimonial, to be played in July 2006; the legendary Dutch forward had announced his retirement at the end of the 2005/06 season, signing off a career which included 315 Arsenal appearances and 87 goals.

Jack, as ever, continued his development at Arsenal's Hale End Academy and was hoping to take full advantage of the club's new-found interest in youth and potential. With the disbanding of the Invincibles and the new financial restrictions placed upon the playing staff at Arsenal F.C., Jack knew it was now or never to make that final step up to the top of the English game. Indeed, the next season at the club would turn out to be one of the most important in the young player's budding career.

7 – UPS AND DOWNS
2006/07

*In which Jack gets an unexpected call – Wenger looks to youth –
Jack finally trains with the Arsenal first team – and says goodbye
to one of the all-time greats*

Jack was on the way up... he could tell.

Fourteen years old and playing at youth level for the recent runners-up of the European Cup certainly wasn't to be sniffed at. He had been captain of the under 11s, 12s, 13s and 14s school football teams and was probably – along with his mate Jake Argent-Martin – the best player currently gracing the playing fields of Hertfordshire. Jack had gone from Whitehill prodigy to Priory hero in the space of five years and he was now looking to take his playing career to the next level both with his school and with Arsenal.

Day in, day out, Jack was demonstrating a remarkable ability with the football. He'd learnt so much since he started with Arsenal only a few years ago and had come such a long way since the days when all he wanted to do was run with the ball and shoot towards the opposition's goal: touch, tempo, intelligence and patience were all new aspects of his game instilled by the coaches at Arsenal, and he was slowly, but surely, developing into one of the most interesting talents in the Hale End Academy. In games against the youth teams of Ajax, Chelsea, and his beloved West Ham, Wilshere excelled against players two years his senior, getting forward all the time and expressing himself as was his wont on the pitch; his ability, furthermore, to change the game – to slow the tempo and dictate the rate of passing – was beginning to shine through, and a real reputation, independent of The Priory school and countless county cup campaigns, was also beginning to develop.

Former Chelsea striker Kenny Swain had been coaching the FA's Under-16 side since 2004 and was in constant contact with club academies up and down the country. He knew Roy Massey well and whenever they spoke on the phone, the Arsenal coach would always refer to a talented kid he had on his books who played the game like it was the easiest thing in the world. Once Jack reached the under-14s age category, Massey thought the kid deserved a chance on a bigger stage and recommended his young player to Kenny.

It was bold of Massey to recommend a 14-year-old kid to the top end of a level two years his senior. But the coach was confident that Jack could make the step up to the next level and hold his own against the young men of the Under-16s. Jack, of course, was used to playing against older opposition – ever since he was drafted in to play for Arsenal at the tender age of nine he outclassed other players in his age bracket, and Massey was one of the first coaches to develop the boy's ability by playing him against more advanced opposition. Swain, on the other hand, was sceptical of Massey's enthusiasm for the young Hitchinian. How many times had Swain heard his friend Roy talk about how Arsenal had unearthed the next Dennis Bergkamp or the next Thierry Henry; indeed, the list of players Massey had talked-up but failed to shine in amongst the dogfight that is international youth football was endless. But there was something about the way Roy spoke with such enthusiasm about Mr Wilshere – from his finesse on the ball to his raw hunger to win a football match – that so intrigued Swain. And with that in mind, the England coach took Massey at his word and visited Hale End to view one of the kid's games.

Ninety or so minutes later, Jack Wilshere was asked to play for England.

The kid, of course, was blown away. Only a few years ago Jack was mucking about with his brother and sister in the garden, re-enacting his favourite Paulo Di Canio goals and annoying his siblings with his constant trickery; but now, only a few years later, a coach from the English Football Association was asking him to pull on the England jersey and represent his country for the first time. It was both a massive surprise and an absolute honour. Jack had spent the majority of his short life playing for teams of varying levels: from his debut games for Whitehill Junior School, to playing for Arsenal week in, week out against teams such as Ajax, Jack understood what it meant to represent a club or institution on the football pitch. But never did he think he would go on to represent his national side at any level of the game. He knew it was only a small opportunity – he was, after all, only selected for a try-out in the Under-16s squad and a starting place in the team was far from certain – but an opportunity is an opportunity and Jack knew it would be foolish to take anything for granted.

After speaking to Massey at Arsenal and conferring with his dad Andy, Jack spoke to Kenny Swain on the phone to gather more information on what the selection meant. According to Kenny, Jack was to be called up for the Under-16 Victory Shield trophy, an FA-funded tournament featuring under-16s from the home nations, including England, Scotland, Wales and Northern Ireland. He'd be in contention for the first team, of course, and would have the opportunity to play each opponent at least once, but Swain couldn't guarantee any game time at all, and emphasised that hard work would get him in the team and not reputation alone. Jack understood: he'd come this far doing hard work, why would he stop now?

Founded in 1925, the first ever Victory Shield was won by Scotland, before being put on hold until 1949 and 1951 when it was won by Wales, and England and Wales (joint holders) respectively; the cup went off the official youth programme throughout the latter half of the 20th century until 1990 when the tournament gained interest from various television channels. Since then it has grown into a premier tournament in the youth season and arguably one of the most significant international youth competitions.

Not only does the Victory Shield represent a chance to play for one's country and a relatively young age, the competition also has a proud tradition of producing regular international players for their respective teams: Peter Shilton, Sir Stanley Matthews, Sir Trevor Brooking and

Duncan Edwards all played for England in various tournaments throughout the Shield's history; Harry Gregg, Norman Whiteside, and Keith Gillespie have all represented Northern Ireland at the Victory Shield at certain stages in their careers; Kenny Dalglish, Graeme Souness and Arsenal legend George Graham all pulled on Under-16 Scotland jerseys and played in the competition, while Welsh legends such as Ian Rush and John Toshack also represented their country at the youth tournament.

It was a massive honour for Jack to even think about playing for the national side, let alone follow in the footsteps of some of the most accomplished players the United Kingdom has ever produced. Jack would have seen names such as Dalglish and Matthews and been overwhelmed by the sense of history and his own place in the bigger footballing picture; he'd have also seen the name Brooking and, being a devout Hammer, thought the whole situation to be completely and utterly unreal.

Yet he took the call-up in his stride and readied himself for the first game of the tournament in October 2006. He returned to school with a spring in his step and told all his mates the amazing news, making sure they knew that the tournament was also going to be broadcast live on *Sky Sports*! Modern-day England internationals such as Michael Owen and Wayne Rooney were first spotted at the Victory Shield and there was major interest in the youth tournament from clubs up and down the country. Jack, of course, wasn't even thinking about a starting place in the team – and certainly wasn't going to be comparing himself with the great Michael Owen or the mercurial Wayne Rooney – but he couldn't help but gloat about the fact that all of his hard work at both school and club level had finally began to pay off with an out-of-the-blue call-up to the England youth team.

As he prepared for the tournament, which began in the autumn, Jack continued to watch his parent club Arsenal compete at the top of the Premier League. He was particularly interested in the youth prospects at the club, hoping their success in the first team might extend Arsène Wenger's sudden interest in the Arsenal youth sides. Cesc Fàbregas was now a regular starter and becoming one of the most integral parts of the team. Other decent prospects such as Gael Clichy and Robin van Persie were also pushing for first-team places, although competition was obviously very tough throughout the Arsenal side.

The manager, of course, had been very busy following Arsenal's loss in the Champions League final in May. He was looking to freshen up the squad and reward some of the 'young players' to whom he had alluded following the game in Paris with brand new contracts. Wenger also wanted to tie down club captain Thierry Henry. The forward, as always, was coveted by clubs the world over, but it was the new European champions, Barcelona, who desired his services the most. Ever the enigma, Henry was coy on his Arsenal future after the Champions League final and admitted no decision had been made prior to the close season. Wenger, conscious of the young talent coming through the squad and the importance of experience spearheading his attack, persuaded the board to stump-up the cash to keep their talismanic captain and ensure the transition on the field from Highbury to the Emirates was a smooth one. The

French striker agreed a new four-year deal and Arsenal could begin to look forward to at least another season with one of the best players in the world scoring from all angles on the pitch.

Henry aside, there were plenty of comings and goings prior to the first kick-off at Ashburton Grove: Sol Campbell, the goalscorer in the final in the Stade de France, was released on a free transfer and signed for Harry Redknapp's Portsmouth; Robert Pires, the outfield player cruelly sacrificed following Jens Lehmann's sending-off, was also released and duly signed by beaten semi-finalists Villarreal. Other exits included José-Antonio Reyes, who was loaned to Real Madrid in exchange for Brazilian forward Julio Baptista, and Lauren, Arsenal's 'invincible' right back, was also off-loaded to Portsmouth for approximately £500,000.

The final – rather protracted – exit of the summer was that of Academy graduate Ashley Cole. The defender had been hankering for a move away from Arsenal for some time and was even involved in a 'tapping-up' scandal with Chelsea boss, José Mourinho. In January 2005, Cole and his agent Jonathan Barnett allegedly met with José Mourinho and Chelsea chief executive Peter Kenyon; what was discussed remains unclear, but it triggered a process of events which saw Ashley Cole go from darling of Highbury to scorn of the Emirates. Following the scandal – for which Cole was fined £100,000 – Wenger and the Arsenal board hoped to contract the defender to the club, offering a slight pay rise on his already considerable wage. Cole, inevitably, declined Arsenal's new offer and opted to sign for Chelsea, and by the beginning of September, Cole was heading to west London while a certain French centre-back came the other way. The centre-back in question, William Gallas, arrived at Arsenal following stints at Marseille in Ligue 1 and with Chelsea. A strong, idiosyncratic centre-half, he was signed with a view to replacing the recently departed Sol Campbell and also to bring in some much-needed experience into what was a rather young Arsenal side.

The outgoing Cole left a rather bittersweet taste in the mouths of the Arsenal management. On the one hand, he arguably turned his back on a club who had nurtured him through his youth development and given him ample opportunity to garner experience on every stage at the top level, before deciding enough was enough and signing for one of Arsenal's closest rivals. But on the other he was, quite simply, the best-ever export from the Arsenal youth academy: from Jermaine Pennant, Jérémie Aliadière, and David Bentley all the way through to the talented Cesc Fàbregas and the enigmatic Sebastian Larsson, numerous graduates of the Arsenal Academy were undoubtedly talented individuals. But Ashley Cole was the most successful player in the history of the Academy. In total he'd made 156 appearances for the club, winning three Premier League medals and three FA Cups, and whatever the club supporters came to think of the Ashley the man, Ashley the player was more or less the original jewel in Arsenal's Youth Academy crown.

Which is why his departure from the club in the close season of 2006 was so perplexing for a young player like Jack: 14 years old and learning his trade at one of the most passionate and well supported clubs in Europe, Jack didn't quite see why a player of Cole's calibre – especially given he was a fan of the club ever since he could kick a ball – would want to leave. Either way, it wasn't Jack's problem and the young central midfielder looked forward to the new Premier League campaign with Wenger's young, new-*ish* looking squad.

Indeed, apart from Gallas and loanee Julio Baptista, and the numerous graduates from the youth and reserve teams, Wenger only added one more member to the side. Creative midfielder Tomáš Rosický was signed from Borrusia Dortmund off the back of a decent World Cup performance within an underperforming Czech Republic team. Another in a long line of creative midfielders Wenger seemed to be keen on stockpiling, the attacking midfielder had won the Czech player of the year in 2005 and had gained the nickname 'Little Mozart' in Germany due to his ability to orchestrate the play on the field. Quick, intelligent, and with a definitive eye for goal, Rosický was certainly a player the young Wilshere could learn from. What's more, he was another short, nimble-footed player with a low centre of gravity, who was able to turn away from his defence and attack in more or less two touches – something Jack had been trying to develop ever since he joined the Hale End Academy.

Rosický was the last player to join the Gunners before the season began in earnest in August 2006. He was also only one of four over-25-year-olds to join the Arsenal playing staff since 2004. Goalkeepers Manuel Almunia (27 when he joined) and Mart Poom (34) were signed in 2004 and 2005 respectively, while the aforementioned Gallas (29) signed the same summer as the Czech midfielder.

What's more, Rosický replaced 30-year-old Robert Pires, an Arsenal player with two Premier League and three FA Cup medals to his name. The Frenchman sought a new contract towards the end of the 2004/05 season, only to be offered a one-year extension to his existing deal. The negotiations with Pires – which were never resolved and concluded with the Frenchman leaving Highbury on a free transfer – coincided with a slow change in transfer policy at the club between 2004 and 2006. Wenger was used to signing slightly more experienced players who could bring something to club regardless of age (relatively speaking, of course). Indeed, the then vice-chairman David Dein was busy behind the scenes throughout 2003-2005 trying to make deals for the likes of Cristiano Ronaldo, Harry Kewell and José Antonio Reyes (who eventually joined Arsenal in 2004). But Dein felt he couldn't make the deals he wanted to due to the lack of funds at the club which was due, in turn, to the building of the new stadium; he said making deals was 'like being in a boxing ring with one hand tied behind my back' and both he, and to a certain extent Wenger, were left perplexed by the direction of the club's finances. Dein, of course, would take his frustrations to the next level by the start of the New Year by leaving the club altogether, but Wenger took a gamble. Speaking retrospectively to *The Guardian* newspaper, he said: 'I believe that the club was at the moment of history [in 2005] where you have to go a step further if you want to become one of the biggest clubs in the world. I told [the Arsenal board] we had good youngsters and that we could still compete at the top level.'

It was a bold statement to make and a gamble for the Frenchman. But Wenger had faith in the likes of van Persie, Fàbregas, Clichy and Rosický and believed they would form what would be his third successful Arsenal side. He was also signaling the importance of youth development within a club of Arsenal's size and argued that Arsenal's future lay not in signing established stars, but *making* them: 'What you always have to consider is how you produce a player,' Wenger added. 'If you want to completely develop a player, ideally you take him at the age of five and you bring him right through to the first team. But the reality is that he arrives at your club at 16 or 17. If you look at the top clubs in Europe, Arsenal are producing more young players than any of them. I have tried to build an academy that will recruit young local lads. At present, we have exceptional under-14s and under-16s. Technically they are extraordinary.' The statement was, unsurprisingly, music to Jack Wilshere's ears.

With a squad primarily made up of under 25s built around the talents of Cesc Fàbregas, Arsenal headed into the 2006/07 looking to consummate their move from Highbury to the Emirates with some silverware. It was a difficult start for the Gunners: the first game at the Emirates ended in a 1-1 draw against Aston Villa (Villa defender Olof Mellberg scored the first ever goal at the new stadium, while Arsenal midfielder Gilberto Silva got the equaliser), after which Arsenal lost to a single Joey Barton goal against Manchester City, before again drawing in their new stadium against Middlesbrough. By the time they registered their first win – a valuable three points against the old enemy Manchester

United – Arsenal were in tenth position and facing an uphill struggle to return to the summit of the Premier League.

The first few months of the season proved to be a difficult period for Wenger and his young team. Coming off the back of an anti-climatic 2005/06 season in which the side struggled to qualify for the Champions League, Wenger was under pressure to make the new group of players gel and gel quickly. Some experience still remained, of course: goalkeeper Jens Lehmann remained at the club along with fans' favourite Freddie Ljungberg. Plus Thierry Henry was still at the club despite constant talk of his imminent departure – and despite the fact he'd only just signed a new deal and committed to the Arsenal *for life*.

The problem for Wenger, though, was that many of his established 'older' players were becoming unavailable due to injury. Thierry Henry, for instance, missed first-team games at the start of the season due to various injuries, including chronic back pain which would go on to mar the rest of his career. The manager was therefore forced into fielding a relatively inexperienced team made up of newly signed players and young first teamers, testing his own assertion that the club could move forward with such a young squad. The aforementioned victory against Manchester United included a handful of seasoned Arsenal players such as Gilberto Silva, Jens Lehmann, Kolo Touré and the relatively experienced 21-year-old Cesc Fàbregas, but the remainder of the team was made up of fresh faces: young Swiss central defender Johann Djourou began the game in the unfamiliar position of left-back, William Gallas partnered Kolo Touré in central defence, Tomáš Rosický started in midfield and winter signing Emmanuel Adebayor began as the lone front man for the Gunners.

It was at this point that the buzzwords of 'youth', 'promise' and 'potential' began floating into the Arsenal ether – a plethora of clichés associated with Arsène Wenger's team for seasons to come. Wenger hadn't made a secret of his desire to build a young squad around the culture of Arsenal F.C., and the press knew that Arsenal's finances were severely limited going into their first season at the Emirates Stadium. Indeed, the directions of Manchester United and Arsenal seemed to be epitomized by the two protagonists on the Old Trafford pitch that day in September: Manchester United's Cristiano Ronaldo, bought in 2003 for approximately £12 million, was a confident, athletic and direct player whose talent was undeniably apparent even during his early games for the Red Devils. Cesc Fàbregas, on the other hand, was brought in by Arsenal at a very young age for a relatively low price and his development coincided with the club's emphasis on development and patience.

However, when Arsenal began to struggle in the first few months of the 2006/07 season, Arsène Wenger rebuked his critics with talk of how his team required time to gel in the short term and how his team had the potential to go on and win 'big things' by the end of the season. After all, the manager wasn't likely to admit publically that the team he was building was to deliver success in seasons to come; Wenger had to keep the team – and therefore the club – competitive in the here and now.

It proved to be a very difficult task. When the Arsenal

manager attempted to draw on the depth of a squad made up of most under 25s, the manager's desire to win things 'with kids' was looking more like a gamble after every single game. For example, Arsenal's fourth loss in the league in 2006/07 came against a Fulham side struggling to keep a foothold in the Premier League. With forthcoming games against Spurs, Chelsea and FC Porto in the Champions League in mind, Wenger opted to rest his first choice full-backs Gael Clichy and Emmanuel Eboué, and instead play Academy graduate Justin Hoyte at right-back with Mathieu Flamini filling in at left-back. He also left Cesc Fàbregas on the bench and played the relatively untested Alex Song-Billong in his wake. Their absences were felt across the whole of the Arsenal team: 'the distribution of Fábregas, a half-time substitute, was sorely missed by Arsenal,' wrote Jon Brodkin in *The Guardian*, 'and the inadequacies particularly of Alex Song and also the stand-in full-backs, Justin Hoyte and Mathieu Flamini, were unmistakable.' Wenger was beginning to come in for criticism from some dissenting Arsenal fans, many of whom were wondering why the manager was compelled to disband the successful team of 2003/04 so quickly.

As the season wore on, it looked as if the Manchester United win in September was going to be the high point of the campaign. A 3-0 home win against Tottenham and a draw at Stamford Bridge against Chelsea remedied some of the ills within the squad, but a lack of form and inability to string more than a few wins together saw Arsenal outside of the top four come the New Year. Even the Champions League wasn't proving any easier for Wenger's men: having qualified for the competition by beating Dinamo Zagreb over two legs, the Gunners contrived to win only three of their six group games, losing and drawing to CSKA Moscow and drawing away to FC Porto. As former Gunner Moritz Volz fired in the 15,000th Premier League goal for Fulham against Chelsea towards the end of 2006 and Jack Wilshere celebrated his 15th birthday at the start of 2007, it looked as if Arsenal, regular conquerors of the Premier League, were heading into the new calendar year in the midst of the dreaded 'transitional season'. And so Arsenal fans began looking to the future to see who was coming up through the ranks.

Jack, of course, had just completed his first tournament playing for the England Under-16s at the Victory Shield, but it was one of the most bittersweet experiences of his young life. After playing his first game in an England shirt, Jack was informed of the death of his uncle James in a car accident. It was devastating news. 'I had just played my first game for England Schoolboys and I was so happy and so thrilled,' Wilshere told the *Daily Mirror* in 2011. 'Then we got the news. My uncle was a passenger in a car that went out of control. It was the worst thing that has ever happened to me.' The kid was very close to his uncle James – indeed, he would later go on to describe him as being like another brother – and Jack naturally found it very difficult to deal with his loss during his time with the young England squad. Uncle James, along with his dad Andy, had been the chief aides in the kid's budding football career and Jack had always confided in his uncle ever since he was a boy. At 16 years old, James was only a few years older than Jack when he passed away and it was the mixture of elation at being picked for England and the sobering reality of the death of a loved one which forced Jack make a vow to achieve his dreams. From then on Jack felt like he was living two lives – that of his own and that of his beloved friend and uncle. He spent a few days at home with his family and reflected on what his uncle would want: for Jack and his family to enjoy life and try to make all of their dreams come true. Jack returned to the England camp with a new outlook on life and would go on to commemorate his uncle in his own special way in years to come.

Back at the competition, Jack's fleeting substitute performances against the home nations allowed him to really consolidate what he'd learnt at Arsenal and try and develop his game amongst relatively anonymous teammates at youth level – particularly during training sessions. His club, Wilshere was beginning to understand, did things slightly differently at Hale End: during training for the Victory Shield, Jack's teammates would frequently train without the ball to enable them to reach peak fitness and increase their stamina. For Jack, football training was all about playing *with* the ball; in fact, 90 per cent of his time on the training pitch was undertaken with the ball at his feet, so he was surprised to see his peers work through different routines.

Either way the experience of playing competitive football for the England Under-16s was massively helpful in the young central midfielder's development. Jack was beginning to sharpen his team skills, learning how to communicate with different players and entertaining different styles; his agility on the ball was coming into play too and his new-found chemistry with his England teammates allowed him to once again dictate the game and demonstrate his unique playing style. Kenny Swain was impressed, and with the Under-16s returning from the competition outright winners (having won the Shield every time since 2001, sharing it with Scotland and Wales in 2003 and 2005 respectively), the England coach sent Jack back to Arsenal with a sparkling review.

Back at his parent club, Jack was eager to kick on following his significant contribution at the Victory Shield. His confidence was sky-high and he'd already marked the England Under-18s as his next international adventure. But Roy Massey, ever conscious of a young player's hubris – he'd seen it countless times before – tried to keep his feet on the ground: confidence was one thing, thought the Arsenal coach, arrogance another. After speaking to fellow coach Steve Bould, both Massey and Bould decided it might be fun – if not rather sobering – to give the young maestro a bit of a surprise for his 15th birthday. Bould popped over to the first-team training pitches and had a word with the club captain. A few hours later, Jack received a message from Bould that the first team required three Arsenal youth players to go over to the first-team pitches for a light training exercise. Jack didn't know what to say; 'well go on then' said Bould, and Jack and couple of fellow Hale Enders slowly ambled over to the first-team pitches. A few years later Jack recalled the story to *The Times*: 'There was [Thierry] Henry, [Ray] Parlour and [Freddie] Ljungberg and they asked for three of the youth team for a training exercise. I was nervous. When Henry shakes your hand you are a bit, "Whoa". We did shooting at the end of the session. Henry stuck the ball down on the edge of the box and put one right in the top corner. Wow!'

From that day on, Jack understood his place at the club and understood what it meant to work your way up to the top of your game. He had returned from the Victory Shield with a surge of confidence bordering on arrogance and Massey wanted to remind Jack of where he was and what team he was playing with. The kid understood perfectly well once he'd returned from the first-team playing fields: he was a uniquely talented kid trying to make his way to the top of a uniquely talented football club in which some of the most well-respected Premier League players were plying their trade. Jack might have been the top dog of the Under-16s Victory Shield, but he had a long way to go before he could count himself an Arsenal first-team player and amongst the elite of the Premier League. Still, from that cold January morning on the first-team football pitches, Jack never looked back.

It was no surprise to hear that Henry et al were putting in extra training shifts with the youth teams at London Colney. By mid-January 2007, Arsenal were 12 points off the pace at the top of the Premier League and were still trying to find some sort of solid form to propel them further than fourth. A home win against league leaders Manchester United certainly helped: after going 1-0 down in the first half, Wenger's side showed character to turn the game on its head and claim all three points. The hero of the afternoon was

Thierry Henry, who – rather surprisingly – leapt up to *header* Emmanuel Eboué's cross, sending the Emirates into raptures. With good reason too: United had arrived at Ashburton Grove in decent form and a win against the league's supposed Champions in waiting was quite a tonic to what had been a relatively dismal season so far.

Indeed, as 2006 became 2007, it became more and more apparent to the Arsenal fans that Arsène Wenger and the playing staff had already begun talking about 'the future' as if the current season was more or less over. The press seemed to agree: 'Arsène Wenger's promising line-up is still at the development stage,' wrote Kevin McCarra in his *Guardian* match report, 'and it appeared that the manager would take no more from this fixture than notes on all the areas needing improvement... All new grounds require folklore to endow them with an identity. Memories have to accrue before fans can feel wholly at home. Henry's finish here could be the first incident to make the Emirates resonant for supporters. It was all the better for the fact that it capped a comeback that seemed beyond reach... The goals for Wenger's side, all the same, were nudges to remind observers of the quality this manager possesses.'

Perhaps more significant for Arsenal, though, was the injury caused to Robin van Persie when he scored the equaliser in the same game. The Dutchman had been the main source of goals for the Gunners over the first half of the season and was finally beginning to look the player Wenger had envisaged when he bought him from Feyenoord in the summer of 2005. Indeed, only a few months earlier the Dutchman scored what the Arsenal manager called the 'goal of a lifetime' against Charlton Athletic, leaping nearly a metre high to volley Emmanuel Eboué's pinpoint cross; the goal was nominated for *Match of the Day*'s 'Goal of the Season' competition and narrowly missed out winning the accolade to Wayne Rooney's effort against Bolton Wanderers (a sumptuous team breakaway goal).

The problem for Arsenal as they geared up for the 'business-end' of the 2006/07 season was that the team seemed to be taking one step forward and two steps back: every time Wenger's side looked to have turned a corner, the team squandered the opportunity to move forward by either losing or drawing against sides they should beat easily. Following their emphatic win against Manchester United at Ashburton Grove, for example, Arsenal travelled to play a Middlesbrough side languishing in 12th position in the league. Arsenal returned to north London with a point following a very drab performance in North Yorkshire, remaining fourth in the league and a massive 17 points behind United in top spot.

The problem, according to pundits and journalists alike, was clear: the Arsenal side of 2006/07 missed the ruthlessness of Wenger's previous teams. Where the Invincible team of 2003/04 looked to counter-attack a team with free-flowing, direct football, the newer Wenger sides placed more emphasis on patient passing and keeping possession of the ball. The 2006/07 FA Cup run was a pertinent example of their profligacy: Arsenal, having beaten Liverpool in the cup at Anfield at the beginning of January (3-1, with two goals coming from a majestic Tomáš Rosický), were drawn against Bolton Wanderers at home.

Coming only a week after Arsenal dispatched Manchester United in the league, the Gunners contrived to send the fixture to a replay after drawing 1-1 with the Trotters at the Emirates; a fortnight later the teams met again and Arsenal managed to squeeze through after winning the game 3-1 following an extra-time goal from Freddie Ljungberg. The Gunners were then drawn against Mark Hughes' Blackburn Rovers at home and again failed to get the result they required, drawing 0-0 in a tense game at the Emirates (Cesc Fàbregas courted controversy after the match when he allegedly told Mark Hughes that he didn't deserve to play for Barcelona following such a cynical display form his Blackburn side). Thus Arsenal travelled up to Lancashire to play yet another FA Cup replay and were duly knocked out following a toothless performance against Hughes' side. It was indicative of the way Wenger was developing his side: the Arsenal fans were used to formidable, direct football but the Arsenal manager seemed to be altering his style to the detriment of Arsenal's results. It was rather galling for the Arsenal faithful, especially given that it was only a few seasons ago that the Invincibles were tearing teams apart and not taking any hostages. The Arsenal of 2006/07, by contrast, seemed reluctant to take their chances and were paying for it in the Champions League, Premier League and, of course, the FA Cup.

The Carling Cup was a different matter, however. In November 2006, Arsenal travelled to play Liverpool at Anfield for a place in the semi-final of the league cup. Throughout the past few seasons, Arsène Wenger used the competition as a platform for the youngsters within the

Reserve Team squad, enabling inexperienced players to gain some valuable experience without the added pressure of league or European football. The team which travelled to Liverpool included youngsters Justin Hoyte, Alexander Song-Billong, Armand Traore, Theo Walcott and Abou Diaby alongside slightly more established players such as Cesc Fàbregas, Julio Baptista and Kolo Touré. Arsenal returned to north London having put six past Liverpool at Anfield, the first time a visiting side had done so since 1929. The score was 6-3 to Arsenal and Wenger's youngsters looked to be growing with every league cup game they played. 'For Arsenal,' wrote Daniel Taylor in the *Guardian*, 'a semi-final awaits against their old friends Tottenham and, beyond that, an exhilarating future for academy graduates such as Alexandre Song and Armand Traoré.' Indeed, the semi-final against Spurs was a similarly enthralling encounter: the first leg at White Hart Lane finished 2-2, but the returning fixture at the Emirates saw Arsenal win 5-3 following an extra-time goal from Jérémie Aliadière.

The Carling Cup run was very rewarding for the Arsenal youth team management. Graduates such as Hoyte, Song, Aliadière, Traore and Diaby were gaining valuable experience in competitive matches across the country; what's more, the majority of clubs were fielding very strong sides and testing Wenger's young side. Not least Chelsea, who booked their place in the final at the Millennium Stadium following wins against Aston Villa, Newcastle and Wycombe Wanderers. José Mourinho was naming close to a full strength first team squad for every Carling Cup game and their semi-final win against Wycombe included a brace for England international Frank Lampard and £30 million man Andriy Shevchenko.

Conversely, youth coaches could see the difference in confidence at Arsenal: with young players coming up against established internationals – and not only holding their own but beating them in the process – the confidence within training sessions was sky-high. Moreover, the opportunities Wenger presented to the youth teams through the Carling Cup created a competitive atmosphere throughout the youth teams from under-16s up. A 15-year-old Jack Wilshere was perhaps slightly too young to be considered for even a place on the bench for the Carling Cup but he knew that the road to the top of Wenger's Premier League team sheet was via the competition.

The Carling Cup team of 2006/07, despite their best efforts, was unsuccessful at the Millennium Stadium in February. Mourinho's Chelsea side – made up of countless first-team internationals – simply had too much for Wenger's young men. The loss left Arsenal trophy-less for the season 2006/07 after the Gunners went on to finish fourth in the Premier League and were knocked out of the Champions League by a very ordinary PSV Eindhoven side. Their underachievement also led to the exit of one of the most iconic players ever to have worn the Arsenal jersey: Thierry Henry, who had only just signed a new four-year contract in the summer of 2006, decided to leave the club in search of new challenges with FC Barcelona. In a tearful goodbye to Gunners, the talismanic captain spoke about his love for the club and the memories he'd shared with all the Arsenal fans. He said he would always follow the Arsenal and that the Gunners would always be in his heart – a big thing to say considering he was going on to play for Barcelona, Arsenal's Champions League nemesis only 12 months before.

For Jack Wilshere, there would never be another player quite like Thierry Henry. Ever since he joined the club in 2001, Henry was more or less the main man in and around the Arsenal training facilities; from the terraces of Highbury and the Emirates, all the way down the ranks through to youth level at Hale End, Thierry Henry's legend was palpable wherever you were at the club, and Jack Wilshere was always a little star-struck whenever he was in the great man's presence. They'd trained together, of course – the kid had had a few training sessions with the first team since his inaugural session on that cold January morning – but Henry continually managed to astound both Jack and his fellow youngsters with his effortless technique both with and without the ball. He was a great player to learn from and an experienced international; he was also evidence of what kind of player you can be if you truly apply yourself.

One of the final goodbyes Henry said was to manager Arsène Wenger. He had played under the manager for nearly a decade, both at Arsenal and at FC Monaco when he was 17 years old (under Wenger's tutelage Henry won French player of the year in 1996). Indeed, the striker also recorded an emotional farewell video message for the Arsenal fans in which he said his goodbyes and thanked them for their amazing support. In the video he speaks of his gratitude to the club for his development as both a player and a man: 'Well guys, I just wanted to tell you you've been tremendous for me. I know you can't see it but I'm shaking right now...you are in my head and in my heart... I hope you do appreciate what you've done for me... and help me grow as a man and be a better football player... Arsenal will always be in my blood and in my heart... once you're a Gooner you'll always be a Gooner.' From an unknown French rookie plucked from the wings of Juventus, through to arguably the most sophisticated player Europe had ever produced, Thierry Henry was the personification of dedication and pure talent. For a player like Jack Wilshere – on the fringes of the England squad and at the top of his game at youth level – Thierry Henry represented everything a player could be if he put his mind to it. One requires time, patience and, above all, talent to reach Henry's level, and Jack Wilshere, following the loss of his Uncle James and subsequent elevation into the England Youth Squad, started to understand the importance of both patience *and* determination in getting to the top of his game.

It had undoubtedly been a massive season for Jack. From starting the campaign as captain of The Priory school football team through to playing at youth level with the England Under-16s, Jack's development had seen a significant jump in its trajectory over the past 12 months. The death of his Uncle James had certainly had an effect on the way he viewed life and his involvement in the game of football; beforehand he took things for granted – he'd always be the captain of his school side, for example – but ever since the tragedy occurred at the start of 2007, the kid realised that you have to fight for everything in life and take your opportunities. Players like Thierry Henry were obviously born with bags of talent but his development as a player hadn't occurred overnight – it took time, patience and drive to get to the top end of your game in football and Jack was coming to realise that he had a long way to go before he could even consider playing week in, week out in the Premier League. First things first for Jack, however: he had to leave school and become an official 'scholar' of the Arsenal Academy. Now it was time to really 'man up'.

8 – SCHOLAR
2007/08

*In which Jack's effort is finally rewarded – Wenger dithers
on the new captaincy – Jack heads off to Malaysia for the
Champions Youth Cup – and Bould hands him an
unexpected promotion*

The most pressing question for Arsenal's first team
following the departure of Thierry Henry was who was
going to replace him as captain? The 2007/08 season was
beginning and Arsène Wenger was yet to name Henry's
successor. The obvious choice was Gilberto Silva, an
experienced defensive midfielder left over from the days if
the Invincibles who had been a vice-captain throughout the
2006/07 season. The Brazilian had been at the club since
2002 and was considered one of the most respected and
renowned players in world football; he was, more
significantly, the most experienced player in Arsenal's
dressing room, and following the departure of Henry in the
summer, Arsenal fans thought Silva's appointment was all
but a formality.

But the Arsenal manager had other ideas. Wenger was

considering a number of players for the role at the club – including Ivorian centre-back Kolo Touré, goalkeeper Jens Lehmann and Catalan maestro Cesc Fàbregas – yet it was another, relatively new member of the squad whose 'leadership qualities' caught the manager's eye. '[The captain] will be William Gallas,' Wenger told *Arsenal TV Online* during an eagerly awaited pre-season press conference. 'There will also be two vice-captains, Kolo Touré and Gilberto. I feel centre-back is always the best position to lead on the pitch and it is Gallas who has more experience at the back. But Gilberto has always been a great captain and Kolo Touré has a stature too... I made a decision that I want all those experienced players, along with Jens Lehmann, to be involved off the pitch... Players like Jens and Gilberto can play the role of a club captain. They can have a very strong impact mentally on the team. I want them to take on that responsibility.'

The announcement came as quite a shock to Gilberto Silva. The Brazilian had been left in the dark about the captaincy and only found out about Wenger's decision after the manager had gone public with the news. 'I was surprised [Wenger] didn't speak to me about his decision,' he told the *Daily Mail*. 'He had the time to do it because I was at the training ground before it was made public. He didn't say anything to me and I just found out about it that evening when I saw it on the Arsenal website.'

Indeed, Wenger's indecisiveness over Henry's successor looked as if it might derail the start of the 2007/08 campaign with the season barely a match-day old. With a dwindling supply of experience in the squad (Freddie Ljungberg was the latest high-profile former Invincibles member to depart from the squad in the summer of 2007, moving to West Ham for an undisclosed fee), press and pundits alike were already questioning Arsenal's potential in the league. 'They are admired across the country for their sweet touches and subtle skills', wrote *The Daily Mail's* Neil Ashton only a few days before the season kicked off at the Emirates against Fulham, 'but the Premier League has Arsenal down as a soft touch. Bully Arsène Wenger's young boys and they will crack under the pressure. Prick at their fragile confidence and they will collapse. Get at Cesc Fàbregas and they will fall apart.' The previous season – a campaign which saw the Gunners struggle away from home and come to rely quite heavily on the youth prospects progressing via the Carling Cup competition – Arsène Wenger's side began to develop a reputation for having a 'soft underbelly' or, as a Ashton says, having 'a soft touch'. It was a criticism which would permeate the club for seasons to come and Wenger's continued faith in youth prospects such as Fàbregas and a particular young central midfielder progressing through the youth ranks certainly didn't allay the press' newfound view of the once 'invincible' team.

But new captain Gallas wouldn't countenance such criticisms and merely called on the younger players of the squad to shoulder a lot more responsibility. 'It was about adaptation last [season],' Gallas claimed in Ashton's newspaper. 'But when I'm on the pitch, I want to win everything... Age cannot be used as an excuse for not challenging for the league any more. The players understand how they have to play sometimes, they are professionals and they've had another year's experience… We've changed as a team and we know we have to fight, to be compact and to defend well… I don't think teams can beat us by kicking us anymore. Our players understand football better. Sometimes football isn't only about playing well. You have to be ready to fight when you're up against teams who play long balls.'

It was quite the rallying cry from the new captain who had already gained over 140 games of Premier League experience with former club Chelsea as well as over 40 international caps. Its principal message was one of 'responsibility' – of every player shouldering the cause and helping each other fight for Arsenal's first piece of silverware since the summer of 2005. The message would have chimed with Arsenal first teamers – both experienced and inexperienced – but his comments also would have had some resonance at the Hale End Academy where the Arsenal Under-18s were also preparing for the coming season.

Jack Wilshere was coming off the back of a sound campaign at junior level, having broken into the England youth setup for the first time and firmly established himself within the confines of his club. He'd been training with the Arsenal first team ever since the start of the year and was eager to kick on as the new youth campaign began at the start of August. Jack noticed how Arsène Wenger had carefully augmented his youth team policy within the club, opting to use the competitive edge of the Carling Cup to 'blood' certain prospects within his youth ranks. The young midfielder was eager to stand up and be counted and, even as a 15-year-old, hope for some sort of inclusion in what could prove to be the breakthrough competition.

One *major* breakthrough for Jack, though, and an even bigger surprise for his parents Andy and Kerry, was Arsenal's offer of scholarship status to the budding central midfielder. Every close season, Under-18s youth coach Steve Bould and Head of Youth Development Liam Brady sit down to discuss which players they would like to 'sign' for Arsenal. They sift through countless Under-17s, separating the good from the not so good and the good from the absolute best, evaluating every player's general fitness and application, technique, passing, and sprinting, shooting and overall reading of the game. The coaches compose reports of each and every single youth team prospect, and Bould and Brady then have to make the very difficult decision as to who they want to let go and who they want to keep at the club. This, obviously, is a tricky situation for both coach and player: on the one hand, Brady and the coaching setup have to choose which player they would like to invest in the future and which player they believe has what it takes to make it at a club like Arsenal (given the remarkable standards first-team manager Arsène Wenger has already set); on the other hand, they have to inform a player – many of whom they've worked with since as young as eight or nine years old – that they do not see their immediate future at the club and perhaps the player might be better served developing his game elsewhere.

Luckily for Jack, Bould and Brady could see the enormous potential in his game and opted to sign him up as a scholar. It was a massive moment in Jack Wilshere's career. Training with Thierry Henry and Cesc Fàbregas was one thing – as was playing a competitive match in an England shirt – but to be asked by the club you love to play for them in a 'semi-professional' capacity was simply one of the greatest honours a young football player could ask for. For the past seven or so years Jack had been training every other day and trying to balance his love for the game of football with the monotony of his school studies. Now it seemed his hard work had finally paid off: he had the opportunity to play football and draw a wage – something he'd been hoping to do ever since he first heard of the term 'professional football player'. He had marvelled at the way players such as Paulo Di Canio could have so much fun with the ball and get paid to do so; now it was his turn to finally substantiate his hard work and actually have something to show for it.

Or so he thought.

Scholars in the Premier League are governed by strict guidelines which are in place to protect both the player and the club. Firstly, along with having a limited amount of scholar placements, clubs can only promote a 'schoolboy' player to 'scholarship' status if he is 16 years old. This meant Jack would have to wait at least six months – until his 16th birthday on 1st January 2008 – before he could make the placement official. Secondly, every scholar has to continue his school studies within the scholarship program; Arsenal, as a club governed by the Premier League, has to offer their scholars the chance to continue their studies – whether that be GCSEs, GNVQs or A-Level qualifications – and the player, of course, has to commit to a certain number of hours of education a week. The third and perhaps most difficult guideline for the new scholar to adjust to is their new home and routine: instead of travelling to and from the Arsenal training facilities with his dad Andy, Jack was expected to move to new 'digs' in and around the London Colney area and fully integrate himself within the culture of Arsenal Football Club. This meant training with the Reserves and occasionally the First teams, attending team meetings with the manager and First team coaches, partaking in social and charity events, and perhaps most galling of all, collecting the First team or Reserve kit and occasionally doing the laundry – all whilst living away from his home on £75 a week!

As when Jack joined Arsenal as a nine-year-old back in 2001, mum Kerry and dad Andy were naturally worried about Jack's school studies, and wondered whether living away from home at such a young age would prove to be such a good idea for Jack in the long run. Andy was used to being a mentor for Jack and was fond of their drives back from games where he and his son would evaluate Jack's performance. It was going to be very strange not being in constant contact with their son and being unable to trace every 'up' and 'down' of his development. But it was also something they had to get used to: not only was Jack going to be living away from home and training every day at London Colney, their son was potentially going to be travelling all over the world to play football – something both Kerry and Andy would never have dreamt of seeing in a million years. Arsenal, of course, reassured them both that Jack's life would be disrupted as little as possible and that his proximity to the coaches and the training facilities were paramount to his continued development as a player. The club also instructed Andy and Kerry on Jack's new dietary requirements and also provided them with information on how players might like to prepare for high-pressure games.

Thus Jack became an 'unofficial' scholar in the summer of 2007, just as Arsène Wenger chose William Gallas to lead out the new-look (and Thierry-less) Arsenal first-team. The coincidence wasn't lost on Jack: he would never admit to anyone out loud, but deep-down he nurtured ambitions to one day be Arsenal captain and he saw Gallas' appointment as something of a lucky omen. He certainly wouldn't admit such ambitions to his teammates, many of whom fell by the wayside when Bould and Brady were drawing up the shortlist for potential scholars. After losing his Uncle James, Jack knew that you only get one chance to make a go of things in life and the opportunity to earn a wage as an Arsenal player wasn't to be sniffed at; nevertheless, he couldn't help but feel for his former youth teammates, with whom he'd shared numerous victories and defeats.

Just as Jack was getting used to life as a (unofficial) scholar and settling into his new home, Steve Bould sprung another surprise on his star midfielder. He had selected Jack to play in the inaugural Champions Youth Cup in Malaysia which was due to begin on 8th August 2007. A competition setup up by the (now defunct) G-14 organisation of European football teams, the Champions Youth Cup featured teams from every major European league along with two teams from South America, a host invitee from Asia and a host invitee from Europe. Arsenal, Chelsea and Manchester United were the Premier League representatives at the competition and appeared alongside European giants AC Milan, Ajax, Barcelona, FC Porto, Internazionale, Bayern

Munich, Paris Saint-Germain, PSV Eindhoven and Juventus. Argentina's Boca Juniors and Brazil's Flamengo represented South America, while a pair of Malaysian youth teams completed the 16-team competition.

Jack was selected alongside a bunch of players he had known since he was a kid: old teammates Sanchez Watt and Jay Emmanuel-Thomas (both talented strikers who joined the club in 1998) featured in the squad, along with left-back Kieran Gibbs who had joined the club from Wimbledon back in 2004. Other players included defensive midfielder Craig Eastmond, powerful centre-forward Jay Simpson, Cedric Evina and gifted 17-year-old goalkeeper Wojciech Szczęsny.

'For the young players [participating in the Champions Youth Cup is] a great experience for them to see another culture and be up against some of the best players in Europe,' Liam Brady told *Arsenal.com* prior to the squad flying out to Malaysia in August 2007. 'They will have to travel a great deal if they become internationals one day and this is the benchmark. They will be able to measure themselves against the best in the world and it will be a big test for them... It looks like being a super tournament. There are all the top teams from Europe, a couple from South America and some local sides. We'll be up against it with the age of our team because in my experience the other clubs will bring under-20 players.'

Neil Banfield concurred. The reserve team coach was also travelling to Malaysia with the Under-19 squad and was hoping to see what Bould's kids might have to offer on what he called a 'journey into the unknown'. 'The names of the teams we're facing speak for themselves,' Banfield told

JACK WILSHERE: ARSENAL D.N.A.

Arsenal.com. 'It's a G14 tournament so you know the standard is going to be high. To win it would be tremendous. Everyone's going with the aim of winning it but we're taking a young side, and we're missing a few players, so we'll just have to see how we get on.'

It was certainly going to be an exciting experience for Jack. Arsenal were drawn in group 'A' alongside the likes of AC Milan, Brazilian stalwarts Flamengo and Dutch side Ajax. He had played teams like Ajax before in friendly youth games but he had never played against such top European sides within a competitive context. Plus the games were going to pretty intense: matches would last for 70 minutes and Bould's team selection was restricted to three substitutes (usually in youth games coaches were allowed at least five changes and occasionally roll-on substitutes). Jack, of course, was hoping for a starting berth, but the coaching staff was particularly concerned about the humid climate in Malaysia and what kind of effect it might have on the players. 'The only thing I am worried about is the heat,' Brady said prior to the tournament. 'Most of the youngsters will have to play in very hot conditions for the first time. We've been to Hong Kong on a few occasions and it's difficult to play in that heat.'

Banfield agreed: 'Playing a game every two days is intense but even more so with the Malaysian climate, the humidity and the temperatures. If it's too difficult we'll take a step back and treat it as a pre-season warm-up. Steve Bould and I are not going to push [the players] too hard. Our first consideration has to be keeping the players fit for the start of the season. Similarly, if we progress from the group we'll just take each game as it comes. The conditions always dictate the game you play. In England we play a pressing game and aim to close down from the front. Over there I think we will have to be tactically very clever and very bright, and Steve and I have worked out the game-plan we will implement... the boys are well-briefed on what to expect so hopefully we'll do well.'

And so it proved for Bould's young guns. Their opening fixture against Ajax tested the Arsenal Under-19s to the extreme: two players (one from each side) were sent off and the Arsenal team failed to impose themselves on what their coach called a difficult playing surface. The game, played at the Darulaman Stadium in the north western area of Alor Setar in Malaysia, finished 0-0, and the high humidity and intense playing conditions certainly contributed to a fragmented display. 'Hand on heart I believe we are a better team [than Ajax], but that has not been proven,' Steve Bould told *Arsenal.com*. 'We did ok but we didn't play as well as we'd have hoped though it was probably a fair result. The pitch wasn't great and it's very hot and sticky out here, but it's a good experience for the kids. In the first 20 minutes we did okay but after that we tired and struggled a little bit. It has been difficult for the kids out here but they've coped admirably.'

Jack didn't feature in the opening game of the tournament. Bould opted for a more conservative approach, selecting slightly more experienced players over the 'rookie' midfielder. Wilshere was unconcerned by the lack of inclusion in the starting lineup; his style of play – particularly his distribution and quick tempo – meant he was only going to be selected for certain types of games. A high-energy, humid and tense opening fixture against a relatively direct Ajax team didn't suit the 15-year-old's open, flowing style and Steve Bould, ever-conscious of preserving a very young squad, opted to keep Wilshere in reserve for a more suitable contest. It was a sensible move, given Arsenal's result against Ajax: despite not taking advantage of the Dutch side's conservative football, Bould was happy to take a point from a relatively difficult opening contest and rest some of his younger players.

The Under 19s' next game was against Brazilian team Flamengo. The *Brasileirão* side were a rather 'unknown quantity' for Bould, Banfield and the Arsenal management. Brazilian football, in general terms, was not known for having the most competitive of leagues, but teams such as Flamengo, Corinthians and Santos had garnered quite a reputation for unearthing some of the most promising young talent in world football. Legends such as World Cup winners Bebeto and Zico both started their careers at the 'red and dark nation' (so called due to the sheer amount of people who support Flamengo), and the *Brasileirão* team also had some involvement in the development of world class players such as Ronaldinho and Romario.

Flamengo, furthermore, arrived at the Champions Youth Cup with Kayke Rodrigues in their ranks, a young player from Brasilia who had garnered quite a reputation back in his home city. As Jack had done with Arsenal, Rodrigues joined the youth ranks of Flamengo when he was nine years old and scored an impressive 200 goals on his way to becoming the first name on the Flamengo Under-19 teamsheet. A fast, tricky forward, Rodrigues was one of the most intriguing talents on show at the 2007 Champions Youth Cup and Flamengo's game against the Arsenal Under-19s was billed as a perfect opportunity to see the Brazilian wonder kid in all his glory.

Steve Bould, meanwhile, was wary of the threat Flamengo posed, particularly given Arsenal's relatively inexperienced squad. A stodgy game against a well-known adversary in the form of the Ajax youths was one thing, but a run-out against an unknown youth team from one of the best footballing nations in the world was quite another. 'The next game will be very tough,' Bould told *Arsenal.com* on the afternoon of the fixture. 'We plan to give all the lads a game out here, so we'll be putting our first years like Cedric Evina and Jack Wilshere out against them. It'll be really tough but it will be a great experience.'

Once again Bould's prediction was proved correct. Jack's first game of the Champions Youth Cup 2007 was both a tough and a great experience, and a game he'd look back on fondly as one which helped him make a real impression on both the Under-19 youth management and reserve team coach Neil Banfield. On the one hand Arsenal lost 2-1 to a rather cynical Flamengo side who were more intent on stopping Arsenal playing football rather than playing their own game. On the other hand, Jack shone in the centre of midfield and left a lasting impression on Bould, Banfield and the Youth Team management. He was calm, intelligent and full of determination, and in his interconnection play between defence and attack raised a few eyebrows within the Arsenal camp.

JACK WILSHERE: ARSENAL D.N.A.

The result left the Gunners in a difficult position in their group and requiring a win in their final game against AC Milan to stand any chance of progressing. With regards to the game against Flamengo, Steve Bould remained pragmatic, although he did have something to say about the way the Brazilian side played: 'All but a couple of [the Arsenal players] were 19 and we played Jack Wilshere [and 16-year-olds] Jay Emmanuel-Thomas, Cedric Evina, and Sanchez Watt, and those boys did really well to hold on considering. It was a completely different type of football too. They were very cynical as well as very talented. It was a new experience because the boys are used to coming up against English footballers who are perhaps more honest.'

Jack was unconcerned about the loss to Flamengo. Obviously he was disappointed to lose the game, but he felt his performance at the centre of midfield did enough to convince Steve Bould and the rest of the Arsenal Youth Team management that he was ready to start at under-19 youth level. A 2-1 loss to an experienced South American side wasn't the biggest disgrace for a 15-year-old midfielder playing in an under-19 tournament, and Jack was particularly heartened to hear Bould's words of encouragement during his post-match review. He was also conscious of the fact that Reserve Team coach Neil Banfield was on the touchline too.

The final group game of the 2007 Champions Youth Cup was against AC Milan. Unlike Flamengo, the Italian giants were known quantities for the Arsenal coaches and featured a number of upcoming players who had garnered reputations in the youth team circles of the G-14 clubs.

Among them was Pierre-Emerick Aubameyang, a player, like Kayke Rodrigues, who arrived at the tournament off the back of numerous impressive performances within the Italian domestic youth leagues. Born in France, the tall centre-forward joined AC Milan in January 2007, and by the summer was being touted as one of the most exciting French players of his generation.

He certainly made his mark. Approximately 30 minutes into the game against Arsenal, the AC Milan left-back floated the ball across the back line where it was met by Aubameyang; off-balance and running at full sprint, the French-Ghanaian poked a first-time volley over the head of the stranded Wojciech Szczęsny and wheeled away in celebration. It was an audacious goal and quite the way to announce oneself to the international youth football scene – particularly against a club of Arsenal's stature. The Arsenal back-line merely looked at each other in disbelief while the ever-confident Jack Wilshere started to feel slightly insignificant playing against an AC Milan side which contained the likes of Aubameyang.

But that wasn't the way Bould or Banfield saw it. Despite losing the game 1-0, the youth team management returned from Malaysia quietly impressed with the Under-19 squad, and unbeknownst to the player, they were rather taken by the quiet, selfless, intelligent central midfielder Jack Wilshere. 'We made some changes to our system at half-time and dominated the second half,' Bould told *Arsenal.com* in the immediate aftermath of the 1-0 loss to Milan. 'Again, we had a great chance to equalise but unfortunately Nacer Barazite miscued. Had we taken our chances we probably wouldn't be coming home – but then everyone could say that. We've got a really good crop of players coming through once again, we're possibly a little bit younger again but that's no problem, in fact it's the way it should be. I think that's the right way to progress and I'm really looking forward to [the coming youth] season.'

After consigning both Arsenal and Ajax to early group exits, AC Milan and Flamengo went on to meet Juventus and Manchester United in the semi-finals of the tournament. Both Rodrigues and Aubameyang scored in their respective semi-finals, but it wasn't enough for either team to make it through to the final which was eventually won by Manchester United's promising Under-19 side (beating Juventus in the final). The two group 'A' sides exited the tournament with their heads held high and with their star strikers' reputations significantly advanced; indeed, it looked to be only a matter of time before the likes of Aubameyang or Rodrigues were snapped up by the AC Milan first team or another top European side.

But if there was one thing that Jack took from the Champions Youth Cup of 2007 – apart from registering in the thoughts of reserve team manager Neil Banfield – it was that reputation alone will get you nowhere. Despite being part of the team which drew once and lost twice in their group games, Jack Wilshere had made a quiet but significant impression on the Arsenal youth management during the competition. Pierre-Emerick Aubameyang might have grabbed the headlines within the international youth scene by finishing as top scorer of the competition with an impressive seven goals from six games, and Kayke

Rodrigues might have found himself a minor star of the fledgling 'YouTube' website by scoring a wonder-goal against Arsenal; but it was the Arsenal central midfielder who had made the biggest steps during the campaign. Both Banfield and Bould were massively impressed with the way Jack held himself together during the competition. As a 15-year-old central midfielder, Jack stood out amongst the average under-19-year-old in many of the squads Arsenal played against in Malaysia, and his versatility on the pitch was slowly becoming a strong attribute of Bould's squad. Players such as Rodrigues may have delivered the more tangible contribution in the form of goals, but Jack's self-assured, subtle, and complete form of football – in which he would slow down or speed up play, use the ball intelligently to play in a forward, or simply make a last-ditch tackle – made much more of a mark.

Pierre-Emerick Aubameyang and Kayke Rodrigues went on to have patchy starts to their careers: the Frenchman had loan spells with Dijon, Lille, Monaco and St Etienne, and played 19 times for the Gabon national side; the Brazilian Rodrigues, meanwhile, found himself pushed into the lower-league wilderness following his display at the Champions Youth Cup, playing with minor club sides Brasiliense and Macaé before ending up at Danish side AaB Aalborg. Whether due to a lack of opportunity or the fact that their talent didn't warrant substantial reward, neither player exceeded the promise of their early-career flourishes. Jack Wilshere, meanwhile, was plying his trade at a club whose resources forced it into investing in youth; having had a solid, dependable performance in the Champions

JACK WILSHERE: ARSENAL D.N.A.

Youth Cup and not – quite significantly – peaked prematurely, Jack returned to England still relatively unknown but as one of the most promising young scholars on Arsenal's books.

It had been a busy close season for Arsène Wenger's Arsenal side: just as the youngsters were kicking off their Champions Youth Cup campaign over in Malaysia, the manager was getting the First team together for the final pre-season training games of the season. The Emirates Cup, a brand new pre-season competition played towards the end of July, was introduced to Arsenal's pre-season programme to provide the majority of the first-team squad with a taste of match-day football prior to the season's start. A showcase competition based on similar models such as Ajax's Amsterdam Tournament, the two-day event gave Wenger the opportunity to measure his squad in a 'semi-competitive' capacity and also allowed the fans of the club to come and view the team for a relatively cheap price. It also allowed the club to tap into 'alternative revenue streams' (such as new fans and increased merchandising) and certainly appeased the companies of some of the club's more lucrative sponsorship deals.

The inaugural competition – held between 27th and 29th July 2007 – showcased some of Wenger's finest young talent and also gave a subtle indication of which players were in the manager's plans for the opening stages of the upcoming Premier League season. Internazionale, Valencia and Paris Saint-Germain were invited to compete in the first Emirates Cup competition and placed into a group of four alongside Arsenal. Since the tournament only lasted a weekend, each team was awarded three points for a win and one point for every goal scored – thus the emphasis was on entertaining the crowd and scoring plenty of goals. Beginning on the afternoon of 27th July, the opening games saw Inter lose 2-0 to a Valencia team boasting the likes of David Villa and Jaime Gavilán, while Arsenal went on to beat Paris Saint-Germain 2-1. Arsenal's first game was a rather stolid affair and didn't really come to life until the second half when Arsène Wenger slightly altered his system. The Gunners team included the likes of utility player Mathieu Flamini (who was entering the final season of his contract), brand new right-back Bacary Sagna and, of course, new captain William Gallas – all three of whom would go on to have some sort of influence on Arsenal's coming Premier League campaign.

On day two, Paris Saint-Germain beat Valencia 3-0, while Arsenal matched day one's score by beating Inter 2-1 with goals from Alexander Hleb and Dutchman Robin van Persie. Wenger selected a slightly altered side to the team who beat Paris Saint-Germain the day before: the talismanic Cesc Fàbregas started in midfield alongside the combative Mathieu Flamini, while experienced players such as Jens Lehmann and Kolo Touré returned to the keeper and centre-half spots respectively. One eye-catching inclusion on Wenger's team-sheet was that of Kieran Gibbs. Wilshere's Champions Youth Cup teammate had impressed in Malaysia and made a real name for himself in Banfield's Reserve Team; rumours were circulating, furthermore, that Wenger was considering giving the talented Gibbs a brand-new professional contract at the start of the new season. Either way, the left-back's inclusion in the Emirates Cup first-team squad was certainly indicative of how the Arsenal manager viewed the player, and his inclusion alongside experienced first-teamers such as Fàbregas, Gallas, and van Persie, spoke volumes about Wenger's plans for the player.

Subsequent editions of the Emirates Cup would go on to play a relatively significant role in Jack's career, but for now the young man was happy to watch from afar and see how his former teammates adapted to the rigours of competitive first-team football. It made for good viewing: topping the group with 10 points (two wins and four goals), Arsenal won the inaugural edition of the competition and William Gallas got his hands on Arsenal's first piece of 'silverware' since Patrick Vieira in May 2005. The victory in the two-day event set-up an optimistic start of the season and Arsenal, replete with a brand-new captain and a young, hungry first team, set about preparing for the first kick-off of 2007/08 in earnest.

Jack returned home from Malaysia just before Arsenal played their first home game of the season against Fulham. He was pleased by his display in the Champions Youth Cup, and despite being knocked out in the first stage he was confident that the experience only served to make him a stronger, more rounded player. More significantly, Reserve Team coach Neil Banfield had shortlisted Wilshere as one of the stand-out players at the tournament and was seriously considering calling him up for the Reserves. The Arsenal coach was impressed by Wilshere's effectiveness on the pitch and was particularly taken by the way he held himself during such intense games in Malaysia.

Bould, however, wanted to keep his star midfielder's feet on the ground. The former Arsenal defender had been well briefed by Roy Massey and the other coaches at the Hale End Academy and instead of massaging the boy's confidence by promoting him to the Reserve Team, Bould knew precisely what might spur on Wilshere to take his game to the next level: more hard work. Thus he sat Jack down and informed him that off the back of his 'okay' performance in Malaysia, Bould was rewarding him with a 'token' promotion into the Under-18s at Arsenal. Jack would begin training with the Under-18s in the next few weeks and perhaps gain a place on the bench for their first game of the season in the third week of August. The Arsenal coach also emphasised that it wasn't necessarily because Jack performed particularly well in the Champions Youth Cup and more that he had lots more to improve upon in his game in general; the bottom line, said Bould, was that Jack still had a lot to improve and a lot more experience to get under his belt before he could even begin thinking about the Reserve Team.

Jack was to participate in the southern division of the Under-18 Premier Youth Academy League. Founded in 1997, the Football Association's Premier Youth Academy League replaced the South East Counties League as the country's most competitive youth competition in the UK. Made up of approximately 16 teams, the competition is split into northern and southern divisions, and teams from each division are scheduled to play each other twice, culminating in a play-off between the two top-ranked teams. Arsenal, naturally, were placed in the southern division for the 2007/08 season, which included the likes of Charlton Athletic, Aston Villa, Fulham and Chelsea. Indeed, it was against the latter of the four that Arsenal kicked off their Under-18 season on 18 August 2007, the day before Wenger took the first team to Lancashire for Arsenal's second Premier League game of the season against Blackburn.

Jack was selected in the match-day squad for the under 18's first game of the season against Chelsea, despite coach Steve Bould insisting he would have to prove himself on the training pitch first. Quite simply for Bould and his fellow Under-18 coaches, Jack was more or less impossible to ignore in terms of playing ability: he was quick, intelligent and combative, and had taken every opportunity to prove himself thus far comprehensively in his stride. The kid had, moreover, proved in Malaysia that playing with opponents two or three years his senior wasn't going to be a problem. If anything, playing against more advanced opposition allowed Jack to excel at what he did best – exerting his own brand of football on the game. As a short, nimble-footed midfielder, Jack was able to navigate around larger, more powerful opponents with both intelligence and grace; his low sense of gravity, furthermore, and his extraordinary athleticism brought a unique side to his game which coaches and opponents alike found rather difficult to fathom. As a 15-year-old boy with no discerning strength or power, Jack appeared on first sight as a pushover or a player who was all style over substance (a criticism which would come to ring true for Wenger and his first team in the ensuing months of 2007/08); but his intelligence and confidence with the ball at his feet allowed Jack to cultivate an extraordinary balance between lightweight and combative which would come to serve him greatly later on in his career.

A number of players from the Champions Youth Cup started the game against Chelsea Under-18s on Saturday 18th August 2007: Wojciech Szczęsny continued his rapid rise through the youth ranks and claimed the goalkeeper spot against a Chelsea side which featured talented, internationally-renowned youngsters such as Ben Sahar (who had already been capped for the Israel senior team); friends Jay Emmanuel-Thomas and Rui Fonte also started the game, the latter – unusually for a 16-year-old – having penned a three year deal with Arsenal in 2006 which would keep him at the club until (at the very least) the end of the subsequent season. Kieran Gibbs also started the game in the now familiar left-back spot, despite having staked a name for himself at the Emirates Cup with the first team only a month earlier; ever the young professional, Gibbs was happy to grind away in the Under-18s and Reserve Team fully aware that it would take a stroke a real fortune to dislodge the talented Gael Clichy from a first-team berth. Abu Ogogo, James Dunne, Paul Rodgers, Håvard Nordtveit, Mark Randall and Nacer Barazite made up the remaining first team squad against the west-London opponents, with Vincent van den Berg, Sanchez Watt and Rene Steer appearing in the game as substitutes.

When Jack arrived at the Shenley training complex on the morning of the game, he wasn't expecting much. He had assumed, given his coach's 'indifferent' opinion of his game, that a place on the bench was the best he could hope for –

especially in the opening match of the new Under-18s season. So when he wandered into the team dressing room and was told by Bould in the pre-game meeting that he would be starting in midfield, Jack was more than surprised – he was overwhelmed. The central midfielder, of course, had played hundreds of football matches, many of which varied in terms of importance and pressure; never before, though, had Jack been presented with an opportunity to mould the history of Arsenal Football Club. However small or insignificant his contribution might turn out to be on that warm Saturday morning at Shenley, Jack knew that the Under-18 results – and, moreover, the outcome of the FA Premier Youth League – were very important to the culture of the club. From the first team right down to the Under-18s (and even beyond), fans of the club liked to see Arsenal be successful in every competition it was involved in – whether that be knocking out European giants in the Champions League, or, more significantly for Jack, beating a local rival youth team in the FA Premier Youth League. For the first time in Jack's career, a tangible cause had presented itself on a plate, and for the first time Jack began to understand what it was like to play purposefully and solely for a cause. And that cause was Arsenal Football Club.

Jack's first foray into under-18s football was a successful one. A goal from Nacer Barazite and a brace from Mark Randall ensured that Arsenal would start the season taking maximum points. The games thereafter came thick and fast for the Under-18s throughout the autumn and early winter of 2007. The Arsenal first team, meanwhile, were picking up valuable points in the Premier League. The Gunners, in similar fashion to their Under-18 counterparts, had started the season in decent form, winning eight of their first nine games in the league (an away draw against Blackburn during the second game of the season being the only blemish on an otherwise perfect start). Two draws against title rivals Liverpool and Manchester United in quick succession didn't stop Arsenal from retaining top spot, however, and for the first time in three or four seasons, Wenger's Arsenal were looking like real contenders.

For players like Wilshere and Gibbs, the first team's progression could only be a positive fillip to the less exciting world of under-18 football. While Fàbregas, Adebayor, Flamini and Gallas were holding the fort in the league, Bould's team of Under-18s were reflecting the first team's form and beginning to make a name for themselves in their respective competition. A 2-2 draw against Charlton Athletic followed their opening day victory against Chelsea and on 1st September 2007 they entertained Aston Villa at home. True to his word, Steve Bould dropped Jack from the team that played Charlton Athletic in the previous match. Not wanting to allow the midfielder to get too far ahead of himself too early on in his budding under-18 adventure, Bould opted to give Wilshere a rest and blood other players in his position. Jack returned for the game against Aston Villa, however, and once again showed everyone – including his coach – what the team was missing. Arsenal won the game 4-1, with goals coming from Fonte, Cruise, Barazite and, inevitably, Wilshere. His first goal of the season capped what was a majestic display and it once again underlined the importance of Wilshere to any footballing side.

JACK WILSHERE: ARSENAL D.N.A.

Bould couldn't ignore such a statement of intent from his young midfield maestro. Wilshere started the majority of the Under-18s games thereafter and in the following match – against Watford Under-18s – he went on to make even more of a mark. 'The [Arsenal] youngsters flew out of the blocks and were 2-0 ahead inside 10 minutes,' read the report of the match on *Arsenal.com*. 'Goals from Jay Emmanuel-Thomas and then Rhys Murphy set the tone for what was a dominant performance. Sanchez Watt followed his debut goal for the Reserves with another one here on 24 minutes before the emerging talent of Jack Wilshere made it 4-0 five minutes before the interval. Watford pulled one back by the break but even with a three goal cushion Arsenal's stranglehold on the game never relented. On 49 minutes Wilshere grabbed the Gunners' fifth and his second before completing his hat-trick six minutes later.' It was, of course, a remarkable feat for Wilshere: at only 15 years of age, Wilshere was already dominating – and scoring – in games against opponents at least two years his senior. Just as he did in the Champions Youth Cup in Malaysia, Jack comprehensively outclassed the majority of his opponents and sometimes even his teammates. Indeed, his first hat-trick in Arsenal colours stole the headlines from an emerging under-18 side which was romping to the top of the FA Youth Premier League: players such as Randall, Emmanuel-Thomas and Barazite were all contributing heavily to the Under-18s' strong start to the season, but it was the 15-year-old Wilshere who made the Arsenal Youth and Reserve Team management sit-up and take notice. Indeed, subsequent games against Millwall, Fulham,

Portsmouth, Southampton, Crystal Palace and Norwich City saw Jack score a remarkable five times in six games.

Things were going well for Jack in the England camp too. John Peacock, the England Under-17s manager, recalled the young Wilshere to the England fold and played him in a few friendlies towards the end of 2007. The England Under-17s had had a remarkable summer at the European Championships: drawn in a group alongside the likes of Belgium, Netherlands (containing the likes of Barazite) and Iceland, the team finished top and managed to qualify for the final against Spain. Unfortunately for Peacock his team couldn't overcome a talented Spanish side containing the likes of goalkeeper David De Gea, Bojan Krkic and Arsenal reserve team (and sometime first team) player Fran Merida, and returned home trophy-less. Nevertheless, Jack joined up with a talented group of potentially world-class players – including the likes of Danny Welbeck, Victor Moses and Arsenal teammate Henri Lansbury – and spent the final parts of the calendar year gaining valuable experience in numerous international friendlies.

On his 16th birthday on 1st January 2008, Jack officially became a scholar at Arsenal. It was a great day for Jack and his family – particularly since his new club were playing boyhood side West Ham United at the Emirates Stadium. The Gunners were flying high at the top of the league and were heading into the New Year off the back of a decent December which saw the first team defeat the likes of Tottenham Hotspur and Chelsea whilst retaining their position at the pinnacle of the league. The latter of the two defeats was particularly satisfying for Wenger's team: given certain pundits' predictions at the start of the season that Arsenal would find it difficult to win against 'top four' opposition, Arsenal's 1-0 defeat of the West London side was a massive statement of intent. Chelsea had been in a relative state of turmoil since José Mourinho – the most successful manager the Blues had ever seen – exited the club in controversy following disagreements with the club's owner, Roman Abramovich. Even so, Arsenal's win at the Emirates over a side now managed by Israeli Avram Grant was seen as a coming of age for Wenger's side and precipitated a greater belief in the side from commentators and fans alike.

The game against West Ham United on Jack's birthday was slightly more straightforward for the Arsenal first team. Goals from Eduardo da Silva and Emmanuel Adebayor in the first-half sealed a 2-0 win for the Gunners and saw Wenger's men retain their two-point lead over Manchester United at the top of the table. It was the beginning of a strong January and early-February for the Arsenal first team: following their defeat of West Ham United, they drew against Birmingham City at home before going on to score 11 goals and concede only once in four games against Fulham, Newcastle United, Manchester City, and Blackburn Rovers. By the time they travelled up to St Andrews for the away game against Birmingham City, Arsenal were still two points ahead of United, having only lost once in the league all season. Wenger's side, furthermore, had a game in hand over their nearest rivals and their recent form suggested they were only going to get better.

Jack, meanwhile, was surprised to learn that Neil Banfield – the coach he was trying his very best to impress back in the summer at the Champions Youth Cup – was looking to promote a few players from Bould's Under-18 side into the Reserves. Of course, players such as Kieran Gibbs were already heavily involved in the Reserves, having taken part in the Emirates Cup only a few months before. But Banfield and the reserve team youth management were interested in also bringing players through who had contributed to such a great first half of the season in the Under-18s. Jack, evidently, was one of those players, but the young man never thought he'd be promoted to the Reserves so quickly; Banfield's team, after all, were the last port of call before a player is promoted to the first team, and Jack wasn't sure if he was quite experienced enough to make that all important step up from youth team football to Premier League reserve standard.

The Arsenal youth team management had other ideas. Wilshere had performed so well with the Under-18s – scoring over five goals in as many appearances and contributing a hat-trick or two against teams two years his senior – that Bould was compelled to recommend him for Reserve team action.

Banfield's Reserve team had had a difficult winter: after drawing at West Ham United and beating Aston Villa in November, the Arsenal Reserves went on to beat an unfancied Derby County Reserves on a cold Monday night in December at the Pirelli Stadium, before going on to lose against Fulham and Birmingham City at the start of 2008. Winning games with the Reserves wasn't paramount to the Arsenal youth team management, however, and come the start of February, Banfield was interested in freshening up his midfield with a set of under-18 starlets who were hungry for experience and eager to develop their game. Players such as Kieran Gibbs, Mark Randall and Fran Merida, furthermore, were all sent out on loan at the start of the year, thus Banfield was in need of new players to blood in preparation for the first team. Coming off the back of a decent campaign with the Under-18s, Jack was certainly one of these players. He was now fully integrated into the Arsenal way and was wholly settled in his position on the pitch as either a deep-lying midfielder or a Bergkamp-esque number-10 playmaker that created more goals than he scored.

It was in the former position that Banfield played Wilshere for his debut for the Reserves on 21st February 2008 – two days before the Arsenal first team played Birmingham City at St Andrews. The Reserves game, against Reading at the Madejski Stadium, was a hard-fought affair, and Banfield's youthful side struggled to assert themselves on a relatively experienced Reading side which included the likes of England Under-21s star Leroy Lita and talented goalkeeper Adam Federici. 'Arsenal were on the back foot for most of the opening quarter,' read the report of the game on *Arsenal.com*. 'Reading's combination of pace and power ensured that any clearance from the visitors came back instantly.' Even so, the hunger and determination of Banfield's side overcame wave after wave of Reading attacks, and as the interval approached, the Arsenal Reserves were hanging on by the skin of their teeth. 'However youthful exuberance and adventure can occasionally outweigh even the most seasoned professionals,' continued the report. 'When the deadlock was eventually broken, it encapsulated so much of what the young Gunners will need to cut it at senior level. The "never give-up" attitude came from Rui Fonte – chasing a lost ball, his mere presence caused an almighty mix-up between three Reading players. The silky skills and vision came from Barazite – benefiting from the mistake, he danced away from the attention of De La Cruz and picked out Wilshere, whose cool finish oozed confidence.'

Suddenly it was the Premier League's turn to sit up and take notice of a young man from Hitchin who, only six or so years ago, was happily showing off against older kids in whilst playing for Letchworth Garden City Eagles. Now, in his debut for the Arsenal Reserves – which was, after all, simply an extension of the Arsenal *first team* – Jack Wilshere was 'nicking a goal' for Banfield's side in the dying minutes of the first half. After plying his trade for the Arsenal Under-11s, 12s, 13s, 14s, 15s, and 16s, after appearing for England at the Victory Shield as a lowly 15-year-old, after becoming one of the players of the tournament at the Under-17s Champions Youth Cup, and after breaking into the England Under-17s a few months before his 15th birthday, Jack was beginning to knock on the door of Arsenal's First team and that of the Premier League. Indeed, it was *only* one goal in a reserve game against average opposition in the Premier League Reserves, but Jack's sheer ascension from unknown youth to a young Arsenal player with the world at his feet didn't happen often. Indeed, the last time it had happened at the training complexes of London Colney was when a young a Catalan signed for

JACK WILSHERE: ARSENAL D.N.A.

Arsenal just after his 16th birthday in the summer of 2003. And his name was Cesc Fàbregas.

It was up to Banfield and Bould to keep their young starlet's feet on the ground. The youth team management were obviously excited by Wilshere's pedigree, particularly given that he was only 16 years old and already outclassing many of his opponents. But they didn't want an arrogant, underdeveloped player on their hands and were wary of Jack starting to believe his own hype and lose all concentration. On the surface they were unmoved by Wilshere's performance, hoping their indifference might fuel the footballing fire that raged within their talented midfielder; privately, however, the Arsenal coaches were tempted to highlight his performances to Arsène Wenger in their monthly Reserve and Youth Team reports. His standard was so high and his hunger for winning games so great they felt the first-team manager should at least be alerted to the talent they had on their hands.

Any praise would have to wait, however, as Wenger was in the midst of one of the most testing periods of his Arsenal career. Two days after Jack's appearance in the Reserves, Arsenal's first team played Birmingham City in the Premier League. Three minutes into the game, Birmingham centre-back Martin Taylor made an over-the-top tackle on Arsenal's Eduardo da Silva; with his studs up and foot clearly raised off the ground, Taylor went straight through the upper part of Da Silva's ankle and broke the striker's leg. Visibly distraught at their teammate's violent injury, Arsenal played with their heads down against Birmingham's 10 men (following Martin Taylor's dismissal) and went in at half-time 1-0 down. They returned for the second half energised and collected after finding out that Eduardo was okay and in the hospital, and put in a commendable shift to bring the score back to 1-2 following a brace from Theo Walcott. But the worst was yet to come for Wenger's team: 'The Gunners seemed guaranteed to take all three points back to north London,' reads the BBC's report on the match, 'before their hopes were shattered by an inexplicable mistake from full-back Clichy. The French defender delivered a pass into no-man's land inside the Arsenal area and allowed Parnaby to seize on the ball before bringing the former Middlesbrough player down. Referee Dean pointed to the spot and McFadden stepped up to smash the ball to Almunia's left.'

Stripped of the initiative in the league and deprived of one of their most consistent strikers following a truly horrific injury, Arsenal trudged off the St Andrews pitch wondering what this might mean for the direction of the Premier League title. Captain William Gallas, meanwhile, drew his own conclusions about the implications of the draw: as his teammates left the pitch, the Arsenal skipper berated the referee and his assistants, and kicked the advertisement boards. Talk of 'mental strength', 'responsibility' and 'fighting as a team' in pre-season seemed a distant memory as Gallas sat in the middle of the St Andrews centre-circle crying, only for the Arsenal manager to come out of the dressing room to fetch his distraught captain.

The game was full of implications both externally in the league and internally for the Arsenal first team. The Gunners remained three points ahead of Manchester United in the league having surrendered the initiative presented by their game in hand; now, however, having played the same number of games as the Red Devils, Arsenal had to keep winning games to ensure Ferguson's team wouldn't overhaul them at the top of the table. This required 'mental strength' – an attribute not wholly apparent in Arsène Wenger's young side. Plus the 'experience' Wenger did have in his side was totally undermined by Gallas' tantrum towards the end of the game against Birmingham City. Indeed, James Nursey at the *Daily Mirror* had his own take on the events at the end of the tumultuous game at St Andrews, questioning whether Gallas was the right man to lead Arsenal to the title: 'Arsène Wenger picked on the wrong target when he called for Martin Taylor to be banned from playing again,' Nursey wrote in his match report. 'Wenger should have trained his notoriously dodgy sights on his own skipper. Because after his histrionics at St Andrews on Saturday, it's legitimate to ask whether William Gallas should be banned from playing for Arsenal again... When your team is in trouble, when your teammates have been sickened by a horror injury to a colleague who may no longer have a future in the game, when you're looking for a leader to steady the ship, you expect your captain to take command.'

It was a shrewd point to make, especially given Arsenal's league run in the games that followed the Birmingham City debacle. Wenger's side more or less capitulated as three draws and a loss at Stamford Bridge left his team third in the league, a point behind Chelsea and a seemingly unassailable five points behind Manchester United. A historic win at AC Milan's San Siro did little to remedy Arsenal's malaise and by the end of April, Arsenal were more or less out of contention for every major honour of the season. It was a difficult period, particularly given the manner in which the first team went from being 'champions in the making' to simply playing catch-up. It was one thing blaming their demise on the horrific injury to one of their best performers (indeed, Eduardo da Silva wouldn't make a return to first team action for over a year and even then it was questionable whether the young Croat would ever be the same player again), but Wenger's side were simply their own worst enemy. As the season reached the 'business end' – in which campaigns are defined on the smallest of margins – the Arsenal first team buckled under the pressure and shunned any semblance of collective responsibility. Just as Gallas sat in tears in the middle of the centre circle at St Andrews, Arsenal were exposed more as a bunch of talented individuals and less a team capable of winning major honours.

It was an endemic problem for Wenger's team and something he had to address as soon as possible. But as April became May and the 2007/08 season drew to its disappointing end, Wenger chose to take his mind of first-team business and observe a Reserves game at Underhill Stadium. With loan deals in the offing for the coming 2008/09 season, Wenger was keen to see what kind of talent was available to the first-team squad. Thus he arrived at Barnet on 21 April 2008 for the Reserve team game against a much-fancied West Ham United side, only to be met by his counterpart Alan Curbishley who was on a reconnaissance of his own.

JACK WILSHERE: ARSENAL D.N.A.

Neil Banfield's team had gone on an unbeaten run since their 2-1 defeat to Birmingham City and were in good form going in to the match against West Ham United. Wilshere, however, had only made one appearance from the bench since his debut goal at the Madejski Stadium and was eager to regain his place in what was turning out to be a very decent Reserves side. Plus he knew – like the vast majority of players in the squad – that the first-team manager was going to be in attendance at the match, and was obviously eager to get on the pitch and show Wenger what he could do.

He was granted his wish and started the game alongside Wenger-bought (and vaunted Patrick Vieira replacement) Abou Diaby in midfield. Twenty-four minutes into the game, Jack 'cut in past a flimsy challenge before threading a glorious reverse pass into Fonte,' said the report on *Arsenal.com*. 'The Portuguese striker duly poked home his second [goal] of the season.' Only a few minutes later, the young Hitchinian demonstrated the other side of his glorious game: 'Arsenal remained on top but failed to find the cushion of a second. Cue Wilshere for one of the season's finest goals. Having been fed by Barazite, Wilshere was faced with a bank of white shirts. Undeterred, he reshuffled his feet and bent an audacious effort high and around the goalkeeper. Via the angle, the ball nestled in the back of the net.'

Creating goals and scoring goals – two most important facets of the game. Jack Wilshere, in the first half of a Reserves match against the club he supported as a boy, demonstrated that he had both attributes in abundance.

Wheeling away to celebrate his goal with his teammates, Jack looked humbled by the moment but everyone knew what such a moment meant to his career. Videos of the game cut to the watching first-team manager after Wilshere placed the ball in the back of the Hammers net: smiling wryly to himself, Wenger tried to hide his true feelings, but he knew he had a truly unique player on his hands.

The first team finished the 2007/08 season in third place following their capitulation at St Andrews. Pundits, as ever, called for Arsène Wenger to invest in experience instead of promoting from within. The manager, though, was as eager as ever to promote internally and spend sparsely in an over-priced transfer market. The Reserves, meanwhile, finished a respectable fourth in the league, with Jack picking up two goals and three assists in just three appearances for the team in 2008. Steve Bould's youth side finished first in the Premier Youth League: Jack, now more or less a Reserve team squad player, had contributed 13 goals in 18 appearances for the youth side and was named one of the Under-18s' players of the season.

In what was a disappointing end to a season which initially promised so much, Wenger was looking to address the mental fragility of the squad and hoping to acquire some much needed drive within the team. Jack, as ever, was happy to provide his services, but Bould and Banfield had other ideas. The Premier League can wait, they told Jack: first you're going to the Atlanta Cup.

9 – THE GREATEST YOUTH TEAM THE WORLD HAS EVER SEEN
2008/09

*In which Jack finally gets a place on the first-team bench –
before making his first Premier League appearance – is
rewarded with his first professional contract – and carries the
team all the way to the cup final*

Jack wasn't in the best frame of mind. He had just come off the back of a fantastic season at both club and international level – in which he created and scored for just about every team he played in – and his two closest coaches were telling him he'd be appearing in yet another Under-16 tournament. After scoring on his debut and setting up countless of chances against players two years his senior, the 16-year-old was being sent back to play against kids his own age. It was difficult to take after such a great season and Jack returned to his parent's house to talk the situation over with his dad Andy.

A month later, Jack was returning from the inaugural Atlanta Cup as Player of the Tournament. After chatting about the ups and downs of such a crazy 2007/08 season with his Dad, the young central midfielder had decided that any opportunity to show what you can do on a football pitch is a *good* opportunity and thus Jack joined the Under-16s and happily participated in the tournament.

Steve Bould had run out of superlatives for his young central midfielder. The 'Player of the Tournament' reward came as no surprise to the Arsenal Under-16 management and some of the coaches even felt slightly sorry for the other players on the pitch when they were up against Wilshere. He had already grown out of playing football like a 16-year-old: gone were the days when Jack would hog the ball and not trust any of his teammates to advance the play. Now he would relish the responsibility in the middle of the park, keeping the ball moving and dictating the tempo of the game. His appearances at the Atlanta Cup merely reiterated to Bould, Banfield and the remainder of the Arsenal Youth management that Jack was ready to begin the journey to the first team. And so they officially recommended him to the manager.

It was a bright, sunny day towards the end of July when Arsenal arrived for their first pre-season game of the coming campaign. Fresh from their holidays, the first team were eager to get back into the routine of playing week-in, week-out and hoping to put the bitter disappointments of the previous season behind them. Arsène Wenger had given extended leave to a couple of players who had participated in the European Championships in Austria and Switzerland, most notably Cesc Fàbregas who won the competition with his native Spain. Togo international Emmanuel Adebayor was also absent from the first team after playing with his national side over the summer months. Apart from a couple of other international players, however, the Arsenal first team were in full attendance in the dressing room when Jack Wilshere arrived to find out if his name was on the teamsheet.

It was tradition for Arsenal to give the first team a run-out against neighbours Barnet F.C. towards the end of July. Arsène Wenger, as ever, treated the tradition as an opportunity to take a first look at his returning squad – particularly the younger players on the fringes of the group. Full-backs Gael Clichy and Bacary Sagna were available for the game, along with other first-team squad players Denilson, Nicklas Bendtner and Theo Walcott; other younger players were hoping to get a run-out too, with Wojciech Szczęsny, Mark Randall and Francis Coquelin all hoping to catch the first-team manager's eye.

Another player Wenger was keen to take a look at was new signing Aaron Ramsey. A talented central midfielder, the Welsh Under-21 captain had arrived at London Colney after courtship from teams such as Manchester United, but opted to sign for Wenger's team after he was given assurances over his continued development as a player. Indeed, Ramsey had followed a rather similar career trajectory to the then relatively unknown Wilshere: just over a year older than the Hitchin midfielder, Ramsey had been snapped up by the Cardiff City Academy at the age of eight where he was advanced through the youth academies. Emerging a skillful and athletic central midfielder, Arsène Wenger signed Aaron Ramsey with a view to developing him as an understudy to – and perhaps even replacement for – Cesc Fàbregas.

JACK WILSHERE: ARSENAL D.N.A.

The Welshman started in midfield for Arsenal in their first game of the 2008/09 pre-season. He was joined in the starting line-up by Theo Walcott, Nicklas Bendtner, Gael Clichy and Bacary Sagna, while Jack resided on the bench alongside the likes of Francis Coquelin and the recently-crowned League One Player of the Season, Jay Simpson. Jack obviously had a lot to be excited about: he was on the verge of playing in his debut first-team game for the Gunners after spending seven years advancing through the rigorous selection systems and grueling youth games; what's more, he had been given the shirt number '19' for the day and naturally took that as a sign of greater things to come.

The home team made the more effective start, knocking the ball around the Arsenal midfield with ease. Barnet's Albert Adamoah came close to scoring midway through the first half, drawing an out-stretched stop from goalkeeper Manuel Almunia. Once the Gunners settled, however, the experience began to shine through: Sagna and Clichy were marshalling a relatively inexperienced defence with ease, while Under-21 Brazilian captain Denilson attempted to keep as much of the ball as possible. Aaron Ramsey, in particular, looked to be a promising acquisition, keeping the ball moving and at one point threading a precise through ball to the energetic Theo Walcott. Indeed, it was the kind of football Wenger was used to seeing from his first team, particularly when a certain Catalan maestro was pulling the strings in the heart of midfield.

Suddenly it was 1-0 to Barnet. 'After [Håvard] Nordtveit had mis-timed a tackle,' read the report on *Arsenal.com*, 'Barnet's Kenny Gillet unleashed a vicious free-kick from 25

At the start of 2010, Arsène Wenger thought it was the right time to send Wilshere out on loan, picking Bolton Wanderers as the young midfielder's 'finishing school'.

Above: The Arsenal midfielder impressed Bolton's manager Owen Coyle during his loan stint at the club, who went on to hail Wilshere as one of the most important young players in the Premier League.

Below: Wilshere certainly learned a lot while on loan at Bolton – not least what took to win ugly and at any cost. He returned to Arsenal in the summer of 2010 having scored his first Premier League goal against West Ham.

Wilshere was called up to the
England senior squad for the
first time on 7th August 2010
and made his England debut
three days later, coming on as
substitute for Steven
Gerrard against Hungary in
the 83rd minute.

Only five days after his first senior England cap, Wilshere made his first Premier League start for Arsenal in a 1-1 draw against Liverpool.

Above: In what was turning out to be the most significant season of his career, Wilshere celebrates with teammates Marouane Chamakh and Cesc Fàbregas following Arsenal's demolition of FC Braga in the Champions League group stages.

Below: Although his run in the team was disrupted after he received his first straight red-card in First Team football for a foul on Birmingham City's Nikola Žigic.

Wilshere was soon back in the team and capped off a wonderful start to the season by scoring his first ever Premier League goal for Arsenal against Aston Villa towards the end of November 2010.

above: Wilshere celebrated his 19th birthday with a brand-new Arsenal contract and yet another solid display against Birmingham City in the League. He continued his progress on the international stage too, sealing his first England start against Denmark on 9th February 2011

below left: It was during the game against Barcelona on 16th Febuary 2011 in which Wilshere showed his true talent, outclassing likes of Xavi, Andreas Iniesta and Lionel Messi to help Arsenal clinch an emphatic 2-1 victory over a team many dubbed the best team of its generation.

below right: Wilshere won 2010/11 Young Player of the Year, capping a memorable breakthrough season in red and white.

After 524 days on the injury list, Wilshere once again became integral to Arsenal
new-look team, helping the club seal Champions League qualification for the 16
consecutive season.

yards that flew blindside round the wall and inside Almunia's near post.' In faint echoes of that cold afternoon against lowly Birmingham City in February, the first team's heads dropped significantly. 'Arsenal were shocked', continued the report, 'and it took until the 35th minute from them to produce anything like a shot at goal.'

One-nil down at half-time, Arsène Wenger made some significant changes to the Arsenal first team: goalkeeper Vito Mannone was sent on for Almunia, while the backline was completely replaced by youth team regulars Rene Steer, Gavin Hoyte, Abu Ogogo, and Paul Rodgers. Denilson, Ramsey and Henri Lansbury, meanwhile, were replaced by reserve team starlets Mark Randall, Nacar Barazite and, of course, Jack Wilshere respectively, while Jay Simpson was given his first run-out of the season following his blistering 2007/08 campaign with Millwall. The new blood made an immediate impact, forcing the Barnet goalkeeper Lee Harrison into a series of saves in the opening 10 minutes of the half. Wilshere and Simpson in particular were growing in influence as the game progressed and the latter was clearly eager to carry over his goalscoring form into the Premier League.

The pressure from the 'young guns' finally paid off when Simpson managed to take one of his chances mid-way through the second half – but this time the goal was all about the creator. Jack picked the ball up in midfield and slotted it through to the sprinting Simpson who smashed the ball into the back of the Barnet net from just outside the area. The majority 5,300-odd capacity crowd then watched in awe as Nacar Barazite – assisted by his majestic midfield counterpart – put Arsenal in the lead. 'Wilshere was the instigator once again,' continued the report of the game. 'The talented youngster wrestled possession in midfield and surged into the heart of Barnet's final third, leaving behind him a flat-footed posse of midfielders. Simpson's clever run created the space and, after Wilshere had picked him out, the former Millwall man bided his time and played in Barazite who coolly dispatched the winner beneath Harrison.'

The result at Barnet was never going to be of the upmost importance to Arsène Wenger, particularly after he made at least 11 changes throughout the fixture. But the application of the win – particularly from the youngsters, many of whom were only just promoted from various youth teams to the Reserves – would have pleased the Arsenal manager. The most important thing for any manager to see from a younger generation is that they play with hunger and determination – attributes the vast majority of promoted players showed with abundance. '[Aaron] Ramsey looked every bit an Arsenal player in the first half,' concluded the report of the game, 'while there was a wealth of talent visible in the second.' Youth team stalwarts such as Nacer Barazite and Mark Randall, furthermore, proved 'that above all else… the Arsenal way runs right through the ranks.'

Jack continued his energetic start to life in the first team, amassing approximately 120 minutes of game time at the Austrian training camp. The young central midfielder began the pre-season programme on the continent by playing 62 minutes against Hungarian side Szombathelyi Haladás, helping Wenger's first team salvage a 1-1 draw in what proved to be a typically stodgy pre-season contest. He then went on to score his first ever goal for the Arsenal first team, scrambling home a first-minute goal against a Burgenland XI in Ritzing, before netting a second from the penalty spot after the half-time interval. His mini-run of pre-season form continued into the final game of the Austrian training camp after he came off the bench to score the final goal in a 3-1 win over VFB Stuttgart in Germany.

All in all, the tempo of Jack's rise was astonishing to both player and club, and there was no doubting that his first pre-season for Arsenal was a massively successful one. After making such a significant contribution to Arsenal's five pre-season games, the young man had made it very difficult for Arsène Wenger to ignore him in his squad plans for the upcoming Premier League season. But there were a few dissenters within the Arsenal management setup who felt Wilshere wasn't quite ready to make the step up to the Premier League first team; a minority of coaches felt that despite his clear technical ability, a player of Wilshere's slight stature wasn't ready for the cauldron that is the Premier League midfield. He was still viewed by some as being too 'lightweight' or 'delicate' on the ball – a criticism which certainly would have chimed with various other Arsenal first-team players given their capitulation in the league towards the end of the previous season – and a small part of the Arsenal management felt that Wilshere needed more time to consolidate his rise and get used to the rigorous style of the English top flight.

Wenger, as ever, kept his cards close to his chest when deciding what to do with his midfield maestro at the start of the new campaign. He obviously had Cesc Fàbregas in the heart of his midfield and had clearly signed the young Aaron Ramsey with a view to playing him either alongside or in the absence of the Catalan. The Arsenal manager also added to his midfield in the close season with the arrival of £12 million signing Samir Nasri – dubbed the 'new Zidane' in his native city of Marseille. The 21-year-old was yet another name on an Arsenal teamsheet which was beginning to look like a roll-call for talented creative midfielders: alongside Fàbregas, Ramsey and Nasri, players such as Under-21 Brazilian captain Denilson and Clairefontaine graduate Abou Diaby also added to the fraught competition for places, and Jack couldn't really see how he might get into the first team at the first time of asking.

But to the young midfielder's surprise, Wenger named him as part of the first-team squad for the upcoming Premier League season and allowed him to stick with the number 19 shirt he had worn in pre-season. It was, of course, a massive honour for Jack to be called up to the first-team squad in the first place, so anything above that – including a Premier League call-up – was the stuff of dreams. With the mass of talent in the heart of midfield and the quality of the squad players on the fringes of the squad, Jack never expected to be selected for the first team as a 16-year-old scholar and was preparing to be selected for a loan move to a Championship club. But the manager called Jack in for a one-to-one meeting and explained to him his intentions for the start of the season, which essentially consisted of playing Jack first in the Carling Cup competition before using him sparingly in the Premier

League. Ever the growing professional, Jack affirmed he was ready for whatever test the manager was prepared to give him and went home to celebrate his astonishing ascent to the Premier League with his family.

Just over a month later Arsenal were kicking off their Premier League campaign against newly promoted West Bromwich Albion. Along with the £12 million signing of Samir Nasri and acquisition of the talented Aaron Ramsey, Arsène Wenger had also strengthened the defensive department of the Arsenal first team by singing French centre-back Mikael Silvestre. The Manchester United defender had found his opportunities somewhat limited at Old Trafford, thus Wenger – ever conscious of the dearth of experience in the squad and William Gallas' potential to go into self-destruct mode – snapped him up for a cut-price £750,000. Conversely, as a few fresh faces arrived to play in the Arsenal red and white (Wenger's signings also included the 'gamble' that was Amaury Bischoff from Werder Bremen), a number of players exited the club: the 38-year-old Jens Lehmann wasn't offered a new contract and returned to Germany to play for VFB Stuttgart; Gilberto Silva followed in the German's wake by joining Turkish side Panathinaikos; former Academy member Justin Hoyte joined Middlesbrough for approximately £3 million, while Armand Traore and Phillipe Senderos were loaned out to Portsmouth and AC Milan respectively. Perhaps the most significant departures during the course of the close season, however, were those of Mathieu Flamini, and to a lesser extent Alexander Hleb. The former had seen his stock rise considerably following a fantastic season alongside Cesc Fàbregas in central midfield; after having a bit-part role in a talented Arsenal squad between 2004 and 2007, the Frenchman used the final year of his contract to make him indispensable to the Arsenal first team, providing much-needed grittiness to what was an otherwise creative midfield. Unfortunately for the first team, Flamini decided not to renew his contract at the end of the season and thus left the club on a free in the summer. Alex Hleb, meanwhile, had his head turned mid-way through the season and decided to push through a transfer to FC Barcelona as soon as he possibly could following the season's conclusion.

Thus Arsenal began the season with a slightly transformed squad and a first team that took a while to resurrect the swagger of the previous season. While they easily dispatched FC Twente in the Champions League qualifying round – with Jack Wilshere on the bench – they found progress in the Premier League slightly more challenging. A home win against West Brom (Samir Nasri scoring the only goal on a fantastic debut) saw the Gunners get off to a winning start, but their next game against an average Fulham side saw them return from Craven Cottage empty handed after a porous display in every department. One win out of two wasn't anything to worry about, but it was telling that pundits and commentators alike were already talking about Arsenal being 'bullied' and 'harried' off the pitch.

Jack, meanwhile, was enjoying his experience in the first team regardless of the lack of game time he was getting from the bench. The young midfielder was learning a lot on the road with his teammates and a number of the Arsenal players were already beginning to take him under their wing. Jack, naturally, knew the vast majority of the Arsenal first-team members quite well prior to joining up with the squad on a full-time basis and obviously got to know them much better as he travelled from game to game. Cesc Fàbregas, in particular, was a welcoming presence in the dressing room and on the training pitch, always giving Jack some extra tuition and helpful tips on the art of the central midfielder. Theo Walcott also made Jack feel welcome and empathised with Jack's lofty position in the team, having been taken to the World Cup finals at such a young age. All in all, life in the first team was – unsurprisingly – just the same as any other team Jack had played in; the quality of football, of course, was much, much higher, but the spirit, character and unity of the team was very similar to what Jack had experienced before at both school and youth level.

Towards the end of September, the Arsenal first team travelled up to Ewood Park for their fourth game of the season. The team had put the Fulham defeat behind them with a 3-0 defeat of Newcastle United in front of the Ashburton Grove faithful and was in high spirits travelling up to Lancashire. The press had painted Blackburn Rovers as one of Arsenal's 'bogey teams' in recent times – particularly since the debacle in 2007 involving the then Blackburn manager Mark Hughes and Cesc Fàbregas – but the contemporary Blackburn Rovers of 2008 were a far less daunting prospect, with Paul Ince's recent appointment setting the tone for a rocky campaign. Indeed, Rovers' season hadn't got off the best of starts, with one win in three games leaving them eighth in the league. Arsenal, on the other hand, were looking to get right back into the title race after riding out their own faltering start to the season.

The team for the Gunners' game against Blackburn Rovers was fairly conventional in outlook, with Manuel Almunia starting in goal and Bacary Sagna, Kolo Touré, William Gallas and Gael Clichy marshalling the Arsenal defence. Emmanuel Eboué and Theo Walcott began the game alongside Cesc Fàbregas and Denilson in the centre of the park, with Robin van Persie and Emmanuel Adebayor leading the line. Jack, meanwhile, took his seat on the bench alongside Aaron Ramsey, Nicklas Bendtner, Kieran Gibbs, Alex Song and Johann Djourou, and settled into watch yet another 90 minutes of football.

The game itself got off to a fantastic start for Arsenal after Robin van Persie slotted home a Theo Walcott pass after eight minutes. It was all Arsenal thereafter and by the interval Wenger's team were 2-0 up and in cruise control. As the team trudged off the pitch, assistant manager Pat Rice told the substitutes to stay on the pitch to keep themselves warm and to knock the ball about in preparation for the second half. Jack did a couple of 'keepy-uppies' and passed the ball back and forth with some of the other subs. He thought back to the time when he would have a kickabout in the park with his brother and sister and dad Andy, and thought about how much football he had played since then. He wasn't sure when the game had changed from something he did with his family to something which paid him a wage, but either way he loved the game and loved playing it. Arsenal, in a funny way, felt like a family to Jack now, and as he stood in the middle of the Ewood Park pitch, he felt a surge of gratuity to all of the coaches and mentors who had allowed him to get to this stage in life. Regardless of whether he ever made a first-team Premier League appearance in red and white, Jack was happy to just be part of Arsenal F.C. and to have the opportunity to play football in whatever capacity both day and night. As the Arsenal first team returned from their half-time break and Jack walked back to his seat, the kid from Hitchin – aged 16 years and 256 days – was simply content at the course his life had taken and the prospect of an amazing future ahead.

Arsenal picked up where they left off in the second half and bombarded the Blackburn goal with wave after wave of attacks. Robin van Persie, Emmanuel Adebayor and Cesc Fàbregas all went close, but it was Theo Walcott who was causing the Blackburn defence the most problems. With a two goal cushion, however, and an away game in Europe against Dynamo Kiev looming, Arsène Wenger opted to take-off Walcott and send on Alex Song to shore-up the midfield. By this time Jack and his fellow subs were running up and down the side of the pitch doing their warm-up drills. Jack could feel the butterflies hovering in the pit of his stomach as he watched the game from afar; for some reason – perhaps it was something to do with the swagger of the Arsenal team picking apart a sorry Blackburn side – Jack had a feeling he was going to make his Premier League debut for the club that very afternoon. As he watched Emmanuel Adebayor score the third goal from the penalty spot, Jack knew that Wenger had the perfect opportunity to send him on fully aware that his inexperience couldn't be exposed with such a big lead.

JACK WILSHERE: ARSENAL D.N.A.

As Emmanuel Adebayor wheeled away to celebrate with the travelling Arsenal support, Pat Rice whistled along the line to the substitutes. Jack's heart skipped a beat as he looked down towards the Arsenal first-team coach. 'Me?' he half-said, more to himself than anyone else. Suddenly Rice pointed just beyond the static midfielder and towards Aaron Ramsey, who immediately began jogging towards the coach on the touchline. Two minutes later, the Welsh midfielder was in the fray and Jack remained rooted to the spot, watching once again from afar.

A couple of minutes later the young central midfielder was still rooted to the spot when he heard 'Jack! Jack!' Pat Rice was motioning for him to return to the opposition dug-out, where he and kit-man Vic Akers were standing. Stuck firmly in auto-pilot mode, Jack began jogging down the touchline. So many things were going through his mind: what if I make a mistake? Who am I going to go on for? Maybe I'll score a goal? Maybe I'm not even going on? But when he arrived at the dugout Pat Rice informed him he was about to be subbed on and told the young midfielder to strip off into his jersey.

Wilshere, of course, was used to the drill, but as he began taking off his tracksuit he could feel his legs turn to jelly and the butterflies in his stomach flapped their wings even harder. By the time he was ready, the referee's assistant was holding up the board on the by-line with the number 19 in green and the number 10 in red. 'Number 10?' thought Jack as he trudged towards the assistant referee who duly asked to check his studs, 'who's number 10 again'? Before he knew it, Robin van Persie was jogging towards him with a smile on his face and it suddenly hit the young man from Hitchin what this moment really meant. As the Dutchman double-high-fived the incoming substitute, it dawned on Jack that everything had built up to this moment – every match for the Under-10s, 11s, 12s, 13s, 15s, 17s, 18s and Reserves, every single school match at Whitehill and The Priory, and every single kick of the ball with his old mates at Letchworth Garden City Eagles and Luton Town Boys. Every single moment had led up to this point in his life, and Jack was going to enjoy *every single minute* of his Premier League debut for Arsenal.

The next day the papers were awash with reports of the game. Commentators were particularly taken with Arsenal's current goalscoring rate which took them to a respectable 11 goals in only three games. A number of other journalists were pointing out the scintillating form of Theo Walcott, who made a significant contribution to Emmanuel Adebayor's headline-stealing hat-trick at Ewood Park. 'Arsène Wenger spoke of "an accomplished performance",' wrote Jon Culley in his match report in *The Independent*, 'but it was difficult to know quite what to make of a facile Arsenal win at a ground where the home side's traditionally robust approach would once have discomforted them more than a little. At the start of eight days in which they also travel to Kiev and Bolton, it was an unexpectedly comfortable warm-up.'

Along with the usual commentary, however, there was a special word for another particular player who happened to make history for Arsenal in his first-ever Premier League appearance for the club. Continued Culley: 'In fact, so tame was the erstwhile Blackburn beast that Wenger felt safe enough later to introduce both Aaron Ramsey, the 17-year-old former Cardiff City prodigy, and Jack Wilshere – in his manager's view, a future England midfielder – who at 16 years and 256 days became Arsenal's youngest player in a league match.'

The *Guardian*, meanwhile, initially lauded the rising talent that was the 19-year-old Theo Walcott before going on to praise a very significant English debut: 'the most incisive piece of distribution arrived much earlier, and courtesy of another teenager,' said Richard Jolly in his match report. 'In the eighth minute, Theo Walcott's dextrous footwork and trademark acceleration enabled him to avoid three would-be tacklers. A wonderfully weighted ball found van Persie, who supplied a finish of casual, and almost disdainful, ease with the outside of his left foot... Nevertheless, Walcott was not the youngest Englishman on show. At 16 years and 256 days, Jack Wilshere became the club's youngest player in league football.'

Perhaps the most significant verdict on Jack's performance came directly from the manager himself. The midfielder was particularly drawn to Culley's affirmation that Wenger believed him to be a future England midfielder. The manager, of course had never been so forthright with the player directly, but for Jack to hear that kind of ringing international endorsement in the press was a massive compliment.

What's more, the fans of the club were beginning to notice the young number 19, many of whom had heard the name 'Jack Wilshere' but hadn't seen the kid play in all his glory.

'He's better than Cesc Fàbregas was when he was 16,' said longtime Arsenal fan and some-time blogger Scott Simons; 'he's got the control of Pires, the stamina of [Perry] Groves, the grace of Bergkamp and the left foot of Brady... plus he's English!' Indeed, only a few weeks after the Blackburn game, Jack started in the more sobering Carling Cup against Sheffield United on 23rd September 2008, and left the pitch to a standing ovation. His performance against Kevin Blackwell's side drew compliments from all quarters of the Arsenal world, not least the some of the club's most diligent bloggers. '*Kids had six appeal as they romp to Carling Cup Win*', said the headline on *Arseblog.com*. Indeed, the Arsenal kids – featuring an in-form Jack Wilshere and free-scoring Mexican Carlos Vela – beat Sheffield United 6-0, with goals coming from the aforementioned Vela, Wilshere and Nicklas Bendtner. 'They had an average age of just nineteen, n-n-n-n-nineteen,' wrote *Arseblogger* after the game, 'making them the youngest ever Arsenal side to represent the club. The opponents might have been a Championship side but they have plenty of experience and a decent manager, and to put six goals past them is really an incredible result.'

The papers, meanwhile, were once again cooing over the performance of Arsenal's second-string side, not least the way Jack Wilshere asserted himself over a sound footballing outfit such as Sheffield United: 'it was to the right of Arsenal's midfield that the eye was constantly drawn,' wrote Sachin Nakrani in his match report for *The Guardian*. 'From there Jack Wilshere conducted proceedings in a manner that mocked his 16 years. He collected and distributed passes with uninterrupted assurance and got the goal his performance deserved with a low drive from the edge of the area.' Even Jack's dad Andy was asked for a comment, telling the *Sun* newspaper that this was hopefully the start of something special: 'Jack has always loved playing football. We first took him along to play for a local side near where we live in Hitchin in Hertfordshire… This is just the start for Jack.'

It was only the start for Wenger too. From this point on the Arsenal manager had to be prepared for questions about his young English starlet, particularly given the way Jack so comprehensively out-shone senior Sheffield United players nearly 10 years his senior. He also had a young, talented side to keep together, and was conscious of keeping their feet on the ground. '[This Arsenal side] might be young but they don't play like kids,' he said after the Sheffield United game. 'I wouldn't be scared to play any of them in the Premier League because they all have the talent to play at the top level. I knew they were good but I did not know how they would react to playing on the big stage. Now the challenge is to keep them all together and integrate them into the first team over the next couple of years.'

The manager didn't stop there. Only a day later he was comparing Jack to a certain former coach and Arsenal legend who first heard about him when he was paying for Luton Town Boys: 'People tell me he is a bit like Liam Brady, because he has good balance and change of direction. I believe later [in his career] he will be a central midfielder or play behind the strikers… He's a natural. He's focused and determined but he's also still very young. I don't think he even shaves yet!' Even Wenger's Sheffield United counterpart Kevin Blackwell had a word to say about the young midfielder, having watched from afar as Arsenal took apart his team to book themselves a place in the next round of the Carling Cup: 'We had him watched for Arsenal Reserves so we had an inkling of what he was about. Even so, his movement and awareness took even some of our most senior players by surprise... I could hardly believe what I was seeing. It is every manager's dream to have players so sure of themselves they want the ball under any circumstances and are able to pick the right pass and play it at the right pace. As I watched him repeatedly demand the ball from more senior teammates, even with someone right up his backside, I had to keep reminding myself he was only 16. It was one of those moments in your career when you have to hold your hands up and say, that was a bit special.'

It was clearly a coming-of-age moment for the young man. He had spent nearly seven years at the club trying to raise his head above the parapet – attempting to stand out in endless youth training exercises – but it looked as if finally Jack was beginning to be noticed by the people who mattered within the domestic game. Endorsements from fans, journalists and opposition managers were one thing, but to be compared to an Arsenal legend by the most successful Arsenal manager of all time was quite possibly the ultimate compliment.

With such amazing comments still ringing in his ears, the games began to come thick and fast for Jack. After outshining the Championship side in the Carling Cup, Jack remained in the Arsenal first team, travelling with them to and from both Premier League and Champions League

JACK WILSHERE: ARSENAL D.N.A.

games. On 25th November 2008, Jack was presented with his European Cup debut, coming on for Carlos Vela in the 76th minute against Dynamo Kiev to become the youngest player to represent Arsenal (at 16 years and 329 days) in the Champions League. It was once again an honour for the young midfielder – particularly since he had 'taken' the record of his midfield counterpart, Cesc Fàbregas. More importantly for Jack, however, was that Arsenal won the game and qualified for the Champions League knockout stages in the New Year.

Things, however, weren't going quite as swimmingly for the remainder of the first team. Throughout Jack's initiation into the team throughout the autumn of 2008, there were grumblings behind the scenes at London Colney involving numerous senior figures at the club. Following the club's capitulation against local rival Tottenham Hotspur towards the end of October, (which ended 4-4 at the Emirates Stadium), captain William Gallas – whose 'tantrum' at the tail-end of the previous season was attributed to be one of the major reasons why the Gunners didn't go on to seal the title – decided to speak out against certain 'individual' issues within the Arsenal dressing room: 'There was a problem at half-time of the 4-4 draw with Tottenham,' he told Associated Press. 'The only thing that I could say at half-time was "guys, we resolve these problems after the match, not at halftime"… When as captain some players come up to you and talk to you about a player… complaining about him… and then during the match you speak to this player and the player in question insults us, there comes a time where we can no longer comprehend how this can happen.'

His outburst coincided with the release of his autobiography in France in which he criticized a member of the Arsenal first-team squad, citing morale-sapping arguments with the player he only refers to as 'S'. This, naturally, sent the national press into overdrive and numerous rumours started circulating on the back pages of a major falling out with a certain young player in the Arsenal dressing room – a situation which seemed to become more and more problematic as the season wore on. The outspoken Gallas was also believed to be frustrated by the application within the first team squad and his comments hinted at an overriding sense of individuality within the playing staff which was contributing to the poor performances on the pitch. 'We are not brave enough in battle', the Frenchman added. 'I think we need to be soldiers. To be champions, you have to play big matches every weekend and fight.'

The comments were a fair assessment of the Arsenal first team – particularly since the club was more or less in free fall in the league with only a handful of wins in their opening 15 fixtures – but manager Arsène Wenger took umbrage with the way Gallas was airing the internal problems of the club in public and was particularly unhappy with the way he was effectively laying the blame at somebody else's door. The problem, which had been boiling over ever since Gallas' emotional outburst on the St Andrews pitch the previous February, culminated in the 4-4 draw against Spurs, and by the time Arsenal played Manchester City at Eastlands, William Gallas was dropped from the Arsenal first-team squad and stripped of the captaincy.

Two days after the defeat to Mark Hughes' Manchester

JACK WILSHERE: ARSENAL D.N.A.

City – in which Jack Wilshere was an unused substitute on the bench – Arsène Wenger wanted to draw a line under the issue and surprised the press by announcing that a certain Catalan midfielder was going to assume the mantle of captain. 'Fàbregas will be the captain, permanently. I do not have to explain to you why,' he told the BBC. 'I believe the captain is the voice of the club towards the outside, and is one of the leaders of the team.' At 21 years and six months, Fàbregas became the second youngest ever captain of Arsenal F.C., only six months older than club legend Tony Adams when he took the armband from Kenny Samson back on 1st January 1988. Gallas, meanwhile, was reinstated into the first team and returned to competitive action for the remainder of the calendar year.

After a difficult autumn, Wenger was eager to forget the incident and was looking forward to continuing the campaign with a new, youthful captain at the helm. But it wasn't to be: just as Arsenal were regaining their rhythm in the league, the new captain was injured in a clash with Spain teammate Xabi Alonso and sidelined for up to four months. Fifth in the league, riddled with in-fighting and struggling to keep up with the chasing pack, Wenger's first team were staring down the barrel at the tail-end of 2008.

But it wasn't all bad news for the Arsenal first-team squad. New number 19 Jack Wilshere had had a fantastic 2008. It had indeed been a strange twelve months for the young midfielder: at the start of the year he hadn't yet made his debut for the Arsenal Reserves and now, only 11 or so months later, Jack was knocking on the door of the Arsenal

210

first team. The Wilshere family had also noticed the change in both their son's life and his prominence within the club. At the start of the year, their kid had a minor reputation as 'one for the future'; now various newspapers were knocking on Kerry and Andy's door asking for comments about their son's obvious talent and how they went about bringing him up. Indeed, as Christmas and the New Year approached, Jack's parents were pleased to have their son back for the festive period, particularly given the amount of time he was spending away from the Wilshere household. With games taking place across the country, Jack had been doing a lot of travelling with the first team and his parents had barely seen him since the summer.

As 2008 turned into 2009 and Jack turned from 16 to 17 years old, the young midfielder was informed that Arsène Wenger wanted him back on the bench for the FA Cup third round game against Plymouth Argyle. The Gunners were drawn against the Championship side a few days after the New Year and Wenger was looking to rest a few of his players ahead of a tricky-looking Premier League tie against Bolton a week later. Thus Jack, having been drafted on to the bench for the game on the bank-holiday, asked his parents to come down to the Emirates to watch what turned out to be yet another record-breaking performance from their son. Arsenal, having gone 3-1 up via goals from Nicklas Bendtner and a brace from Robin van Persie, were in cruise control, and the Arsenal manager decided to send on his young Arsenal starlet to provide a little more energy in midfield. The ever-faithful Arsenal crowd cheered on Wilshere's arrival as if he were a brand new signing and his parents watched in awe as Jack Wilshere became – once again – the youngest ever player to represent Arsenal in a competition, this time the FA Cup. His six minutes against the Pilgrims on that crisp, cold January day in the FA Cup third round wouldn't live long in the memory for many Arsenal fans, but Jack's first game of 2009 in front of 60,000 people at the Emirates stadium was hopefully the start of what might be his best year yet.

The great start of the calendar year wasn't to stop there, however. Only two days after his FA Cup debut, Wenger called Wilshere and his dad Andy into to his office at London Colney to sign a brand new professional contract at the club. After turning 17 on New Year's Day, Jack, who signed on as a scholar at the club just before he flew to Malaysia with the youth team for the Champions Youth Cup in the summer of 2007, was pictured with the manager before and after signing the contract and was elated that he had finally put pen to paper at the club he had grown to love. 'We are delighted that Jack has signed a professional contract with us,' Wenger told *Arsenal.com* after the young midfielder signed the new deal. 'Jack is a player with great potential, with an ability to find the final ball and also score goals. Jack is a passionate and committed young player, he is not afraid of tackles and I am convinced he will have tremendous penetrative power in a few years. We have already seen Jack's qualities in both his first-team performances and in training on a regular basis, and we look forward to Jack being an important part of our first team for years to come.'

But Wenger's words were very different to his actions

indeed. With Jack finally signing his first professional contract and looking to 'kick on' in the Arsenal first team, the manager wanted to keep his young midfielder's feet firmly on the ground. Conscious of Arsenal's busy schedule and the need for stability for a player at such a young age, Wenger allowed youth team manager Steve Bould to select his former midfielder for youth team games, fully aware that a return would keep his confidence in check. Bould was looking to take his young, talented squad on a decent run in the FA Youth Cup and was thus looking to reinstate the club's classiest 17-year-old in central midfield. With the likes of Craig Eastmond, Henri Lansbury, Francis Coquelin and Jay Emmanuel-Thomas up for selection in midfield, the former Arsenal centre-half was hoping Jack would bring the missing creative ingredient to what was turning into a very talented Under-18 squad.

Thus, with Wenger's permission, Bould spoke to Jack and asked him to return to the squad in between supporting the first team in the Premier League. Jack, of course, jumped at the chance to continue to prove himself and joined up with his old teammates in mid-January 2009, ahead of their next fixture. The Arsenal Youth team had had a sound season so far: after progressing well in the league at the back end of 2008, they knocked out a decent Aston Villa youth side to reach the fourth round of the FA Youth Cup. With Jack back in the team, however, Bould was looking to take the youth team to the next level, particularly given the calibre of some of the players he had on his books: Islington-born James Shea was a talented goalkeeper who was already proving himself in the Arsenal Reserves; Craig Eastmond and

Thomas Cruise were both very capable full-backs, flanking two talented centre-halves in the form of Kyle Bartley and Luke Ayling. Lansbury, Frimpong, Coquelin, Emmanuel-Thomas and Wilshere made up the midfield, while Sanchez Watt and Gilles Sunu provided the firepower up front. The most important factor for Bould and his team, however, was the fact that the majority of this talented side had known each other for around seven years: the spine of the team –Ayling, Eastmond, Frimpong, Emmanuel-Thomas, Wilshere and Watt – had all played together in various youth teams at Arsenal and were good friends outside the game too.

Jack's first game back in the Under-18s was against Wolverhampton Wanderers in the fourth round of the FA Youth Cup on 13th January 2009 – a mere 10 days after his senior FA Cup debut against the Pilgrims. The youth side went into the match in decent form, having won 10 of their first 12 games of the Premier Academy League season, and many of Bould's players were looking to stand out in what was turning into an eye-catching season. Jack, as ever, was also hoping to turn a couple of heads – particularly since it was barely a week since he had been breaking records for the Arsenal senior side – but he was also looking forward to making a return to a side which had come on in leaps and bounds since they all first started playing together over five years before.

The game itself was played at Barnet F.C.'s Underhill stadium on a very cold January evening. Indeed, 'the recent sub-zero temperatures had made way for a slightly soggier North London evening,' recalled the match report on

Arsenal.com, 'and a healthy serving of rain, in the lead up to kick off, provided a perfect surface for passing.' The pitch suited Wilshere's game and Bould also took note by playing the young midfielder in the 'Bergkamp' role just behind lone striker Rhys Murphy. The latter was having a fine season at Arsenal and was hoping the return of his friend Jack might compliment his hard running and intelligent movement off the ball. The weather conspired against him, however, as Murphy was substituted off after 35 minutes after acquiring what turned out to be a serious ankle injury whilst turning on the rain soaked floor.

With Gilles Sunu taking Murphy's place, the game began to open up for Arsenal and before the Underhill crowd could catch their icy-cold breath, the substitute had put the Gunners 1-0 up. Jack took a corner from the right hand side of the pitch and delivered the ball into the danger zone of the Wolves penalty area; the alert Sunu, after much dithering from the opposition defence, found the ball at his feet and turned to smash it into the Wolves net from close range. *One-nil to the Arsenal* – and it was the least the Under-18s deserved after a decent, if uneven, first half.

The second-half began much in the same way for Jack and his talented youth teamers: he was having a decent game in the supporting striker role, playing 'dinks' here and 'lay-offs' there, and at one point playing in Frimpong for what could have been a second Arsenal goal. Around 12 minutes into the half, however, Arsenal took their chance and doubled their lead: 'Wilshere's cute flick on the halfway line was collected by Lansbury, who powered down the line and into the box before delivering low to the waiting Sunu,' continued the match report. 'The Frenchman shook off the attention of his marker before slotting past Woolley from eight yards. It was a goal that Arsène Wenger's seniors would have been proud of.'

Two-nil and the Arsenal Under-18s still didn't ease the pressure. Making sure their names were in the hat for the fifth round of the FA Youth Cup, Bould's side put the icing on the cake by knocking in the third goal towards the end of the game. Gilles Sunu, once again, was the man at the end of the through-ball, though this time it was Frimpong's intelligent pass which set up the talented French substitute. Leaving the pitch 3-1 after a late Wolves consolation goal, Wilshere and his mates were treated to a rousing applause from the small crowd at Underhill, while Steve Bould looked ahead to what could be a tasty fifth round tie against Sunderland.

The Arsenal coach kept much of the same team for the Black Cats tie at the end of January. With Giles Sunu scoring freely and Rhys Murphy out injured following the Wolves game, Bould felt the combination of the young Frenchman supported by Wilshere in the 'Bergkamp' role worked well. The youth team coached also noted how Francis Coquelin and Emmanuel Frimpong provided a solid foundation upon which Jack could weave his magic, and with Lansbury and captain Jay Emmanuel-Thomas supporting the forwards from the flanks, the Arsenal Under-18s were beginning to look like a force to be reckoned with.

It was the Sunderland Under-18s, however, who conspired to shoot themselves in the foot at the start of the game. The Black Cats' goalkeeper Michal Misiewicz clattered into Sunu and the referee pointed to the penalty spot. Lansbury – on the cusp of heading to Scunthorpe for a month-long loan – smashed the ball into the Sunderland net and the Arsenal youths never looked back. Lansbury scored a second goal from the penalty spot, before Emmanuel-Thomas and debutante Benik Afobe sealed an impressive 4-0 win for Steve Bould's boys in the north-east.

The Gunners returned to London Colney in high spirits and particularly excited about the next round of the cup. While the Arsenal youths were busy knocking out the Black Cats from the competition, Tottenham Hotspur demolished Plymouth Argyle to set up a quarter-final draw to savour. With Jack and his fellow Gooners playing some of the best football of their youth careers, the prospect of playing the club's greatest rivals – at White Hart Lane – was a mouth-watering prospect.

And so it proved. The game, in front of a relatively vociferous crowd for a youth team fixture, was intense to say the least. Arsenal started the game brightly and showed real purpose in what was becoming an intense north-London derby. But six minutes in, Spurs went 1-0 up. The unfamiliar formation proved to be a hindrance in the opening stages of the game and the Gunners went to sleep as Spurs' Andros Townsend delivered an intelligent cross from the left by-line. Jonathan Obika met the cross with his head and planted the ball in the back of the net.

'The goal,' said the report on *Arsenal.com*, 'provoked an Arsenal onslaught. First, Wilshere bustled into a shooting position but saw a weak effort saved before Watt speared a sizzling drive just over the bar from 20 yards.' With Arsenal beginning to turn the screw on their local counterparts, Tottenham looked to be tiring and by the 51st minute Arsenal were level. A Coquelin free-kick was met by Tottenham defender Adam Smith who only managed to nod the ball into the back of Arsenal centre-back Kyle Bartley before it trickled into the Spurs net.

The game continued in its high intensity with both teams close to taking the lead: Jack was slowly turning the screw for the Arsenal Under-18s and John Bostock was looking particularly effective for the Tottenham Youths. But it was the Arsenal captain Jay Emmanuel-Thomas who made the difference. 'Both sides had given everything but there was no dip in pace and the game became almost basketballesque in nature with chances coming and going at both ends,' continued the match report. 'And with 18 seconds left on the clock, one would finally stick. Emmanuel Frimpong slid in a low pass to Emmanuel-Thomas who wriggled free of two Tottenham defenders on the edge of the area before lashing a left-foot strike past the despairing Jansson.'

The returning Rhys Murphy put the icing on the cake for the Arsenal youths, nicking another stoppage time goal to make it 3-1 in what was a thrilling North London derby. As the referee blew his whistle for full-time, the Arsenal Under-18s headed over to celebrate with the Arsenal fans on the far side of the stadium. Jack and his fellow teammates danced around the White Hart Lane pitch, joining in with renditions of Arsenal chants and congratulating one another on what was an excellent display against a massive rival. As they jogged back in to the dressing room, Bould patted each and every member of his side on the back: he was proud of his

Under-18s and knew that a win such as the one over Tottenham would have a massive say in how far his side could go in the FA Youth Cup that season.

Standing in the way of the final, however, was a daunting two-legged tie against Manchester City youths. The senior team at City was going through a somewhat transitional period at the club. Since his takeover of the club in June 2007, Thaksin Shinawatra was slowly investing in the first-team playing squad in the hope of bringing more success to the club both on and off the pitch. Just as Chelsea had a few years before, the owner's money simply raised the expectations and heaped even more pressure on the youths coming up through the ranks. Current and former youth team players such as Joe Hart, Michael Johnson and the talented Dedryck Boyata – all of whom had travelled through the ranks at City and were on the cusp of gaining starting places in the first-team squad – were forced to raise their game if they were going to break into what was fast becoming one of the most competitive first-team squads in the Premier League. Thus a place in the FA youth final – against a talented under-18 side such as Arsenal – represented a massive opportunity for the young players at the club.

Arsène Wenger's Arsenal first team, meanwhile, were struggling to find any kind of consistency in the league. After a relatively dreadful autumn, in which they lost five in 14 games – which included a 3-0 loss at Manchester City and the culmination of the William Gallas affair – the Gunners were in fourth position in the league and finding it difficult to keep up with the leading pack. Indeed, a set of five 0-0 draws in the league against teams such as West Ham, Sunderland and Fulham, represented a real problem for Wenger, particularly in the creative, goal-getting areas of the squad. The first team simply weren't creating or putting away chances and the Arsenal manager was in desperate need of a creative spark in the middle of the park, particularly following Cesc Fàbregas' untimely injury at the back-end of 2008. Wenger hoped new signing Andrei Arshavin – who had shone in the playmaker role at the 2008 European Championships – might bring a creative drive to the heart of the Arsenal midfield, but with Chelsea and Manchester United battling it out at the top of the league, it looked as if a Champions League spot or domestic cup success would be the only realistic outcome for a season blighted by injury and infighting.

The Arsenal Youths, on the other hand, were in the ascendancy, and just as the first team were struggling to overcome Hull City in the senior FA Cup, the Under-18s were beginning to show real swagger in the league and in their own FA competition. The first leg against Manchester City took place at the City of Manchester Stadium on 18 March 2009, a little over 24 hours after the senior team beat Phil Brown's Hull side at the Emirates. The youths had gone on a decent run since their quarter-final win at White Hart Lane: nine goals in two games saw the team pick up wins against the Chelsea and Fulham Under-18s and they travelled to Eastlands in decent shape with the majority of Bould's squad available for selection.

The game followed a similar pattern to previous outings in what was turning out to be a legendary Under-18s cup run:

the Arsenal youths started the more brightly of the two sides, but went 1-0 down following good work from City striker Alex Nimely. A half-time team talk from Steve Bould energized the flagging Arsenal side, however, and Frimpong, Jack and Ayling all went close to getting an equalizer. The coach also restructured his formation, moving Jack back into the 'Bergkamp' role at the tip of the altered system: 'We put Jack Wilshere just behind the front two and moved Sanchez Watt up one into a diamond shape', said Bould after the game. 'We passed the ball better and found some little pockets of space high up the pitch. We were a bit deep first half and it was all a little bit pedestrian.' As the game wore on, the Arsenal youths began to assert themselves physically and Bould's change in system began to pay dividends. A Wilshere set piece in the 72nd minute finally restored the balance on the scoresheet: Jack fired in a sublime in-swinging corner which was glanced in by Emmanuel-Thomas beyond the Manchester City 'keeper, triggering a frantic finale to the game. Ten minutes later, Sunu tipped the tie on its head. The Frenchman powered into the area and smashed the ball across the Manchester City keeper, in turn condemning the Sky Blues to their first defeat of an otherwise stellar youth season.

Two-one up in a two-legged tie wasn't to be sniffed at and the Arsenal Under-18s returned to North London fully aware that they had one foot in the FA Youth Cup final. Bould, as ever, was gracious in defeat and issued a reminder to his Arsenal boys that a 2-1 advantage wasn't a foregone conclusion. 'It will be a tough second leg at the Emirates,' the Arsenal coach told the club's website, 'and I just hope our kids don't get too carried away thinking the game is won because it's far from over. That will be the difficult part with this group.'

Just over a month later, the Arsenal Under-18s hosted their City counterparts at the Emirates. Jack, who was carrying a knock from a league encounter a few days before, was Bould's only injury worry, but the young midfielder managed to shake off the injury prior to the game on 22 April 2009. Bould selected the same team to finish the job they had started at the City of Manchester stadium, although this time Bould started Jack once again in the 'hole' behind the two centre-forwards. The coach wanted Jack to get on the ball a lot more and was hopeful that his creativity and guile would stretch a somewhat static City midfield. Frimpong and Coquelin, meanwhile, continued their esteemed partnership in the centre of midfield, with Sunu and Watt once again leading the line in attack.

It was the latter who made the difference in the first three minutes of the game, latching on to a Jay Emmanuel-Thomas through ball and smashing it beyond Joe Clegg in the Manchester City goal. By half time, Arsenal were out of sight: Jack converted a penalty following a Clegg foul on Watt; Bartley made it three after nodding in Jack's in-swinging corner; and Watt completed the first-half rout by sliding the ball under the City keeper to make it 4-0 to the Arsenal.

Despite a consolation for City in the dying embers of the first half, Arsenal booked themselves a place in the final of the FA Youth Cup against Liverpool. A 6-2 aggregate win was a massive result for Bould's team and a trip to Anfield for the two-legged final was no more than the boys deserved for what was fast becoming one of the most successful youth teams Arsenal Football Club had ever produced.

It wasn't the only taste of progression in and around the London Colney training complex. Members of the first team also had a spring in their steps after beating Villarreal in the quarter-finals of the Champions League to set up a semi-final meeting with Premier League rivals Manchester United. There was good news for captain Cesc Fàbregas too: after nearly four months out, he was given the all-clear to play at the beginning of April and was instrumental in knocking out the Spanish club, although he couldn't prevent the side going out of the FA Cup at the hands of Chelsea.

Only a week after the Under-18s demolished City in front of the Emirates faithful, the Arsenal seniors began their quest for Champions League glory at Old Trafford. The first leg of the semi-final took place on a mild spring evening on 29th April 2009, and Cesc Fàbregas proudly led out the Arsenal first team in the hope of repeating 2006's emotional rollercoaster to the final. It was not to be, however: after a tiring first leg at Old Trafford – which Arsenal lost 1-0 – Manchester United tore the Arsenal first team apart at the Emirates, with Cristiano Ronaldo and Wayne Rooney redefining the concept of counter-attacking play for a new generation.

The club, it seemed, would have to settle for Champions League qualification for the fourth season running, so it was rather fitting that the Arsenal youths – *the future of the club*, as Wenger would never tire of pointing out – would have the last say by playing Liverpool in a two-legged cup final at the very end of the season. The first leg of the final took place at the Emirates stadium on 21st May 2009 and featured the same team which knocked out Aston Villa, Sunderland, Tottenham and a highly-rated Manchester City on their way to final. A strong Liverpool side, meanwhile, were just edging their London counterparts with the bookies as the teams prepared for the game.

Jack, as ever, was looking forward to it. He had had a varied and exciting 2009: from playing against Plymouth Argyle at the start of the year, through to rekindling his fire alongside some of his closest mates playing for the Arsenal youths, he was hoping a trophy at the end of the season would be a fitting tribute to the progress he and his teammates had made since they arrived at the club all those years ago. Following the once again callow demise of his campaign, Arsène Wenger was already looking into strengthening his squad in the summer transfer window and there was yet more talk of the young man from Hitchin being redrafted into the senior squad. But for the time being – in preparation for what could be one of the most exciting appearances he had ever made at the club – Jack was merely thinking about the next game: the FA Youth Cup final against one of the domestic game's greatest institutions. Still, it certainly didn't help that the first-team manager was in attendance at the Emirates for the first leg of the tie!

Indeed, the final was a pair of fixtures Jack would never forget. The teams kicked off at a packed Emirates Stadium in the first leg, with Jack in particular showing his pedigree by once again teeing up his goal-poaching teammates. Inevitably, after 20 minutes, Gilles Sunu put the home side ahead. Then, only 14 minutes later, Jack made it two, scoring once again from the penalty spot after a foul on Sanchez Watt. Arsenal were certainly in the ascendency but suddenly the opposition found a breakthrough: the inventive Chris Buchtmann cut back for Alex Kacaniklic to volley the ball beyond James Shea and into the Arsenal net.

Two-one and all to play for – but Jack Wilshere wouldn't lie down. 'Once again Wilshere was the architect,' read the match report on *Arsenal.com*. 'The young midfielder played the ball through to Sanchez Watt – on for the injured Emmanuel Frimpong – who took the pass in his stride before delicately chipping the advancing Bouzanis.' The goal oozed maturity and Watt celebrated with a delighted Wilshere by sprinting towards the home-team dugout. Meanwhile, just as he did during Jack's reserve team debut against West Ham United over a year before, Arsène Wenger merely smiled and applauded, careful not to show too much of his true feelings. But he knew that it was only a matter of time before the young midfielder could do the same for the first team in the Premier League.

The game at the Emirates finished 4-1 after the captain Jay Emmanuel-Thomas capped an amazing evening for the Gunners. The Arsenal Under-18s left the Emirates Stadium knowing that they had one hand on the trophy and only a huge upset at Anfield would prevent them lifting the trophy away from home in four days time. Bould, meanwhile, attempted to keep the focus on the game in hand and implored his young guns not to take their eye off the ball in their quest for cup glory. Only a professional job would see them through the difficult game that was Liverpool away from home and Bould knew that a tight, organized approach to the game would be the only way to steer clear of any kind of complacency. His midfield whizz kid agreed: 'I think complacency is the biggest danger for us,' Jack told Setanta Sports prior to the game. 'Steve [Bould] will let us know it's not over and we'll go there and look to do a job. We want to go to Anfield to get a result. We've done well so far but it's not over.'

And so, twenty years after Michael Thomas put Liverpool to the sword in the final First Division game of the 1988-89 season, the Arsenal Under-18s emerged from the tunnel replete in yellow and blue, hoping to resurrect the spirit of their predecessors. With Frimpong failing to shake off a groin injury, Bould named Jack in the centre of midfield alongside Coquelin, while the rest of the first team remained unchanged from the game four days before. As 'You'll Never Walk Alone' belted out of the loud speakers, Jack posed for a team photo just in front of the away team dugout; with so many youth games under his belt, Jack couldn't help but think this was just another game in which he had to prove himself to someone in the crowd – a watching manager or diffident scout. But as he turned away from the photographers and wandered on to the Anfield pitch, the young midfielder was reminded as to the purpose of this game: to win silverware and to win it in style. 4-1 up on aggregate and 90 minutes away from his first ever cup success, Jack was ready for the next test.

The hosts, inevitably, started with real purpose and very nearly took an early lead. Centre-forward Lauri Dalla Valle latched on to a dodgy Thomas Cruise back pass only to see his shot parried by an alert James Shea. Arsenal, meanwhile, seemed to be fairly content to pass the ball around, fully aware that the opposition had to bring the game to them. Along with Dalla Valle's early scare, both Jack and Gilles Sunu went close in the opening stages of the game – their attempts repelled by Dean Bouzanis in the Liverpool goal. Then suddenly, seemingly out of nowhere, the Arsenal Under-18s went ahead. Sanchez Watt, according to *Arsenal.com*, 'scurried onto Jay Emmanuel-Thomas' high up-and-over and nonchalantly prodded a low effort' beyond the onrushing Liverpool goalkeeper, to score a goal that felt like 'game, set and match' for the visiting side.

Unfortunately for Arsenal, however, this particular set of Liverpool Under-18s didn't know when they had been beaten. Following a half-time team talk, a sprightly Liverpool emerged from the tunnel and finally got what they were looking for within seven minutes of the restart via a textbook finish from Dalla Valle.

Bould's talk of complacency before the game suddenly came into focus and Jack and his fellow Arsenal teammates were forced to keep their heads in what was turning into an uncomfortably tight contest. With Liverpool bombarding the Arsenal goal it was up to the Arsenal back five and a little defensive discipline from the likes of Wilshere and Lansbury to see out the game and finally ensure victory. It was a frenzied 10 minutes and Arsenal emerged from Liverpool's attacking spell with their lead intact and with FA Cup glory in their sights.

And then finally the victory was sealed: 20 or so minutes from time, Arsenal scored again. 'Watt was the instigator with a typically bullish run to the byline,' said the match report. 'His low cut-back was heading towards Wilshere in the area but [Liverpool defender Daniel] Ayala inadvertently diverted the ball home before it got to the young Englishman.' With their coach's words ringing in their ears, the Arsenal boys didn't lose their composure and saw out the remainder of the game professionally – taking the ball to the corner flags and ensuring that victory was theirs both in the tie and on the night itself.

As the referee blew for full-time, the players on the Arsenal bench erupted and rushed onto the Anfield pitch. Jack, who was busy shielding the ball by the corner flag when the referee blew, turned away and celebrated with the travelling Arsenal support. He danced around with his fellow teammates and nicked an Arsenal scarf from the one of the fans in the crowd. It was a great moment – and one he would come to cherish right through his senior career at the club. Indeed, speaking after the game to *Arsenal.com*, the young midfielder tried to put everything that had happened in the season into some sort of perspective. 'If you think about it, we've been together since we were nine and we've wanted to win things together ever since then. Now we have gone and won the Youth Cup – it's unbelievable. We knew we had the strength in depth in this team to do it and it's just great really to win them both. We always had belief we could do it. We just carried on showing what we could do and the cups came. It's great; this is basically what we've been working for all season. It's just an amazing feeling.'

For Jack, playing for the club was one thing, but winning a trophy for the club he had been with since he was nine was by far his greatest achievement to date. As he congratulated his fellow teammates – hugging team captain Jay Emmanuel-Thomas and his good friend Sanchez Watt – the young midfielder was overwhelmed by how far he had come with this group of players. He recalled his old mates from Luton Town youths and thought back to his time at Letchworth Garden City Eagles and thought about how he was so anxious about moving away from them all when the Gunners came calling. Suddenly, on that balmy night at the end of May – in front of some of football's most influential spectators – Jack felt like he was an important attribute of one of the most successful youth teams in the country. His Reserve Team goals, his Premier League and Champions League appearances – even his FA Cup appearance against the Pilgrims the previous January – each of his milestones were brought into perspective after being part of a team which had won a solitary piece of silverware. Jack and his mates from the Hale End Academy were *by far the greatest Youth Team the world had ever seen* – and didn't he just know it.

10 – FINISHING SCHOOL
2009/10

*In which Jack shines in the Emirates Cup – gains a call-up
for the England Under-21s – antagonises a former
Arsenal youth player – joins up with his 'finishing school'
– and scores his first ever Premier League goal*

'Owen Coyle is God' read the banner at Turf Moor at the start of the 2009/10 season. The Clarets had just been promoted to the English top flight for 33 years and the Burnley faithful felt they had to repay their talented manager with some sort of revered respect. Indeed, Coyle had masterminded a very challenging Championship season to take his side up to the Premier League via the play-offs and his stock as one of British football's most promising managers had risen significantly. He had also taken the Lancashire club to the heady heights of the League Cup semi-finals – no mean feat given the resources at the young Scot's disposal at the start of the 2008-09 campaign. But as the new season began in earnest during the long summer days of August, the Burnley manager knew that the previous campaign would have nothing on the perfect storm that awaited him: steering the Claret ship through the high seas of the Championship was one thing, navigating his talented side through the murky waters of the Premier League was quite another.

Arsenal manager Arsène Wenger knew of Owen Coyle's growing reputation. The two managers had met only a few years before during an FA Cup third round tie in which Arsenal humbled Coyle's side 2-0 at Turf Moor. Wenger had also monitored Coyle from afar, admiring his ability to get the best out of players who weren't particularly talented football players. Since the manager had taken over the Lancashire side from Steve Cotterill in late 2007, Coyle had set about trying to get the best out of a relatively aging squad whilst blooding and developing decent young talent at the club. Twenty-three year-old Chris Eagles, for instance, was signed from Manchester United and was immediately placed into a starting lineup which also included veteran Brian 'The Beast' Jensen between the sticks. Promising players such as Wes Fletcher (who won Young Player of the Season at the club in 2009) and England Under-21 striker Jay Rodriguez were also part of a Burnley side which many pundits said might have over-achieved as they reached the Premier League for the first time in over a quarter of a century. Either way, Coyle seemed to be a coach keen on the development of young players and that was a quality Arsène Wenger could certainly admire.

Indeed, the Frenchman's own reign was looking rather subdued as Wenger entered his 14th full season in charge at the club. With teams ranging from champions Manchester United to plucky Burnley waiting on the 2009-10 Premier

League fixture list, Wenger was conscious of overworking an already stretched squad. The previous season had been quite an anti-climax. After an autumn from hell and more or less conceding the Premier League as early as March, the only hope for the Arsenal first team was in the domestic and European competitions – neither of which reaped much reward. The Gunners reached the FA Cup semi-finals but were beaten 2-1 by an aging Chelsea side at Wembley stadium, despite having taken the lead through a first-half Theo Walcott goal, and were humbled by a rampant Manchester United who dumped them out of the Champions League semi-finals with an aggregate scoreline of 4-1. Whichever spin the French manager wanted to put on it – and two semi-finals did represent a small hint of progression with his current project – Arsène Wenger was a man under pressure to bring some silverware back to the red and white half of north London.

Thus, as the pre-season began, Wenger went about rejuvenating his ailing squad. His first piece of business was to bring in Belgian international centre-half Thomas Vermaelen who had impressed for Ajax a few years earlier at Dennis Bergkamp's testimonial in the first game at the Emirates Stadium. With defensive fragility a bug-bear of the previous season, the Arsenal manager was certainly conscious of solidifying his back four and the Belgian captain's purchase was seen as the first step on the long road to making Arsenal formidable again. There was much movement going the other way too, with a long list of Arsenal players either heading out on loan or making their way to the exit: Emmanuel Adebayor left the club with his reputation more or less in tatters after a falling-out with the Arsenal fans; long-serving defender Kolo Touré, meanwhile, followed the Togo international out of the door and joined him at Manchester City to be part of the Sky Blues' rich revival. There were also a number of slightly lower-profile moves, with FA Youth Cup winners Jay Emmanuel-Thomas and Henri Lansbury both heading out on loan – to Blackpool and Watford respectively.

Jack, meanwhile, was now part of the first team. The workaholic FA Cup winner had just returned from the 2009 UEFA European Under-17 Football Championships, in which he impressed playing in the centre of midfield. His campaign was cut short, however, after he picked up an injury against Germany, forcing him to miss out on the final games of the tournament. Still, he was named as one of the '10 future stars' of the tournament – despite only gaining approximately 180 minutes of game time!

With the new season looming, the Arsenal senior returned to his parent's house in Hitchin to recuperate before the season began. He took part in the majority of the pre-season friendlies – against Barnet in the traditional friendly at Underhill and in a few games at the Austrian training camp – and felt he was in decent condition going into the Emirates Cup in the first week of August. Indeed, the Arsenal manager clearly agreed and gave Jack some game time in each of the competition's fixtures, the first of which was against Atletico Madrid on 1st August 2009. Jack – on the bench for the first half – came on as a substitute to more or less turn the game on its head and astound the near-capacity crowd. Three minutes into the second half Jack sent Sagna clear on the right and the full back's low cross was flicked back towards goal by van Persie only for John Heitinga to knock the ball off the line. 'Almost immediately,' read the match report on *Arsenal.com*, 'Bendtner controlled Wilshere's lofted cross at the far post and blazed over when, at least, he should have employed the keeper.' Despite the profligacy, Arsenal won the game 2-1 and Wilshere took all the plaudits for what was turning into a very strong pre-season for the young midfielder.

What's more, Jack's influence was growing and growing, and the next game saw an even more influential performance from the young midfielder. In a *Daily Telegraph* article that posed the question, 'Just how good can Jack Wilshere become?', Jeremy Wilson hailed the most influential first-team game Jack had ever played in red and white: 'Arsenal's superiority against [Glasgow] Rangers was established by Wilshere after less than two minutes. Cesc Fàbregas, playing just behind Eduardo in an advanced midfield position, fed Andrei Arshavin, who cleverly flicked the ball into the 17 year-old's path. Wilshere's left-footed finish was precise although he was also aided by some unconvincing goalkeeping from Allan McGregor... Wilshere then sealed the victory with an emphatic half-volley from Aaron Ramsey's cross.' It was a pleasing display, particularly given the fact that a certain England manager was being entertained in the executive seats of Ashburton Grove the very day Jack was showing Rangers how to play football. Wilson noted: 'Fabio Capello was among those present and, given the England manager's commitment to selecting his squads on current form, it is not beyond the realms of possibility that Wilshere could find himself being considered for the friendly against Holland in 10 days' time… Wilshere is already among the players earmarked for fast-tracking into the senior squad and, while he is still only 17, Wenger does not regard next year's World Cup as an impossibility.'

Despite an impressive Emirates Cup display, Capello opted against calling up Wilshere for England duty. Clearly the England manager felt he was slightly too raw to be thrown into the gauntlet that was international football. Stuart Pearce, however, disagreed: the Under-21s manager cast a watchful eye over Wilshere during his pre-season activities and was considering calling him up for the junior fixture against Holland on 11th August 2009. Pearce could see the clear potential in Wilshere and was looking to patch up his squad following their heroic display in the European Championships the previous June, when they finished runners-up to Germany's champions. Yet he wasn't wholly convinced Jack could make the grade – the player was, after all, only 17 – and thus left it to the last minute before calling up the young central midfielder after Bolton midfielder (and fellow Arsenal graduate) Fabrice Muamba was injured in training only a day before the game.

Jack's debut for the England Under-21s came as no surprise. The youngster had featured at every level of international football so his step up to the next grade was seen as only inevitable. What wasn't inevitable, however, was the manner in which the young midfielder took his debut by the scruff of the neck and once again gave the England senior side something to think about. Indeed, by the end of it, Stuart Pearce had to rebuff questions that the senior manager was thinking about taking the Arsenal youngster to the World Cup in South Africa in less than 10 months time: 'I find it a little bit sad that we over-hype players, because I know what is around the corner,' Pearce told *Telegraph Sport* following the Under-21s' 0-0 draw against the Dutch. 'It just shows the folly of it. From our "golden generation" to our "lost generation", I have seen it many times. It is very unfair on the player – you should just let the player develop. People are talking up his chances, but how many of them have watched [Jack] at the Under-17 or Under-19 championships? I have, and he needs to be allowed to blossom in his own time. I will look after him, as will Fabio.' Jack, meanwhile, had only a good word to say about his Under-21 coach: 'Stuart Pearce is a good coach and I like him,' he told Arsenal's match day programme. 'He's a bit like the boss [Arsene Wenger] in that he is focused and wants to win.'

With talk of World Cups and 'lost generations' ringing in his ears, Jack returned to the club looking forward to the start of the season. The Arsenal first team travelled up to face Everton at Goodison in what was – on paper at least – a tricky opening tie. But Arsenal hadn't read the script: after a competitive opening 20 or so minutes, the Gunners suddenly turned on the style and by the end of the first half were 3-0 up. 45 or so minutes later, Arsenal had doubled their lead and with many pundits writing off the Gunners' chances of silverware at the start of the season, a 6-1 win at what was always a tricky away ground to get a result was an auspicious way to start the campaign.

JACK WILSHERE: ARSENAL D.N.A.

Jack unfortunately wasn't included in the first-team squad for the trip to Everton; Arsène Wenger had informed his young midfielder that he was going to use him sparingly throughout the season and thus he remained back at the first-team training ground. He did make the bench for the next game however – an away trip to Celtic for a Champions League qualification game – and stayed on the bench for the return leg a week or so later. His involvement in the Premier League was less forthcoming: despite making the bench for the trip to Manchester United at the end of August, Jack hadn't made any contributions to Arsenal's league position which had dropped as low as eighth by the time Arsenal lost to United's local rivals Manchester City at the start of the new month. Even so, he was happy to wait for his chance and knew that any kind of injury or loss of form would present the young midfielder with the opportunity he needed to stake a claim in the team.

The best chance for Jack to stake such a claim was in the Carling Cup. Arsenal had done well in recent seasons and Wenger typically used the competition both to blood youngsters coming up through the ranks and to give game time to the remainder of his first-team squad. Jack fell into both categories and was thus guaranteed a start in the third round tie against West Bromwich Albion on 22 September 2009. Roberto Di Matteo's side were having a very good season in the Championship and arrived at the Emirates on top of the division. With a talented line-up which included the likes of Simon Cox, Luke Moore and ex-Arsenal winger Jerome Thomas, the Baggies were looking to take full advantage of the unfamiliarity in the Arsenal ranks and cause an early-season cup upset. It wasn't to be, however, as Arsenal picked off their Brummie counterparts, winning the game 2-0 following goals from the Mexican star Carlos Vela and FA Youth Cup hero Sanchez Watt. The game wasn't without incident for Jack, however: on 37 minutes, Jerome Thomas, who had been an Arsenal youth graduate from 2001 to 2004, went in on a challenge on Jack which was spiky to say the least. With Wilshere lying on the deck, Thomas put out his hand to apologise and was immediately shunned by his Arsenal counterpart. Words were exchanged and suddenly the Baggies' midfielder pushed Jack in the face back onto the ground, right in front of the referee. He was duly sent off and West Bromwich Albion played the remainder of the game with 10 men. 'It was a red card,' conceded Di Matteo to the press after the game. 'My player went to shake the Arsenal player's hand and he refused and reacted. There was an exchange of words and then there was a reaction. I know what was said, but I'm not saying that. I'm disappointed that Wilshere didn't accept his hand. He wanted to help him get up, actually.'

Whatever was said, the incident represented another side of Jack's game which had been creeping in for some time. Steve Bould had noticed it from Wilshere's days with Arsenal Youths. On a few occasions Jack would get the 'red mist' and antagonize opposition players (many of whom were already frustrated about not being able to retrieve the ball from a kid two years their junior!). 'When I was younger, around 14, I was being sent off four or five times a season,' Jack admitted to the Arsenal matchday programme. 'Sometimes I'd lose my head and make a bad tackle straight after I'd been fouled.' Indeed, it was only a few months later that Jack was 'giving as good as he got' to Craig Bellamy in the same competition – a game which Arsenal went on to lose 3-0 away to Manchester City. 'Craig Bellamy is certainly the mouthy type,' he added in his interview in the Arsenal matchday programme. 'But he was mucking around and smiling as well so it was no problem. On one occasion I just laughed at him and that wound him even more!' It wasn't the most obvious side of his game – he kept the negative aspects covered up by his enthralling talent with the football itself – but it was a side Bould and now Wenger were hoping to keep in check as they developed Jack into the world-class player they knew he would eventually become. Besides, said Jack, you have to look after yourself on the pitch: 'Opponents can try and take advantage of you if you're younger or smaller than them, so you have to stick up for yourself.'

The Arsenal first team, meanwhile, had an eventful autumn, though not quite as eventful as the season before. After back-to-back losses against the Manchester clubs, Arsenal went on a seven-game unbeaten run before being stopped in their tracks by a stubborn Sunderland side at the Stadium of Light. Chelsea duly beat them 3-0 the following weekend and by the end of the calendar year Arsenal were staying the course and third in the league.

Just over two weeks after Jack's 18th birthday, in January 2010, Arsenal played Bolton Wanderers twice in the Premier League. The awful weather in and around the UK had caused a number of games to be snowed off and a small quirk of the fixture list meant that Arsenal had to play the Trotters twice in three days. Wanderers had had a very strange season thus far: the first five months of the season had been one of desperation, with the club bouncing in and out of the relegation zone after losing four of their first eighteen fixtures. Just before the New Year, however, the Bolton chairman Phil Gartside decided to sack Gary Megson in the hope that a fresh start at might ignite a first team which were slowly heading towards relegation. And two weeks later he appointed Burnley manager, Owen Coyle.

The appointment raised a few eyebrows – not least from the Burnley faithful who thought their manager was going to successfully lead them through the unchartered terrain of the Premier League and ensure survival. But with Burnley floundering at the foot of the table alongside Bolton Wanderers – and with the latter having the funds to keep themselves afloat in the wealthy world of the Premier League – Coyle felt that the opportunity to work within an established Premier League club was one not to be passed up: 'If you look at the infrastructure of the club [Bolton], the academy, the training centre, everything is geared for top-flight football and my job as manager is to make sure that happens,' he told the BBC following his appointment. 'I must say, Burnley have still got a Premier League team as well. We really galvanised the club and took them to a level that is always going to be difficult.'

After the double-header against Arsenal (which the Gunners won with an aggregate score-line 6-2 to send them to the top of the Premier League), Coyle's next piece of business was to rejuvenate his ailing squad with some fresh legs. He firstly acquired Vladimír Weiss from Manchester City and Paul Robinson of West Bromwich Albion before tentatively putting in an offer to sign on loan the services of one Jack Wilshere.

The Arsenal star was still on the fringes of the Arsenal first team and apart from occasional starts in the league and Champions League (plus a satisfying appearance against West Ham in the FA Cup third round) he was looking to get some substantial game time under his belt to aid in his development into a fully-fledged Premier League player. Wenger, too, wanted to give Jack a little more experience of the Premier League but felt the pressured boiling-pot of a title-chasing first team wasn't the right place to do it. With Bolton struggling to stay in the league and with Owen Coyle now at the helm, Wenger decided it was a good time to send his young midfielder out on loan to finally gain some gritty experience of the league. Indeed, Wenger also intended Jack's loan-move to be his 'finishing school', where everything he had learnt from the age of nine would be consolidated by the new environment that was a north-west club in the throes of a relegation battle. From playing alongside the slightly more aesthetically pleasing players such as Cesc Fàbregas and Robin Van Persie at Arsenal, to battling alongside Premier League veterans Kevin Davies and Kevin Nolan, a new way of playing the game and thinking abut the game would only add to Jack's already impressive footballing CV. 'Jack is a talented, young, hungry player who I think has got a really bright future,' said Coyle after Jack agreed to join the Trotters. '[He] has got an abundance of quality and will enhance our squad.'

A truism from the Bolton manager: even before Jack could find a place to rent in the north-west, he was drafted into the first team and was playing nearly 90 minutes a week of Premier League football. He made his first league start against Manchester City on 9th February (which the Trotters lost 2-0) before playing a set of 14 fixtures against the likes of Everton, Manchester United, Aston Villa and Chelsea. On 6th March, Jack scored his first ever Premier League goal against the club he supported as a boy. Latching on to a Kevin Davies centre in the West Ham box, the young midfielder scored what turned out to be the winning goal against the Hammers, lashing the ball into the net after Tamir Cohen headed the ball down to his feet.

With every game a battle for three points, and every minute of every match looking to be decisive as Bolton struggled to stay in the league, Jack was sharpening his style as a Premier League football player. The Arsenal midfielder, who had been brought up in the comfortable confides of a relatively successful 'top four' outfit, was beginning to understand the importance of a team ethic and playing to one's strengths – two components he had developed at Arsenal, but not two sides of his game he had seen as explicitly valuable. During the half-time interval in a game against Stoke City, for example, Owen Coyle derided his Bolton team for playing like 'men who had never met in their lives' (according to the *Guardian* match report). After the break, he elected to drop Jack into a central role at the base of the midfield and play Ivan Klasnic alongside captain Kevin Davies upfront. He also brought on another loanee, Vladimír Weiss, to provide extra pace to an otherwise stagnant attacking line. It worked wonders for the team, with each player using their strongest attributes to bring out the best in each other and grind out a 2-1 win over the Potters.

After the game, Coyle had to acknowledge the ability of his young Arsenal loanee and admitted that changing his tactics halfway through a game had been a gamble which had paid off. 'Sometimes you get lucky with changing things, and that's what we did,' Coyle told the press. 'We brought Wilshere back into midfield because I knew he would go and take the ball regardless of who his opponent was, because he has got so much ability and he's brave and he's tough and everything you would want of a player, and to think he's only 18.' Jack, in other words, was the first cog in a mechanism which allowed Bolton to turn the game on its head and come away from the ground with an invaluable three points.

Talking towards the end of the campaign, Coyle only had good words to say about the young Arsenal starlet. 'He is a total footballer,' he told the *Daily Mail* during the midfielder's time at the Trotters. 'He can play wide, he can play in the middle or he can play as a second striker. Everything he does oozes class.' Indeed, his time at the club also sharpened him physically and the athletic side of his game significantly improved: 'The first day's training he took a whack off Kevin Davies in a tackle and straight away was happy to give him one back,' added Coyle. 'I thought, "If you're willing to go toe to toe with my captain, son, you'll do for me!"'

With Bolton safe in the league and Jack back at his parent club, the midfielder turned his attention to the next season.

With Arsenal failing to secure any kind of silverware again – after coming very close once again in the Premier League – he was hoping that Arsène Wenger might consider him for a starting berth in the Arsenal first-team lineup for 2011/12. But with the exertions of the previous season still fresh in Jack's bones, the young midfielder went on a well-earned break with his family to reflect upon what had been an amazing season.

11 – BREAKTHROUGH
2010/11

In which Jack scores his first ever Premier League goal for Arsenal – gets himself into trouble both off and on the pitch – signs a new contract – receives his first international cap – and beats the best team in the world at their own game

On 27th November 2010, Arsenal went top of the table. After a nail-biting game at Villa Park, in which the hosts came close to grabbing all three points, the Gunners scraped through 90 nerve-racking minutes to regain top spot in the early stages of the 2010/11 campaign. Their win at Villa Park might have sent them top for a mere half an hour – the game, after all was an early kick-off and both Manchester United and Chelsea were due to kick-off at the traditional 3pm – but the result sent a statement of intent to the other title challengers that Arsenal were a force to be reckoned with during the current campaign.

And that's all that mattered really to Jack Wilshere. He might have scored his first ever Premier League goal for the club during the game – becoming, furthermore, one of the youngest ever players to have scored for Arsenal – but the most important aspect of Jack's first goalscoring contribution was that it sent his team to the Premier League summit for the first time that season. He was 'buzzing' after scoring his first goal for the club, according to his *Twitter* feed, but he was quick to point out that it was a good win for the team which kept the club on course for its first piece of silverware since 2005.

His first goal for the club wasn't the way Jack pictured it: he didn't round three defenders – à la Thierry Henry versus Spurs in 2002 – and fire the ball into the back of the net. Instead, recent signing Marouane Chamakh dinked the ball across the face of the goal for Jack to dive in and nod into the back of the Villa net. It was a special moment and Jack wheeled away to celebrate with the travelling Arsenal support, happy to have chalked his first Premier League goal for the club he had played for since the age of nine.

It was the high-point of what had been a bittersweet start to the season for the young midfielder. In August, at the start of the season, Jack was surprised to hear that his manager was going to hand him his first ever start in the Premier League. He would have the honour against Liverpool at Anfield – the stadium, of course, where Jack and his under-18s put the Liverpool youths to the sword in such thrilling fashion in the FA Youth Cup only a year before. Some four months later, Jack Wilshere was a regular starter in the team – the Aston Villa game becoming Jack's tenth of the season – and he was competing alongside the likes of Andrei Arshavin, Cesc Fàbregas, Abou Diaby, Alex Song and Samir Nasri for a place in the heart of Arsenal's midfield.

His rise to the top of Arsène Wenger's midfield priorities

also coincided with his profile on the international stage: after helping Owen Coyle's Bolton Wanderers stay in the Premier League and being named one of the Trotters' players of the season in the process, England manager Fabio Capello decided the time was right to promote Jack to the senior national squad. Indeed, Jack's rise to the senior post at Arsenal couldn't have been better timed: coming off the back of a terrible World Cup campaign in South Africa (in which they were humbled and eliminated by a young, talented Germany side at the quarter-final stages), Fabio Capello was under extreme pressure to blood some fresh, upcoming talent and to draw a line under the lumbering under-achievement that was the so-called 'golden generation'. With Jack playing a fresh, energetic, technically-minded brand of football, his inclusion in the England squad was the silver-lining on the otherwise dark rain cloud that was the England football team.

Joining up with the likes of Steven Gerrard, Frank Lampard, and Arsenal teammates Theo Walcott and Kieran Gibbs, Jack trained with the senior England squad before making his first appearance for his country in a friendly game against Hungary on 10th August 2010. The midfielder – capped, of course, at more or less every level since he first arrived on the international youth scene at the Victory Shield over four years before – was substituted on for Steven Gerrard and put in a solid performance in the heart of his country's midfield. It was, naturally, a great moment for Jack and his family: ever since he could pick up a football Jack was obsessed with the game and never was it more apparent than when he would watch an England World Cup or

European Championship game on TV with his dad back in their living room in their semi-detached house in Hitchin. From Michael Owen's thrilling run against Argentina in 1998 to David Beckham's graceful, qualification-saving free-kick against Greece in the run up to the World Cup in 2002, Jack had followed England throughout his young life and was just as much an England fan as he was a Gunner. His call-up to the senior side was thus a massive honour and yet another highlight in what was turning into a fantastic 2010 for the young midfielder.

Or so he thought. August had been a great month for the Arsenal and England player and Jack was flying: along with his international call-up and first Premier League start, Jack had also played in the 6-0 home win against Blackpool on 21st August 2010, contributing an assist to Theo Walcott's hat-trick. It seemed as if his rise to the upper echelons of his chosen profession was being accelerated by the day – and it was becoming more and more apparent that he was a pivotal figure in Arsène Wenger's first-team plans for the foreseeable future.

Yet Jack found himself in trouble towards the end of August and looked as if his flying start was about to hit a brick wall. On 29th August, Arsenal travelled to play Blackburn Rovers in the third gameweek of the new Premier League season. The Gunners were looking to string together a series of wins and capitalise on their drubbing of Blackpool the week before. Jack started the game on the bench and came on in the 83rd minute to replace goalscorer Andrei Arshavin in what turned out to be a decent, ground-out 2-1 victory against the Lancashire side. In celebration of his team's success that afternoon, Jack returned to London and headed out with his mates to a few bars in West London, ending up in a the fashionable Amika nightclub on Kensington High Street. At approximately 2.30am on the morning of 30th August, the police were called to intervene in a fracas which had broken out between Jack's friends and a group of other men outside Amika. The incident, which occurred on the steps of the *Daily Mail* offices in Kensington, allegedly materialised after Jack and his friends left the nightclub and an argument broke out between the two groups. Jack, though, was seen to be the peacemaker in the scuffle. 'Security guards at the nearby Kensington Roof Gardens nightclub rushed across to try to separate the two groups of men fighting,' read the *Daily Mail* article, complete with CCTV images. 'One doorman said: "It was chaos. They were scrapping at each other viciously. There was a girl screaming on the floor and more girls came rushing out of the club. We tried to separate them but they kept trying to hit each other."'

Jack and his friends were taken to a nearby Metropolitan police station and remained in custody for approximately 10 hours while the police pieced together what had happened outside the nightclub. It was quite a shock to the system for Jack, particularly since he was a teetotaller and hadn't had a drink all night; his mates, on the other hand, were all drinking and it was difficult for the police to work out which individual in each group was responsible for the attack. What became clear early on, however, was that Jack was the peacemaker and had tried to intervene after the two groups came to blows. Even so, the police had no option but to arrest the Arsenal midfielder and he was released on bail pending further investigations into the incident.

The next day, Jack and his dad instructed Wasserman Media Group – Jack's media representatives – to issue a statement to the press to clarify the situation. The statement read: 'Jack Wilshere was arrested by police in the early hours following a fracas but was released on bail later. The police have made it very clear that he is an important witness to the incident and played the role of peacemaker and is unlikely to face any charges as a result. Jack has made it very clear he will cooperate fully with the police investigation.' The midfielder, meanwhile, returned to his parent's house to reflect on what was an unnecessary dent in his budding reputation.

It went from bad to worse for the Arsenal man. Following Jack's debut in the senior side, England manager Fabio Capello gave the Under-21 manager Stuart Pearce permission to use the talented midfielder in the upcoming Under-21 friendly matches against Portugal and Hungary. But barely a week after the fracas outside Amika, the England Under-21 manager dropped Jack from his first team, relegating him to the bench for crucial European Championship qualifiers against the likes of Portugal and Lithuania. The young Arsenal midfielder, according to Pearce, had 'taken his eye off the ball', and needed to regain focus before he was to be included in the Under-21 first team. 'Leading into the Portugal game,' said Pearce, 'he was swapping phone calls with his agent and one or two other people in regards to newspaper articles which were going on. We just did not feel it was right for him to start in Portugal.'

Arsène Wenger, however, was slightly more sympathetic to Wilshere's situation, although he did echo Pearce's stern assessment by declaring that Jack should have 'been at home and in bed' instead of hanging out in nightclubs until the early hours of the morning. 'You don't make a career at the top without knowing how to behave,' the Arsenal manager said to the press a few weeks after the incident and day before his team were due to meet Bolton Wanderers in the Premier League. 'If you are a football player and you stay out half-an-hour longer than you should, it is a massive problem.' Wenger added a word of support for his young midfielder, though, conscious of the need for perspective in what was slowly turning into a difficult situation for Jack. 'Jack is focused and I believe he was always focused. He wants the ball and he wants to play. It could have been a concern for Pearce, but I believe Jack Wilshere is a happy man on a football pitch.'

He had the chance to prove his manager right the very next day when he was named in the starting line-up for the Premier League fixture against his old club Bolton Wanderers. The return of Owen Coyle's side proved to be good timing for Jack; his former manager swept the past few weeks under the rug in the pre-game interview with the press, reminding a packed media room that, despite his problems off the pitch, Jack was still one of the best young players plying his trade in the Premier League. 'Maybe he was a bit immature when he came [to Bolton Wanderers] but when he left he was a real man,' declared Owen Coyle at the Bolton press briefing before the game. 'Jack is such a talented player; he improved by leaps and bounds [at Bolton

Wanderers]. It doesn't surprise me that he is involved [in Arsenal's first team]; he really took his game on when he came here. We like to think we played a part [in his development] but ultimately that was down to Jack with the ability he has got.'

It served as a timely testament for the Arsenal player, who started the game alongside Alex Song and Cesc Fàbregas in midfield. By the end of the afternoon, Arsenal had knocked in four goals and put a largely average Bolton Wanderers side to the sword. Jack, meanwhile, left the field on 63 minutes to a standing ovation, after being substituted to keep him fresh for the upcoming Champions League tie against Braga in the week. With a capacity crowd's applause ringing in his ears and his former manager's endorsement serving to underline his importance to the future of English football, it looked as if by the second week of September, Jack had finally put the 'Amika episode' to bed.

Indeed, doubts about Jack's 'focus' off the pitch were well and truly out of sight towards the end of that month. Following on from his solid performance against his former club, Jack went on to play in all six games in September and featured in a 4-1 thrashing of old rivals Spurs in the Carling Cup. In a game which resurrected the ghosts of the FA Youth Cup some two or so years before, Jack, Kieran Gibbs, and Henri Lansbury (with a little help from Andrei Arshavin and Samir Nasri) comprehensively outclassed a Tottenham side which featured first-team members such as Aaron Lennon, Sandro, and Robbie Keane. A few days later, Jack was at it again, playing in Andrei Arshavin with the back of his heel to tee up his goal against Partizan Belgrade. What's more, the 18-year-old England international was now keeping out the likes of Tomáš Rosický (who had returned from injury only the previous season to see his place in the team dominated by the young Englishman), Denilson, and Abou Diaby (who had, admittedly, been plagued by injury problems). Not even Arsène Wenger could have predicted Jack's prodigious rise to the top; the Arsenal manager, after all, had estimated that Jack would only play around 20-25 games of the 2010/11 season. But by the end of September 2011, with nearly nine appearances under his belt, Jack was beginning to seriously surpass expectations at the club. This was underlined when the Arsenal fans voted him Player of the Month after what had been an instrumental 30 days in the heart of Arsenal's midfield in all three competitions.

Another month, another milestone reached. Yet Jack's purple-patch was brought to an abrupt end on the afternoon of 16th October 2010. Hosting Birmingham City in the Premier League, Arsenal were looking to bounce back from defeat against Chelsea the previous week and a fixture against Alex McLeish's gritty boys in blue looked to be a real test of the Arsenal character. The Gunners went behind after Nikola Žigić scored from a Sebastian Larsson pass, before Samir Nasri converted a penalty for Arsenal to put the Gunners back on level terms. With everything to play for in the second-half, Arsenal came out with all guns blazing and were rewarded after Marouane Chamakh converted a lovely Jack Wilshere assist to make it 2-1. So far, so good for the Arsenal; but they required maximum concentration to see out the game and take all three points. Before they knew it, they were defending deep and Birmingham, with the big centre-forward Žigić providing the thrust for the Blues' route-one attacks. Arsenal peppered the Birmingham goal with shots – with Samir Nasri and substitute Nicklas Bendtner both going close – but the elusive third goal never arrived. As the 90th minute approached, Arsenal were increasing in confidence and looked more and more assured at the back. Then Jack tried a bit too hard to tackle Žigić; a minute later he was trudging down the Emirates tunnel having received the first red card of his senior career.

After the game, Alex McLeish tried to make a point about Jack's tackle, citing the fall-out after the infamous Martin Taylor tackle on Arsenal's former striker Eduardo. 'We've had to put up with the "Eduardo stuff" for the last couple of years every time we play Arsenal,' said the Birmingham manager. 'It's scandalous. Martin Taylor is not a dirty player, but it was a mistimed challenge. We're not citing Jack Wilshere as dirty, but that tackle could have caused Žigić terrible damage. It just shows that anyone can mis-time things in this hurly burly modern football.' It was a sorry end to a very competitive game of football and Jack was disappointed to be sent off – particularly after having such a decent month in an Arsenal shirt. He certainly didn't mean to injure Žigić, and despite McLeish's misgivings, was genuinely sorry that the whole sorry mess had happened in the first place. A three-game domestic ban followed for the young midfielder, and with the exception of a comfortable 5-1 home win over Shakhtar Donetsk in the Champions League, Jack could rest up and prepare for his Premier League return.

In the meantime, the young midfielder was approached by

Arsenal with a new, improved contract offer. The club felt that his acceleration through the ranks, his long service at the club and his astonishing start to his first-team career deserved a long-term deal and duly asked him in to Arsène Wenger's office to sign his new contract. It was a momentous occasion and Jack was obviously very proud and excited to have signed a long-term deal with the club that had nurtured him through nearly 10 years of football development. Just like he did in 2007 before he was whisked away with Steve Bould and the youth team to play in the Champions Youth Cup in Malaysia, Jack posed for a picture with his manager, who went on to say some very positive things about Jack signing for the club. 'It's such great news that Jack has committed his long-term future to the Club,' Wenger told *Arsenal.com*. 'Jack is a fantastic footballer with a huge amount of potential, and we have all seen with his performances so far that he is a very gifted player, who could be an extremely influential player at the top level of the game.'

The man himself was truly honoured and went on to thank some very special people who had helped in his formative years at the club. 'Arsenal Football Club has been like a second home for me and my family since I was nine years old,' Jack said to to the club's official website. 'To be offered a new contract means everything to me. At this point in my career, when I'm only 18 years old and still learning so much about the game and myself, this is the perfect club, the perfect teammates, the perfect fans, the perfect backroom staff and most importantly, the perfect manager to help continue that. I've got a long way to go before I can become the player I dream of becoming and I'm sure I'll keep making the odd mistake, but it is a massive help for me having a special manager like Arsène Wenger and so many quality teammates and the unbelievable Arsenal fans around me. I believe there is a lot more to come from me. I've been at the Club for almost 10 years already, so I would like to thank everyone that has been part of getting me this far, especially people like Liam Brady, Roy Massey and all his staff at the Hale End Academy. Also Neil Banfield, Steve Bould, Academy Coach Steve Leonard, Academy Scout Bob Arber, Assistant Head of Youth Development David Court, all the backroom staff, Arsène Wenger, all my teammates and, of course, my family.' It was a fantastic moment in Jack's career and one which formally confirmed him as an Arsenal legend in the making. Indeed, Arsenal fans were already thinking up 'Wilshere Songs' to chant on matchday and his continuous Tweeting and online banter with anyone from Arsenal players to Spurs fans immediately endeared him to the Gooner faithful.

The games came thick and fast for Jack after his suspension and before he knew it he was nodding in Chamakh's assist with glee in front of the travelling Gunners at Villa Park. With an official 'caution' from the police after the Amika fracas the only blip on an otherwise stellar start to the season, Jack was now playing some of the most effective football in his life and was turning into an undroppable player in the centre of Arsenal's midfield. Indeed, it looked as if the Amika episode simply served to underline the importance of dedication in Jack's game and his form since the fracas in Kensington was anything but unfocussed. 'If I could give any advice to young players now', the young midfielder would go on to say to the Arsenal matchday programme in an interview towards the end of the season, 'it would be to listen to what people tell you, and live your life off the pitch how you do on it – always be professional and live your life as a footballer.'

December came and went, and with it a 3-1 battering of Chelsea at home which once again revived talk of another Arsenal title push. As the Arsenal first-team entered the New Year – and Jack turned a sprightly 19-years-old – they were fighting for trophies on four fronts and chasing Manchester United and Chelsea at the top of the Premier League. A congested January saw Arsenal play Leeds United twice in the FA Cup (beating them comprehensively on the second attempt 3-1), before dispatching Ipswich Town in the Carling Cup semi-final to book a place in the final at Wembley against old foes Birmingham City.

Progress in the Champions League also brought massive opportunities for the Arsenal first team. After finishing second in their group they were drawn against the mighty Barcelona in a two-legged fixture played towards the end of February and the beginning of March. It was a massive fixture and a game that would on to define Arsenal's and Jack's seasons in more ways than one. But firstly there was a small matter of international friendlies to get out of the way – and Jack was once again called up by England manager Fabio Capello to represent his country in midfield. This time he started the game as a holding midfielder – a similar role to one he was playing at Arsenal throughout the 2010/11 season – and Capello singled out the player for praise after the game, impressed by his confident performance in the midfield of the park: 'Wilshere did well and showed confidence on the ball,' the England manager said after the game. 'It is too early to say if he will play in [the next game] but certainly it was an important game for him and for me to see him.' Jack, meanwhile, was happy to have gained his first full cap for the Three Lions and was also pleased with the 2-1 victory over Denmark: 'I'm glad to get my first start, even if was for 45 minutes,' he told the press after the game. 'I'm pleased how it went. The main thing is that we won and we'll take a lot from it.'

But this wasn't the whole story. Prior to the game, Fabio Capello made some comments in the press which would have made even the ultra-confident Wilshere sit up and take notice. The Scudetto and European Cup-winning coach admitted that Jack was now foremost in his plans for the international side and his presence in the team would only get more and more important in years to come: 'Wilshere represents the very best of the young players,' Capello said in the *Metro* newspaper on the eve of the game. 'I know [he] is only 19 but I remember the best players I managed; [Franco] Baresi, Paulo Maldini, Raul... It is the same talent.'

Quite the compliment from the England manager – but Jack knew that Capello's words would mean nothing if he didn't produce the goods on the pitch. With his first full England cap under his belt, he returned to his club to play in a crucial fixture which would go on define what kind of debut season Jack was to have at the club.

Barcelona were the favourites to win the Champions League, let alone the two-legged fixture against Arsenal.

BREAKTHROUGH

Arsène Wenger and his Arsenal charges were making the right noises going into the game – affirming that 'this season would be different' to the previous season's humbling at the hands of Lionel Messi – but nobody really believed Arsenal had any chance of beating the side many were calling the greatest ever. There were numerous subtexts, of course: the Arsenal captain Cesc Fàbregas was playing against his boyhood side – and a club he had been continuously linked to for the past four or five seasons; Arsène Wenger, furthermore, had his own personal reasons to want to beat the Catalan outfit. It was only five or so years before that he had sent his Arsenal side out to play Barcelona in the Stade de France, only for Jens Lehmann to be sent off and see his team lose thereafter. There was unfinished business at the core of this fixture and whatever anyone said about Arsenal's brittleness (it was, after all, only a few weeks since they had conceded a four-goal lead away to Newcastle United), Wenger, Cesc, Jack and the rest of the Arsenal team were ready to show what they were made of.

Ninety minutes later, Arsenal walked off the Emirates pitch after what had been one of the most exhilarating games of football the stadium had ever witnessed. They won the game 2-1, with Robin van Persie and Andrei Arshavin turning the game on its head with two invaluable strikes. The atmosphere inside the stadium was white hot and the players congratulated each other for a victory well-earned against the most feared side in Europe. Jack, meanwhile, removed his jersey after putting in the shift of a lifetime. Xavi Hernandez, Andres Iniesta, Lionel Messi, Sergio Busquets: they'd danced around him all night but Jack kept his head and proved he was a match for them all. With his jersey in his hands, Jack was about to ask little Lionel Messi if he'd like to exchange shirts but then had a sudden crisis of confidence. Even after playing in one of the biggest and most intense games on the planet, Jack balked and asked club captain and Messi's mate Cesc Fàbregas to request the forward's shirt; playing world-class football was one thing, but talking to the world's best player was quite another thing entirely.

Humbled and overwhelmed with the atmosphere inside the stadium, Jack trudged off the Emirates pitch, got changed and emerged to find his dad waiting for him outside the player's entrance. Jack hopped in the car, sent a quick Tweet on his Blackberry, and settled in for the journey back to Hitchin. His dad Andy was silent. For the first time in over 10 years, he didn't have a word to say about his son's performance.

12 – SETBACKS
2011/12

In which Jack experiences the disappointments of the top flight – is consigned to the injury table – watches from afar as two players leave the club – and sees Arsenal pip the old enemy for a place in the Champions League

The victory over Barcelona back in February 2011 was in some ways the peak of a season which had promised so much but returned so little.

Arsenal, so full of confidence after beating the best team of its generation, couldn't repeat the feat in the second leg against Barcelona. Blighted by injuries and replete with a half-fit Cesc Fàbregas, Wenger's side returned to the Camp Nou only to be shafted by a dodgy red card and a Lionel Messi double. Jack, as ever, tried to have his say in the matter: towards the end of the game, he poked a perfectly weighted through-ball into the path of the advancing Nicklas Bendtner. With only Valdes to beat, the Dane fluffed his lines and the ball bounced off Valdes' arms and into the path of the retreating Carlos Puyol. 'Sadly we couldn't do the job away,' said Jack upon reflection, 'but that was possibly more down to a big decision from the referee than us. But the home game [against Barcelona] was an amazing night. The fans were brilliant and we played brilliantly as well, especially in the second half. To be a goal down and win against a team like that is great.'

It wasn't to be in the Carling Cup either. In their first Wembley final in what seemed like an age, Arsenal contrived to blow their chances to win a first piece of silverware in over five years. A lapse of concentration and a big mix up between goalkeeper Wojciech Szczęsny and defender Laurent Koscielny allowed Birmingham City's Obafemi Martins to smash the ball into the back of the Arsenal net, winning it for the blues in the dying minutes of the game. 'We were 1-0 down and when we equalised it was more of a relief because we knew we could create chances to get the winner,' continued Jack. 'Obviously then there was a mistake from a couple of our players and that happens in football. It was a freak moment in the final... but had we won that game, then maybe...'

The remainder of the 2010/11 season didn't get much better for the Gunners. Out of the Champions League and beaten finalists in the Carling Cup, their league form took a turn for the worse and Wenger's side slipped down to fourth position – below champions Manchester United, second-placed Chelsea and Manchester City, the North West's new financial and footballing powerhouse. With Cesc Fàbregas making noises about leaving the Emirates stadium for good and certain players having their heads turned by the riches on the blue side of Manchester, it wasn't the best time to be a Gooner.

SETBACKS

On 17th April 2011 – just as Arsenal were in the midst of a major crisis of confidence – Jack Wilshere won the Professional Footballers Association Young Player of the Year Award, following in the footsteps of Tony Adams, Paul Merson, Nicholas Anelka and Cesc Fàbregas to become the fifth Arsenal player to have done so. It was a big surprise, given the targets the young man had set himself at the start of the season: 'My target at the start was to play 20-25 times for the first team', Jack confided to the Arsenal matchday programme. 'The boss said that to me as well in pre-season. I had just come back from Bolton and wanted to establish myself at [Arsenal]. I obviously had more targets – I wanted to score more goals for example… I used to score a lot in the youth team and there's no reason why I can't take that into the first team…but I'm only 19 so I'm working on everything.'

Picking up his award, Jack acknowledged those who had supported him and gave particular praise to the club which had nurtured him ever since he was a boy: 'It is my first full season and it is a massive award, especially from my fellow players,' he said at the ceremony. 'It is amazing. I am very proud to be the fifth recipient from Arsenal; it is good to keep this history going. Arsenal is a good club for bringing youngsters through and they keep proving it so I would like to thank the manager as well. I am delighted just to be in the team.' It capped what had been a wonderful year in Arsenal and England colours for the young midfielder. A month later he was crowned *Arsenal.com*'s Player of the Season, taking 41 per cent of the total vote and beating the likes of Samir Nasri and Bacary Sagna to the prize. 'The thing that is different about Jack is that he is very consistent. You hardly ever see him have a bad game,' said teammate and long-time friend Emmanuel Frimpong. 'We have got lots of players in the Reserves that are very good players, in my opinion even as good as Jack on their day. But they don't have that day as often and that is where the difference is.'

Consistency, as Frimpong rightly pointed out, was the key to Jack's game. As the Arsenal first team slipped down the Premier League during the dying days of the season, there was only one player who would consistently give 100 per cent to the team. Every minute of every game, Jack was either on the ball or looking to get on the ball and his manager, his teammates and anyone who watched the game could see that Jack had something special in him – a sense of pride and determination to take full advantage of his opportunities at the club. Indeed, not much had changed since Jack first arrived to meet Roy Massey at the Hale End Academy back in 2001; he'd grown up, of course – he even found out his ex-girlfriend was expecting his child in October 2011, a shock which only reinforced his sense of responsibility at a relatively young age – but Jack was still essentially the same young player, the same young kid who simply wanted to score goals and win football games. By the end of the 2010/11 season, Jack had played in 35 games in the Premier League, assisted in 3 goals and scored one himself. He was slowly but surely turning into the metronome of the new Arsenal side and was beginning to look like a captain in the making as he played with his heart firmly on his sleeve.

Indeed, it was the shining light for a team which had come

so far yet achieved very little. As the season came to a close, fans and players alike began a post-mortem of where exactly things had gone wrong for the club. At one point, Wenger's team were challenging at the top of the Premier League, keeping Barcelona at bay in front of their home support and only 90 minutes away from regaining the League Cup for the first time in nearly 20 years. Then suddenly the confidence and momentum began to topple in front of their very eyes: the Carling Cup debacle sapped the squad of any self-belief, and after they had faced Barcelona in the European Cup and Manchester United in the FA Cup, they were left with only the league to play for.

By the end of the season, the majority of the Arsenal support couldn't take any further dissapointment and for the first time in his reign fans began to seriously question Arsène Wenger. With reigning champions Manchester United rebuilding, Chelsea bringing in a top-class new manager in the form of Andre Villas-Boas, Manchester City flexing its limitless financial muscle in an overvalued transfer market, Spurs in the ascendancy and Liverpool back under the stewardship of 'King' Kenny Dalglish, people were beginning to ask where Arsenal might fit into such a transformation in the Premier League landscape? Nobody quite knew what would happen – not the fans, not even Wenger. And the problem for the Arsenal support was that nobody seemed to want to take responsibility on the pitch. Fàbregas was close to leaving, Vieira was long-gone, Henry was in the USA and Adams was managing a team somewhere in Azerbaijan.

At the end of August 2011, after a protracted and frustrated summer of wrangling and financial mind-games, Cesc Fabregas and Samir Nasri left Arsenal Football Club. Jack, meanwhile, was now a regular guest at Arsenal's refurbished rehabilitation centre at London Colney after picking up an injury in Arsenal's pre-season game against the New York Red Bulls. 'It is not very serious,' Wenger said of his young midfielder's knock after the game on 31 July, 'he is a quick healer usually and a tough boy, so I hope he will be quicker than the medical prediction.' Only a few weeks later, though, Jack was told that he would miss the start of the 2011/12 season as the original diagnosis of a minor 'inflammation' had uncovered a more serious, previously undetected injury. 'I can confirm I will be out for two to three months!' he told his followers on *Twitter*, 'I am working hard in the gym to stay fit and I am gutted but I will be back stronger!'

The injury wasn't the only the only thing on the young midfielder's mind as Arsenal played out their pre-season program. He was also keeping a keen eye on the comings and goings at the Emirates stadium, with Fàbregas's and Nasri's transfers of particular interest. After seeing the pair of midfielders have such a productive season, Jack was keen to see both Nasri and Fàbregas stay on at Arsenal and help him and other emerging talent (such as his good friend Emmanuel Frimpong) learn the trade. But the more the summer went on, the more it looked as if his midfield counterparts had made up their minds and by the time Jack was asked about it during Arsenal's pre-season tour of Malaysia, he couldn't keep his thoughts to himself. 'Loyalty is a big part of football and it shows if you are a real man or not,' Jack said when pressed on the issue by a Malaysian journalist, before adding, 'there have been a few players who have shown Arsenal great loyalty and, hopefully, we will get a few more like that. Then we will see if we can get a trophy or not.'

It seemed as if the moves of Nasri and, to a far lesser extent, Fàbregas were grating on Wilshere, and by the time they departed Arsenal at the end of August 2011, the young midfielder was consigned to the treatment table with only the media as a platform to fight Arsenal's battles. And there were countless battles to fight as the Gunners began the 2011/12 season: justification for a last-minute round of 'panic buying' in the transfer market; a tight Champions League qualification round against plucky Italian side Udinese; a hammering at the hands of Manchester United; and a capitulation at Ewood Park against relegation favourites Blackburn. What's more, the old enemy Tottenham Hotspur were beginning to wake from their slumber and despite a trouncing at the hands of the Manchester clubs at the start of the season, were beginning to look like the team to beat to regain Champions League qualification.

Indeed, by the time the first North London Derby of the season rolled round, Jack and his fellow Gooners were on the back foot, trying to disprove countless assertions that power between the two rivalries – a power which had been nestled in Arsène Wenger's pocket since he arrived at Highbury some 16 or so years ago – had shifted. And despite losing the first derby 2-1 and Tottenham powering above Arsenal as the season rolled into the winter months, Jack was convinced that the Gunners would still finish above their rivals and took to *Twitter* to put his money where his mouth is. 'All Spurs fans are buzzing they are ahead of us in the league' he told his *Twitter* feed before going on to add: 'at the end of the season if Spurs finish above Arsenal I will give £3,000 to charity and if Arsenal finish above Spurs every Spurs fan that follows me must send me a pound which I will send to charity.'

It was all fun and games for Jack and he seriously believed that despite being nearly 10 points off their rivals in the New Year, Arsenal would finish above their North London rivals. But as 2011 became 2012 and Jack turned the ripe old age of 20, his expected return to the Arsenal first team fold was becoming more and more protracted. His rehabilitation had gone to plan and the Arsenal faithful were looking forward to seeing Wilshere back in an Arsenal shirt as soon as possible, but Arsène Wenger had reservations about Jack's return, and despite a 'miraculous recovery' at the end of January 2012, Wenger remained cautious with the development of his midfield star.

Indeed, only a few weeks after the *Guardian* newspaper published an article entitled 'Jack Wilshere's imminent return to full training stuns Arsenal doctors' in January, the midfielder picked up another injury in the same troublesome ankle. 'It is true I have had a setback... I can't tell you how long I have been set back because I don't know!' he told his concerned followers on *Twitter*, 'I am very annoyed but will stay strong.' It was a big blow for the young midfielder and he was even more disappointed after Wenger said he may not be fit in time to play at the

European Championships in Poland and Ukraine. Asked how Jack was feeling about his situation, the Arsenal manager said: 'How do you say in English? Gutted.'

Wenger might as well have been describing how he felt about the situation too. By the time Wilshere's new diagnosis had reached the press, Arsenal were struggling to keep up with the chasing pack in the race for the top four. Tottenham Hotspur were still the favourites for third, whilst Chelsea, Liverpool and Newcastle United were looking to nick the final qualification place for the European Cup. Wenger was relying on the same core players – Alex Song, an in-form Robin van Persie, a re-energised Tomaš Rosický and an overworked Aaron Ramsey – and was desperate for more energy in midfield, particularly given the lack of depth in the squad. 'I like to have a left-footed player in midfield,' Wenger told the *Guardian* in reference to his injured midfield star. 'We miss that little burst from Jack.'

Fortunately for Arsenal, his first team squad responded with a run which propelled them into the top three for the first time in over a year. Wins against Blackburn, Sunderland, Newcastle United, Everton and Aston Villa, and massive victories over Liverpool at Anfield and Tottenham Hotspur at home, sent Arsenal above their nearest rivals and prompted Wenger to declare the achievement one of the most impressive during his tenure at the club.

Jack, meanwhile, was declared unavailable for both the European Championships and the Olympics in London. Wenger emphasised the importance of Jack's rehabilitation and pre-season programme over the summer of 2012 and, despite opposition from the Olympics coach Stuart Pearce, confirmed that Jack will not be playing at any competitive tournament before the start of the 2012-13 season.

As for Arsenal, a top-three finish was indeed a massive achievement, given the fact that Arsenal were 15th after the first North London derby back in October. Some nine months later, the Gunners were 'crowned' the best club in London and could begin their transfer business secure in the knowledge that they definitely will be playing Champions League football in 2012-13. There were, of course, still questions to be answered: what of Robin van Persie's contract situation? Where will the newly crowned Premier League Player of the Season be plying his trade in next season? What of Theo Walcott (who Wenger said had his best season at Arsenal in 2011-12) and Alex Song, both of whom were due new contracts? And what of Arsenal Football Club? After a 'summer from hell' and a roller-coaster-ride of a season, where was Wenger going to take them next?

13 – ARSENAL D.N.A.
2012/13

In which Jack inherits the Number 10 shirt – makes a
thrilling return from injury – signs up for his boyhood club –
and captains the Arsenal first team

'It's such an honour for me,' Jack said to the Arsenal website just before a Premier League ball was kicked in earnest in August 2012; 'Getting the number 10 shirt at the club means so much to me as I wore it through all the youth teams at Arsenal.'

So much had changed at Arsenal Football Club since Jack strolled off the Emirates pitch after beating Barcelona back in February 2011. Then he was the plucky 19-year-old in the number 19 shirt; now, over a year later, Jack was preparing to begin a new season at the club, but this time he'll be wearing a shirt worn by 'legends' of the club. 'It has a special place for all attacking or creative players,' he added. 'I feel proud to wear it now after some real club legends have worn it, such as Dennis Bergkamp.'

Jack's choice of words was rather telling. The same month,

JACK WILSHERE: ARSENAL D.N.A.

August 2012, Robin van Persie, the club's captain, talisman and holder of the legendary number 10 shirt, signed for Manchester United in one of the most poisonous transfers of recent times. On the surface it was business as usual for Arsène Wenger and the Arsenal board: a player who was approaching 30-years-old, whose contract expired within 12 months, refused to sign the offer that was tabled by the club, so Arsenal had no choice but to move him on. But Arsenal fandom – and Jack Wilshere would certainly consider himself an Arsenal fan – saw it differently. For the majority of the Arsenal faithful this was betrayal at every level: from the player, the manager and even the owner of the club, Stan Kroenke.

On the one hand Robin van Persie had repaid the faith the club had shown him over the past eight seasons: he'd scored goals for the club and contributed significantly to its Champions League qualification in the preceding 2011/12 season; he'd also spent eight years at the club and won only one trophy (the FA Cup back in 2005), and would later go on to admit that such a return caused genuine hurt and remorse. Professionally, too, it looked as if Van Persie had outgrown his teammates, and some of his performances in his final season at the club illustrated the gulf in quality between the Dutch forward and some of his red and white counterparts.

But it hurt. It hurt the Arsenal fans, the Arsenal players and it certainly hurt the Arsenal manager who had picked-up Robin van Persie from Feyenoord on the 'cheap' back in 2004 and developed him into one of the most potent forwards on the planet. But Wenger was optimistic about the future of the team: 'We lose great players,' he told the *Guardian*, 'but I

274

want to show that we have great players at the club.' And the manager didn't have to look far to see there was one player in particular who stood out from the rest of the current playing squad: 'By giving Jack the No10 [jersey] I want to show I am confident he will be the one who will lead the team one day. At his age, one year out is not easy to take and every day he comes in at 8 o'clock on the morning and works out but he didn't get anywhere. I want to show him that I believe in him and that he will come back quickly.'

Unfortunately for Wenger, Jack continued to be sidelined until October 2012, by which time Arsenal had only won three of their opening eight fixtures. New signings Santi Carzola, Lukas Podolski and Olivier Giroud were still getting used to their new roles and positions in the team, and it appeared Arsenal were still reeling from the after-effects of Robin van Persie's acrimonious departure. It also seemed as if the Gunners were still getting used to life without their previous club captain Cesc Fàbregas, whose range of passing and vision allowed the team's fluid 4-2-3-1 system to work effectively. Alas, without the Spaniard in the middle of the park or Van Persie's goals papering over the cracks, Arsenal's standing in the league was beginning to look rather precarious.

Jack finally returned to first team action on the 27th October 2012 against Queens Park Rangers. After 524 days on the sidelines, Jack started the game alongside Mikel Arteta and Aaron Ramsey in midfield and put in a 'man of the match' display against the West-Londoners. 'It felt amazing to be back,' he told *Arsenal.com*; 'all the hard work and long days at the training ground have paid off.' Indeed, his drive and tenacity simply underlined what Arsenal had been missing over the past 12 to 18 months: a player not only with startling natural ability, but a player who seemed happy to take responsibility and drive the Gunners forward. The game ended 1-0 and Jack left the pitch to a standing ovation when substituted in the second half.

A week is a long time in football, however, and Jack's return to the Arsenal first team wasn't heralded for long. Little over seven days later, Arsenal travelled to Old Trafford to face Manchester United for the first time since Robin van Persie decamped to the north-west. It was always going to be a tense affair: Arsenal were struggling in the league to find any kind of consistency, while their former captain was riding high at his new club, pretty much picking up where he left off at the end of the previous season and firing the Red Devils to the top of the Premier League. Jack's return to the Arsenal first team, meanwhile, looked to have re-invigorated the Gunner faithful, with many Arsenal fans hopeful that his return – coupled with a ground-out victory the previous week – might be a turning point in the season, and that a victory at Old Trafford would be the perfect way to remedy what had been a rather frustrating season so far.

But it was to be the same old story for Arsenal, who began the game very nervously. In the third minute Thomas Vermaelen, the new captain of the side, panicked when clearing the ball and fired it straight at Robin van Persie. The Dutchman didn't think twice and smashed the ball past Vito Mannone and into the Arsenal net. The Gunners found it difficult to get into the game thereafter and an insipid performance by Arsène Wenger's men culminated in Jack's dismissal in the 68th minute following a second bookable offence. 'The midfielder had done well to stay out of trouble after picking up an early caution for a scything tackle from behind on [Tom] Cleverley,' read the *Guardian* match report; 'but when [Wilshere] caught [Patrice] Evra on the ankle with raised studs he knew the referee had little option but to produce another card.' The Gunners went on to lose the game 2-1 after Santi Cazorla scored a late consolation goal with the last kick of the game; the match was lost in the third minute, however, when Robin van Persie put United ahead and turned his back on his former team once and for all.

Arsène Wenger defended his combative midfielder after the game, arguing that Jack took part of the ball when he attempted to tackle Patrice Evra: 'His game is commitment,' he told the press when pressed on Jack's second yellow card. Yet the manager was criticised by some after the game for refusing to substitute Wilshere following his first booking in the 13th minute, opting instead to keep him on in the hope he might keep his discipline and help the team win the game.

Whatever the reason for the loss, Arsenal's inconsistency in the league was beginning to take its toll. Despite Jack's return, this new-look Arsenal first team seemed as if it was perpetually taking one step forwards and two-steps back. There was an endemic problem within the heart of the team – a psychological issue Wenger was finding difficult to iron out: indeed, Vermaelen's mistake at Old Trafford which led to Van Persie's goal was the latest in a long line of unforced errors which allowed opponents a strong foothold in the game, and it was errors such as these which were stopping

JACK WILSHERE: ARSENAL D.N.A.

Arsenal progressing in the league and keeping up with the chasing pack for a Champions League spot.

In fact it was in the Champions League itself where Arsenal were most confident and at ease. Drawn in a group with Schalke, Olympiakos and Montpellier, Arsenal began the first round well, beating Montpellier away from home before dispatching an average Olympiakos 3-1 at the Emirates. But by the time they played back to back fixtures against German side Schalke, Arsenal were once again tormented by the aforementioned problems at the back and were duly beaten 0-2 at home before salvaging a 2-2 draw away at the Veltins Arena. Jack, meanwhile, took his Old Trafford dismissal in his stride, opting to see it as a chance to rest-up following his lengthy injury lay-off. It seemed to work: by the time he returned to first team action the young midfielder seemed re-invigorated and sharper, and proved he was ready to help the Arsenal in all competitions by scoring his first goal since returning from injury against Montpellier in the Champions League.

Yet the Gunners' league form left a lot to be desired. November 2012 proved to be a disastrous month for Arsenal, with three draws bookended by the loss away to Manchester United and a shock defeat at home to Swansea City (a 5-2 home win against the old enemy Tottenham Hotspur notwithstanding). December didn't fare that much better either: despite a string of wins in the league (including a Man of the Match performance from Jack against West Bromwich Albion), Arsenal were knocked out of the League Cup by Bradford City in what was one of the most disappointing results of Arsène Wenger's Arsenal career.

Despite the pressure in the league and the growing scepticism of large parts of the Arsenal fan base, Wenger pulled off a minor coup towards the end of the year, tying down five young, British players to brand new, long-term deals at Arsenal Football club. Aaron Ramsey, Alex Oxlade-Chamberlain, Kieron Gibbs, Carl Jenkinson and, of course, Jack Wilshere all put pen to paper to keep them at the club for the next five or so years. 'The plan is to build a team around a strong basis of young players, in order to get them to develop their talent at the club,' a bullish Arsène Wenger told the press. 'Jack is certainly the best known, the leader of this group – but the other four are exceptional footballers, and we're very happy that we could conclude their new deals at the same time.'

It was a real statement of intent from Arsenal after seeing a 'core' of young foreign players decamp to various clubs across the continent after failing to achieve their own personal ambitions at Arsenal. Wenger, though, was keen to emphasise that the new backbone of the Arsenal squad were 'local', home-grown lads who wanted to win things at Arsenal and bring glory back to a club which had failed to win anything since leaving Highbury stadium six years ago: 'We could not keep the core of foreign players [at the club] but I hope we can build a team around these players,' Wenger declared. 'We have gone through a period of restricted financial potential when we moved into the new stadium but we have gone over that and, hopefully, we can be a bit more convincing now.'

Indeed by the start of 2013, Arsenal were beginning to look slightly more convincing in the league, coming off the back of December which saw them pick up four wins in five. Jack, meanwhile, celebrated his new deal at the club by scoring the winning goal in the third-round FA Cup replay against Swansea City in front of a packed Emirates crowd. Running on to Olivier Giroud's measured lay-off, the 21-year-old smashed the ball on the half volley beyond Michael Vorm in the Swansea goal, before sprinting to the corner flag to celebrate with his teammates. After the game he was interviewed alongside club captain Thomas Vermaelen and was quick to emphasise the importance of the win not just in terms of his own personal contribution but also of the team's effort and work ethic during what turned out to be a tough FA Cup tie: 'It was important we got the goal', Jack said; 'we've got a tough game coming up at the weekend [against Chelsea] and then next week [against West Ham United] so it was important we got the win in 90 minutes.' His captain, though, when asked about Jack's contribution, was a little more forthcoming with his comments: 'For me [Jack] is a world class midfielder,' Vermaelen told the interviewer, 'he showed that today, he played really well; he's really important to us.'

Vermaelen's comments were brought into greater focus a week later when the defender went off injured in a league game against West Ham United. In the absence of vice-captain Mikel Arteta, the Belgian centre-back handed the arm-band to Jack who duly strapped it to his right arm and put in yet another man of the match performance against his 'second team'. The irony wasn't lost on the young midfielder who had dreamt of captaining West Ham after his dad took him to see the Hammers as a boy; now, over a decade later, he was the captain of the team that taught him everything he knew, playing against a side which first introduced him to the game he came to love. His manager, furthermore, had a few rather telling things to say following Jack's temporary stint as club captain: 'Jack was an interesting choice [of captain]. Honestly, Vermaelen made that choice and I let him make it. It is always interesting to see when Vermaelen is out who he feels spontaneously should be captain. I did not want to stop him. It is interesting because the players know on the pitch. [Jack] is naturally a guy who is not scared of anything on the football pitch and that is usually the sign of a leader. He wants to win and shows you that. Of course he will be one of the leaders of this club – in fact he already is on the pitch. A leader is somebody who does everything on the pitch to help his team to win. And he does that. If you are asking me if I will take the captaincy away from Vermaelen, no. It is not a question that holds me at the moment. I think Jack will be captain of this club this day – yes, of course. First of all, because of the quality of the player. Second, his commitment and desire to win.'

Jack's tenacity, however, and desire to win would inevitably take its toll on the young midfielder. Having been out of the game for over a year and a half, the midfielder was beginning to feel the strain of playing nearly a game every three days, and by the time the full-time whistle blew in what was another full-blooded North London derby, Jack was struggling to to keep up. Indeed, the 2-1 away loss to Spurs proved to be Jack's last game for Arsenal for approximately six weeks after he picked up another injury on his ankle (although the club was quick to emphasise that it was a minor strain and the midfielder should be returning to the first team squad within four weeks).

By the time he did return to the squad – on 13th April – the Gunners had hauled themselves above Tottenham and Chelsea and into third place in the Premier League, beating Swansea City, Reading, and West Bromwich Albion (and Bayern Munich at the Allianz Arena in what turned out to be a fruitless victory in the Champions League round of 16). In fact, Arsenal had played themselves into such startling form some commentators were beginning to question whether Jack was still part of Arsenal's current strongest 11. Other commentators, on the other hand, saw the situation rather differently: many were touting Jack as the captain in waiting, and the fluctuating form of Thomas Vermaelen – who was dropped from the first team following the defeat to Spurs in March – left many wondering whether the manager might stay true to his word and promote Jack from someone who 'does everything on a football pitch to help his team win', to the captain of the club.

Indeed, by the end of the season it was one of many questions laid at the door of Wenger and the Arsenal board following the club's success in reaching the Champions League for a 16th consecutive season. With the Gunners sealing qualification by the skin of their teeth again, and failing, no less, to get past the first knock-out round of the Champions League, many fans were beginning to question the ambition of the club and the direction in which it was heading. Were they ever going to challenge again for the Premier League title? Was the self-sustaining business model – and self-styled antidote to the sugar-daddy spending of modern-day Premier League – the most efficient way of remaining competitive both domestically and on the continent? With Chelsea flexing its financial muscle once again and Bayern Munich re-emerging as a European powerhouse, how will Arsenal cope against teams that hoover-up talent and spend their way out of trouble? And will the Gunners ever get the chance to show Nasri, Adebayor, Van Persie et al that they *could* win things at Arsenal Football Club?

Amid such a myriad of uncertainties, there was, of course, hope on the horizon: a player who would emerge from the ashes of the 2011/12 and 2012/13 seasons and revive the club from its sorry slumber; a player who would dominate the midfield as Brady, Vieira, Parlour, Pires, Gilberto and Fàbregas had once done; a player who would wear the cannon on his heart with pride and class; a player who would play every pass, head every ball, make every tackle and score every goal like it was his last; a captain in the making who takes games by the scruff of its neck and shows his teammates what it really means to 'play for the shirt'. 'I've been at the club since I was nine and learned to love it. From the [Patrick] Vieira days, to [Dennis] Bergkamp, [Cesc] Fábregas, I've watched them come through and move on. There's a crop of new players, [Aaron] Ramsey, myself, Kieran Gibbs…hopefully we can really create something special. I love the club and I want to be part of its future.'

His name is Jack Wilshere, and he has *Arsenal D.N.A.*

ACKNOWLEDGEMENTS

Firstly, I would like to thank the John Blake Publishing team for giving me the opportunity to write this book – it was great working with you all. I would also like to acknowledge the excellent work of my copy-editor Jake Ellwood, whose help and guidance transformed a 'beast' of a manuscript into this much 'smaller' tome. Thanks also to Mum and Mike, and Dad and Kevin for all their help and encouragement throughout the past year or so.

Finally, I would like to thank my partner Thea for her help and support – without your encouragement and endless patience I don't think this book would have ever been written.

Joe Jacobs
Crystal Palace, 2013

ACKNOWLEDGMENTS